It's Another Ace Book from CGP

This book is for 14-16 year olds.

First we stick in questions on all the <u>really important stuff</u> you need to do well in GCSE Biology.

Then we have a really good stab at making it funny — so you'll <u>actually use it</u>.

Simple as that.

CGP are just the best

The central aim of Coordination Group Publications is to produce top quality books that are carefully written, immaculately presented and marvellously funny — whilst always making sure they exactly cover the National Curriculum for each subject.

And then we supply them to as many people as we possibly can, as <u>cheaply</u> as we possibly can.

Buy our books — they're ace

Contents

Section One — Cells

Life Processes 1
Cells 2
Specialised Cells 3
Diffusion and Osmosis 4

Section Two — Plants

Plant Structure 7
Leaf Structure 8
Transpiration 10
Transport Systems in Plants 12
Photosynthesis 14
Food and Plants 16
Hormones in Plants 17

Section Three — Human Biology Part One

The Digestive System 19
Digestive Enzymes 21
Absorption of Food 22
Food Tests 24
Circulatory System 25
The Heart 26
Blood Vessels 28
The Blood 29
Lungs and Breathing 30
Respiration 32
The Nervous System 34
The Eye 36
The Digestive System 19
Digestive Enzymes 21
Absorption of Food 22
Food Tests 24
Circulatory System 25
The Heart 26
Blood Vessels 28
The Blood 29
Lungs and Breathing 30
Respiration 32
The Nervous System 34
The Eye 36

Section Four — Human Biology Part Two

Hormones 38
The Use of Hormones 39
Insulin Diabetes 40
The Menstrual Cycle 41
Hormones in the Menstrual Cycle 43
Disease in Humans 45
Fighting Disease 47
Drugs 48
Alcohol 50
Tobacco 51
Homeostasis 52
Homeostasis and the Kidneys 53
Kidneys 54

Section Five — Genetics and Evolution

Variation in Plants and Animals 55
Genetics 56
Genes, Chromosomes and DNA 58
Mitosis and Meiosis 60
Fertilisation 62
Mutations 64
X and Y Chromosomes 65
Monohybrid Crosses 66
Cystic Fibrosis 68
Genetic Diseases 70
Selective Breeding 72
Cloning 73
Fossils 75
Evolution 76
Natural Selection 77

Section Six — The Environment

Population Sizes 78
Communities (Adapt and Survive) 80
Acid Rain 82
The Greenhouse Effect 84
Farming and its Problems 85
Pyramids of Number and Biomass 87
Energy Transfer 89
The Carbon Cycle 90
The Nitrogen Cycle 92

Section Seven — Answers 93

Published by Coordination Group Publications Ltd
Typesetting and layout by The Science Coordination Group

Coordinated by Paddy Gannon BSc MA

Contributors :
Dr Nigel Saunders
Carol Graves
Chris Christofi

Design editor: Paul Thompson BSc (Hons)

Updated by:
Chris Dennett BSc (Hons)
James Paul Wallis BEng (Hons)
Dominic Hall BSc (Hons)
Suzanne Worthington BSc (Hons)

With thanks to Colin Wells, Claire Thompson and Glenn Rogers for the proof-reading

ISBN 1-84146-605-0

Groovy website: www.cgpbooks.co.uk

Printed by Elanders Hindson, Newcastle upon Tyne
Clipart sources: CorelDRAW and VECTOR

Text, design, layout and original illustrations © Coordination Group Publications 2001
All rights reserved.

Section One — Cells

Life Processes

Q1) The diagram opposite shows some of the life processes of a cow.
  a) Name one life process that is not shown in the diagram.
  b) Explain this life process.

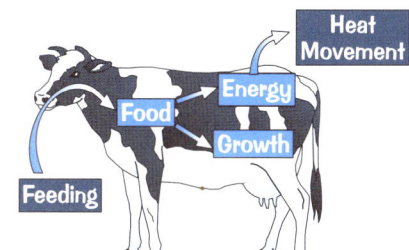

Q2) Next to each statement fill in the correct life process.

Observation	Life Processes Involved
a) One amoeba splits to form two individuals.	
b) When a gardener measured his bean plants, they had all increased in height by at least 5cm.	
c) After taking a plant out of a dark cupboard and shining light on it for at least 24 hours, there was starch in the leaves.	
d) On a kitchen window, cress plants bend towards the light.	

Q3) Draw lines to join the correct *life process* with the correct *description*.

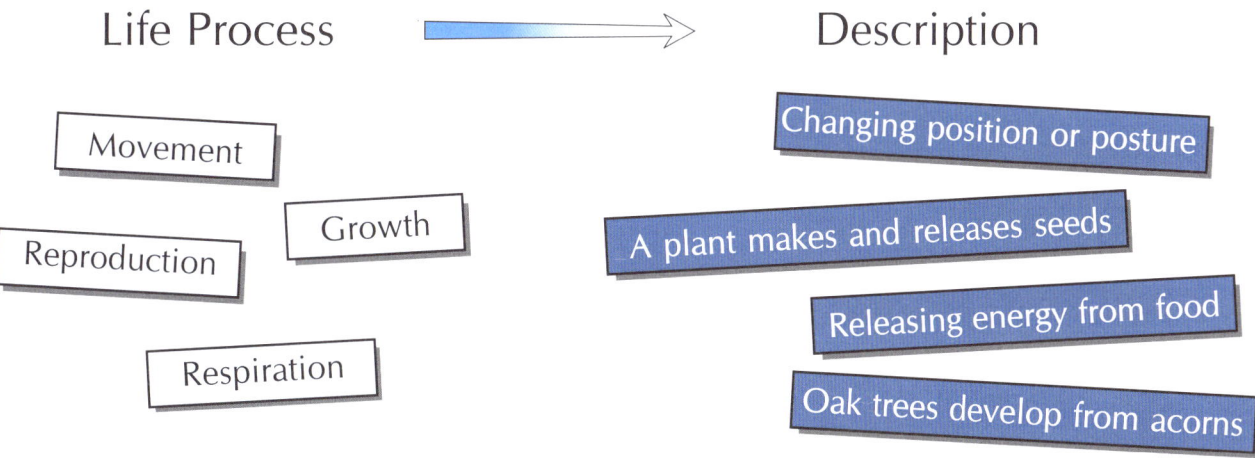

Q4) Use the words to fill in the spaces.

move   reproduce   sensitivity   nutrition
excreted   respiration   grow

For living things to keep their species going from one generation to the next, they must _____. Animals also need to _____ in order to find food, find a mate and escape from predators. Living things produce new individuals that _____ to become adults. To carry out the process of living, energy must be released from food. This is called _____. We call the process of making or taking in food _____. Inside our bodies we produce waste from chemical reactions. This is _____ from the body. Living things must detect and respond to changes around them. This process, known as _____, is very important for living things to survive.

Top Tips: Let's face it, the Seven Life Processes are pretty easy. Mind you, it can be quite tricky **remembering** them all — but that's what **MRS NERG** is for. Make sure you learn **more** than just the names though — learn what they **actually mean**.

Cells

Q1) These are two single-celled organisms that swim in water.

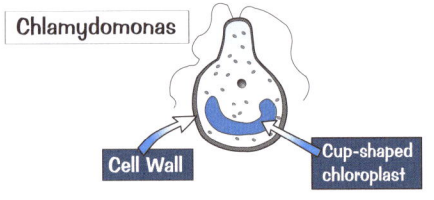
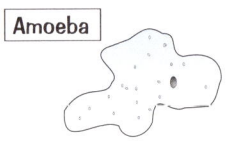

a) Which one is more like a *plant cell*?
b) Give *two* reasons *why* it is more like a plant cell.

Q2) Name three structures that both plant and animal cells have.

Q3) This is a diagram of a leaf cell.   a) *Add* the following *labels* to the diagram:

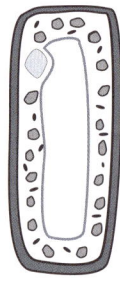

cell membrane   cell wall   chloroplast
cytoplasm   nucleus   sap vacuole

b) What structures *enable* the leaf cells to make *sugar*?
c) What is the name of this *process*?
d) What is the name of the *green substance* found in leaves?
e) What is the *function* of the *cell wall*?

Q4) Complete the blanks using the words below (words may be used more than once).

cell membrane   cell wall   chloroplasts
cytoplasm   nucleus   sap   vacuole

Virtually all plant and animal cells have a _____, cytoplasm and a_____ _____. Plant cells are strengthened by a cellulose _____ _____. They also have a large, permanent _____ which contains _____. This is a liquid that contains stored substances and water. The water provides support for the cell. Chemical reactions take place in the _____ of the cell. A _____ controls the activities of the cell. It contains chromosomes which carry genes. The genes control characteristics. Plants make food in their leaf cells by photosynthesis. To do this, plants absorb light with chlorophyll which is found inside _____.

Q5) This is a diagram of a human sperm cell.

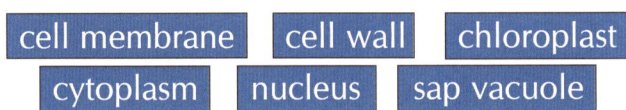

a) Name *two structures* found in the sperm cell that are not commonly found in animal cells.
b) Label two structures that are typical of *animal cells*.

Q6) *Cells are grouped into tissues. Tissues are arranged together to form organs. Organs make up the systems.*

a) Name the different *systems* in which you would find blood cells, brain cells, and the uterus.
b) What is *glandular tissue*?

Top Tips: Two main things to learn — 1) the **four structures** that all cells have in common, and 2) the **three structures** that **only** plant cells. Oh, and you'll need to know this sequence: **cells → tissue → organ → organism** — that's not much to ask is it.

Specialised Cells

Q1) *An ostrich egg could be considered to be the largest cell in the world. Which three main features does it share with a cell in the human body? What is the function of the egg?*

Q2) A, B and C in the diagram below are different types of cells.

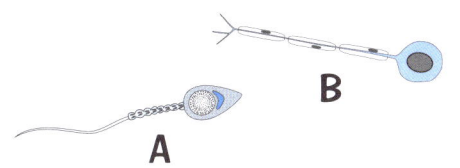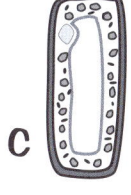

a) Name each type of cell.
b) What is the function of each type of cell?
c) Give one feature of each type of cell and say how that feature helps the cell to carry out its function.

Q3) Cells in animals and plants perform specific functions. An example is the jellyfish which has stinging cells to protect itself from predators.

a) The diagram opposite shows a jellyfish cell. Label three different structures that are present.

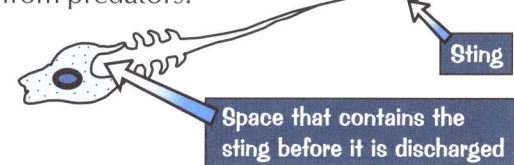

b) Name one other example of an animal cell, stating the special job it does.

Q4) On the surface of roots there are special cells called *root hair cells*.

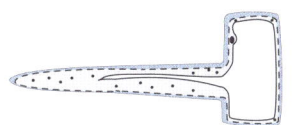

a) How are these cells adapted to perform a specific function? Explain how the adaptation helps them carry out this function.
b) Name two features shown in the diagram that tell us that this is a plant cell.

Q5) The diagram below shows how endothelial cells make up the structure of a blood capillary.

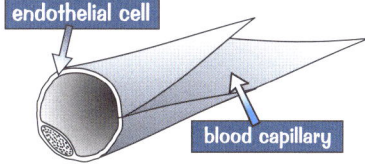

Blood capillaries are fine blood vessels that allow substances to move across the endothelial cells. Substances like oxygen, sugar and other useful materials are passed out of the capillaries and into surrounding cells.

a) From the diagram, explain how endothelial cells are adapted to carry out their function.
b) Name one substance that enters the capillaries from surrounding cells.

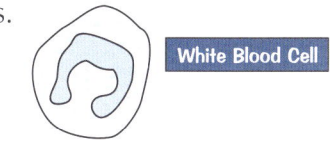

Q6) White blood cells move inside blood vessels. What function(s) are these cells adapted for and how do they carry them out?

Q7) Red blood cells are biconcave in shape — they curve inwards on both sides. They are also unusual because they have no nucleus. Oxygen diffuses across the membranes of red blood cells, which then carry the oxygen to different parts of the body. These cells travel down capillaries which are only slightly wider than the cells.

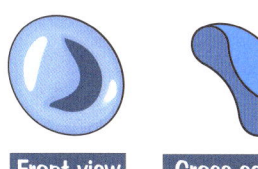

a) Red blood cells are specialised cells. What does this mean?
b) Give one possible reason for: (i) the shape of the cell.
(ii) the lack of a nucleus.

Top Tips: Specialised cells are just cells with **jobs to do**. Exams are bound to ask you what that job is, or what makes the cell so good at it. Look at all the bits of the cell, and see where they're different — the **shape's** a good place to start. Learn these seven in particular: **palisade** leaf cell, **phloem** cell, **xylem** cell, **root hair** cell, **muscle** cell, **nerve** cell, **sperm** cell.

Section One — Cells

Diffusion and Osmosis

Q1) An experiment using the equipment on the right was set up.

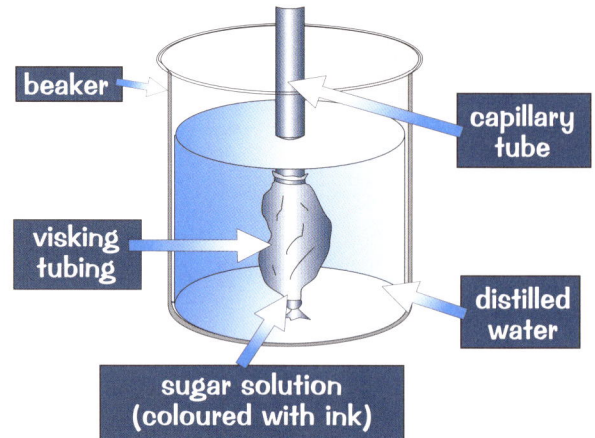

a) Explain why the distilled water in the beaker became coloured.

b) Explain why the sugar solution moved up the capillary tube.

Q2) Livadia is a Mediterranean village by the sea. In spring, there is flooding and the sea water rises and covers some of the nearby farmland owned by farmer Antonis. When this happens, Antonis has noticed that his crops begin to shrivel and die. Explain why this happens.

Q3) For each of these sentences, indicate whether the process involved is *diffusion or osmosis*, by putting a "D" for *diffusion* or an "O" for *osmosis*.

a) Oxygen crosses the alveoli of the lungs and enters the blood.
b) Water enters guard cells in the leaves from surrounding cells.
c) Water moves from the moist stomatal space to the drier atmosphere.
d) Water enters blood capillaries from surrounding body cells.
e) Water in the soil crosses into the root hairs.
f) Water is absorbed out of the kidney tubules and back into the blood stream.
g) In the blood vessels in the lungs, oxygen enters red blood cells.
h) Carbon dioxide enters stomata for photosynthesis.

Q4) Kelly set up an experiment. She placed one prune in a beaker of distilled water and another in a very strong sugar solution (syrup).

Kelly returned to her experiment 24 hours later. Explain what you would expect to have happened to Prune A and Prune B.

Section One — Cells

Diffusion and Osmosis

Q5) *Luke carved a boat out of a potato, and played with it in the kitchen sink. He placed salt inside the boat as his cargo and then left it sitting in the water for an hour while he had lunch. When he returned to his boat, he found that it had water inside. The water was not there before lunch and nobody interfered with his boat.*

Explain how the water got into the boat.

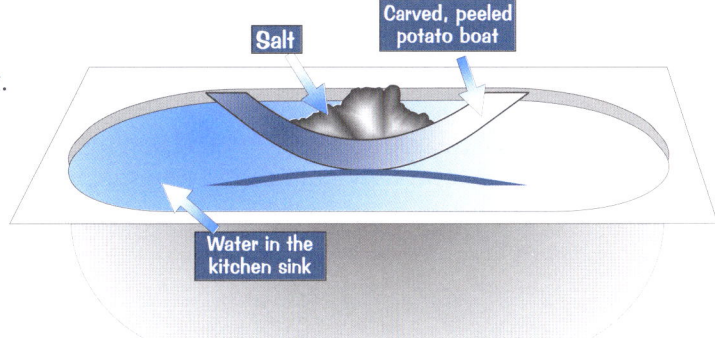

Q6) Complete the blanks with these words.

osmosis   diffusion   partially permeable   water molecules
high water   low water

Osmosis is the movement of _____ _____ from a region of _____ _____ concentration to a region of _____ _____ concentration. In _____, water molecules move across a _____ _____ membrane. Osmosis is sometimes called a special case of _____ because water molecules move from a high to a low concentration of water molecules.

Q7) This is a diagram of a *guard cell*:
Guard cells are found in leaves and form pores called stomata between them.

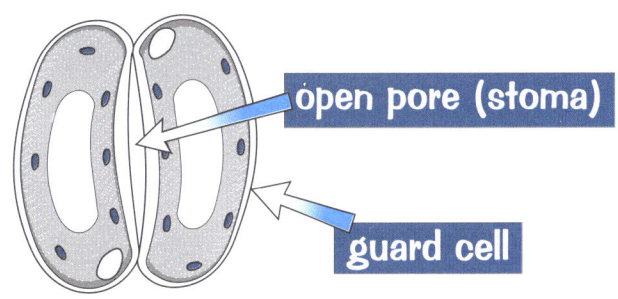

a) To bend and open the pore (stoma), guard cells must take up water from their surrounding cells.

    i) What process is involved when water *enters* the guard cells?

    ii) *Explain why* this process happens.

b) Gases can move through the stoma.

    i) Name *two gases* that can enter leaves through the pore.

    ii) What is the name of the *process* when molecules move in this way?

Diffusion and Osmosis

Q8) By pushing a cork-borer into a cut potato, two identical cylinders of potato were obtained. One cylinder was placed in a 20% sugar solution (a strong solution) and the other was placed in water.

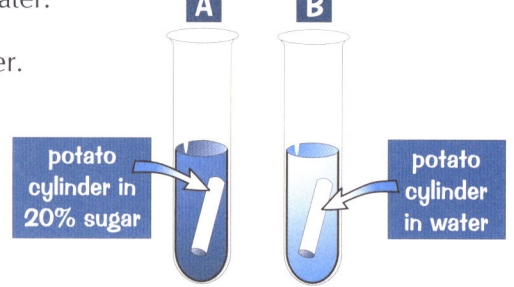

a) *Explain* what happens to the *length* of each potato cylinder.

b) In another experiment, a range of different concentration solutions were made, from pure water to 20% sugar. It was noticed that the cylinder in one of the middle test tubes *did not change* length. Explain this result.

Q9) *An amoeba is a single-celled organism found in pond water. Water from the pond continually enters the body of the amoeba. To prevent the amoeba bursting, it has vacuoles that collect water and release it to the outside.*

a) By what *process* does water enter the amoeba?

b) *The pond water also contains the oxygen that the amoeba needs.*
   i) What is the *oxygen* needed for?
   ii) How does the amoeba get the *oxygen* it needs?

c) i) Name one waste product that would be harmful to the amoeba if it could not get rid of it.
   ii) By what process does this waste product get into the water?

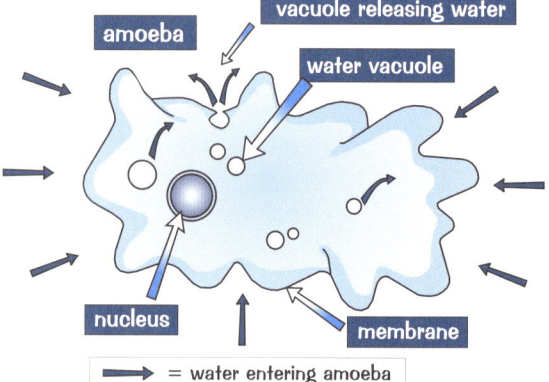

d) *Some amoebas live in the salty sea, but they do not have vacuoles. Why don't these organisms burst?*

Q10) *Joseph's mother showed him how she makes fruit salad. She cut fruit into a bowl and then sprinkled sugar all over the fruit. She placed the bowl in the fridge overnight. When she took out the bowl the following day, Joseph noticed that the fruit had liquid all around it. His mother then placed a few drops of food colouring in the middle of the bowl and again returned it to the fridge.*

a) i) What is the *liquid* in the bowl?
   ii) Where did it come from?
   iii) By what *process* did the liquid appear in the bowl?

b) Later that day, Joseph noticed that the food colouring had spread through much of the liquid. What *process* had occurred?

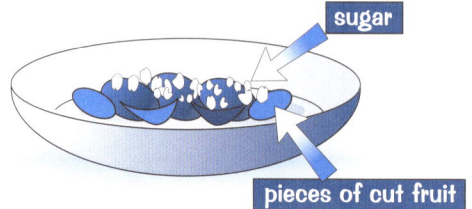

Top Tips: Things tend to **spread out** — that's all diffusion is. Osmosis is just a special case of this — when you're talking about **water molecules**, moving across a **partially permeable membrane**. They're both **random** processes — so the organism doesn't expend any energy. If the **concentration gradient** is in the wrong direction, it'll use **active transport** instead — which **does** need energy.

Section Two — Plants

Plant Structure

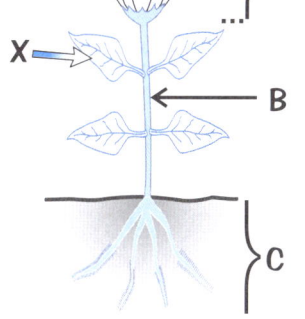

Q1) Look at the diagram on the right showing a typical plant. A plant is made up of four main parts.

   a) Label parts A, B and C.
   b) Give the name for the part of the plant marked with an X.
   c) Name the function of each part of the plant you have identified.

Q2) Leaves are important organs in the plant. The diagrams below show three different types of leaves (these are drawn to scale).

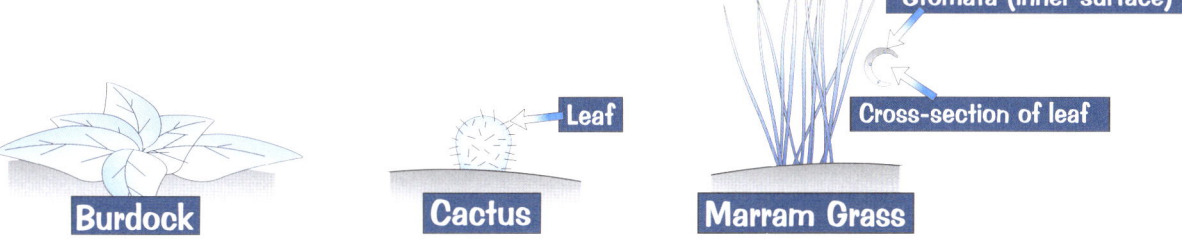

Fill in the table

Name of Plant	Possible type of habitat	Leaf Adaptation	Reason for adaptation

Q3) The roots are the parts of the plant that are found below the ground.
   a) Give two functions of roots.
   b) How have roots adapted to increase their surface area?

Q4) Use the words to fill in the spaces (the same word may be used more than once).

   flower   leaves   mineral salts   roots
   seeds   stem   water   xylem

Plants can be divided into three parts; the _____, the stem and leaves, and the _____ under the ground. The roots hold the plant firmly in the ground. They also absorb _____ with dissolved _____ _____ from the soil. The water travels in the _____ cells to different parts of the plant. The _____ has the function of holding the plant upright. This helps the leaves to capture more light. The _____ are organs responsible for making food.

Top Tips: You need to know the names of the various bits and what they do as well. It helps to think of the functions and which bits of the plant carry them out. Try these — storage, reproduction, anchorage, growth, support, and transport of food and water.

Leaf Structure

Q1) The diagram opposite shows a section across a leaf.

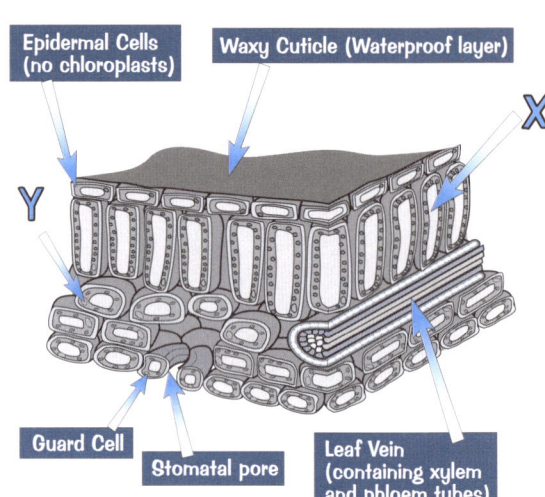

a) i) Give two functions of a leaf vein.
   ii) Name the cells carrying out each function.

b) i) What name is given to the pores in the leaf?
   ii) What controls the size of the pores?
   iii) Why are there more pores on the underside of a leaf?

c) i) Give the name for cell X.
   ii) What is the main function of this cell?
   iii) Give one way in which this cell is adapted for its function.

d) i) Give the name for cell Y.
   ii) These cells are rounded, creating large air spaces between them. Why is this useful for the leaf?

e) What is the function of the waxy cuticle?

Q2) Most plants have more pores on the lower surface of their leaves.

a) Water lilies have more pores on their upper surface. Give a reason for this.

b) Name a gas that the lily needs for photosynthesis.

c) From the diagram, describe one adaptation of the water lily for photosynthesis.

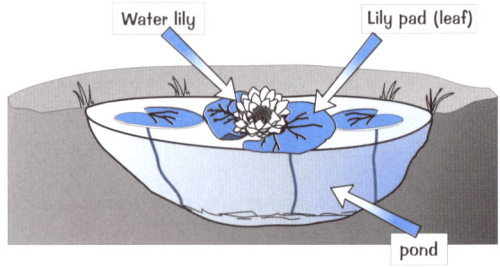

Q3) Greenfly sit on leaves and pierce leaf cells with their mouthparts. They use their hollow mouthparts to extract food from the transport cells in the leaf. If a lot of greenfly are feeding on a plant, the plant can start to die.

a) What part of the leaf do greenfly pierce?
b) What type of cells do they take food from?
c) Give the name of the food the greenfly are taking.
d) In which cells is this food made?

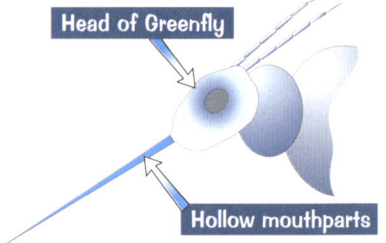

Q4) Match the statement with the correct part of a leaf, for example **A) — ii)** or **B) — ii)**.

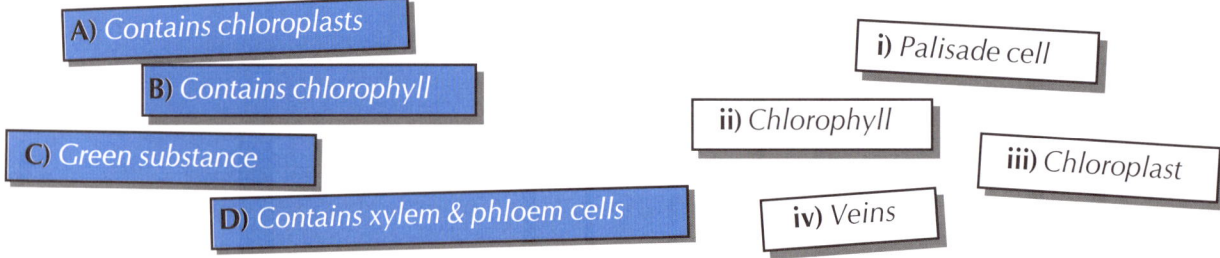

A) Contains chloroplasts
B) Contains chlorophyll
C) Green substance
D) Contains xylem & phloem cells

i) Palisade cell
ii) Chlorophyll
iii) Chloroplast
iv) Veins

Section Two — Plants

Leaf Structure

Q5) Below is a cross-section of a marram grass leaf. Marram grass lives on sand dunes, where it is windy and there is a shortage of water.

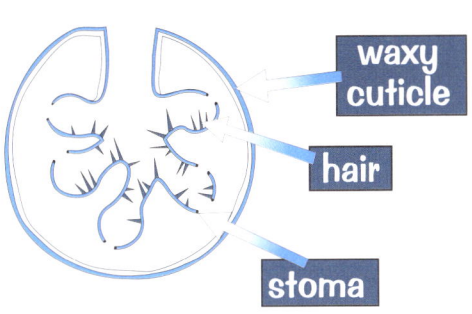

a) What does the waxy cuticle do?

b) i) How does the position of the stomata help this plant?

ii) Why are there no stomata on the outer surface of the leaf?

c) Explain the function of the hairs on the inner surface of the leaf.

Banksia marginata is an Australian shrub. It is found in dry conditions and has sunken stomata.

d) Explain how having sunken stomata will affect gaseous exchange in the plant, and why this would be an advantage to the plant.

e) How would you expect the waxy cuticle of marram grass and *Banksia marginata* to be different from that of a plant that is found in damp places?

Q6) A variegated geranium has both green and white areas on its leaves.

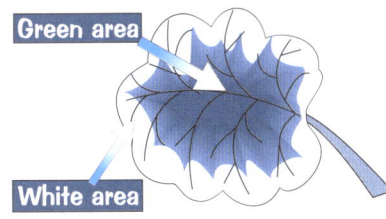
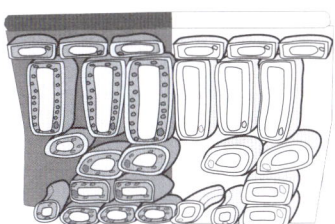

a) If the diagram were not shaded, how could you tell which cells were the green cells?

b) What substance makes these cells green?

Q7) Complete the blanks with these words:

    carbon dioxide   chlorophyll   chloroplasts   guard cells   mesophyll
    palisade   stomata   veins   waxy cuticle   xylem

The leaf is the organ where food is made in a plant. Its _____ cells are packed closely together. These cells have many _____ which contain the green substance _____. This substance absorbs light. The spongy _____ is so called because it has many air spaces. _____ diffuses easily through these spaces to get inside the leaf cells. To make sugar, water is also needed. Water is transported to the leaf cells by _____ vessels. The transporting vessels are inside the _____ of the leaves. To prevent water loss, the surface of the leaf is covered by a _____. To allow gases to move in and out of the leaf, there are many _____, mainly on the lower surface. The size of the stomatal pore is controlled by the _____.

Top Tips: Knowing your leaf structure boils down to knowing the various cell types. There's only a few — but you've really got to know their functions and how they carry them out. Practise drawing them — so you can recognise them when they come up in the Exam.

Section Two — Plants

Transpiration

Q1) The diagram shows how water is lost from a pore in a leaf.

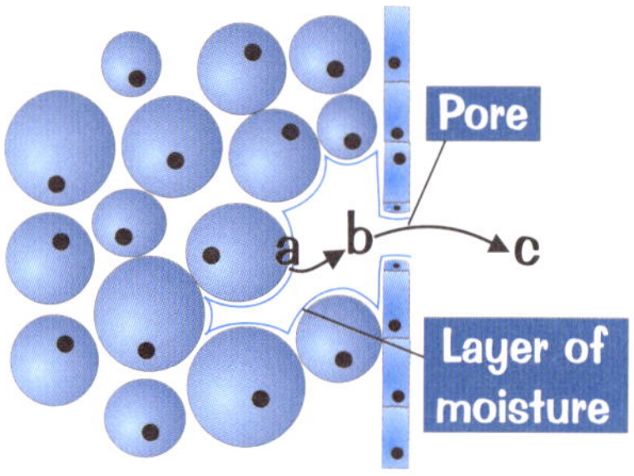

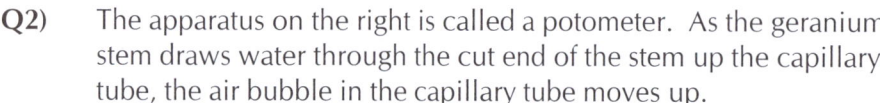

a) Give the name of the process that occurs
   i) between a and b.   ii) between b and c.
b) What name is given to the pore?
c) What controls the size of the pore?
d) Which surface of the leaf has more pores? Give a reason for your answer.

Q2) The apparatus on the right is called a potometer. As the geranium stem draws water through the cut end of the stem up the capillary tube, the air bubble in the capillary tube moves up.

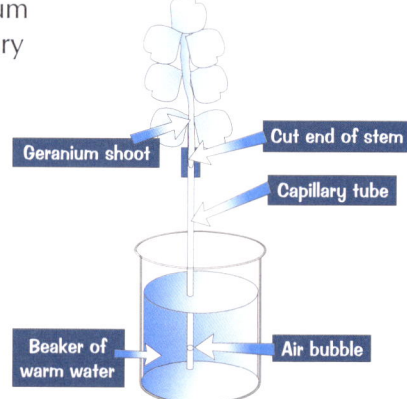

a) Explain why the amount of water lost from the leaves is not the same as the amount of water taken up by the stem.
b) By what process is water lost from the surface of the leaves?
c) What type of cells does the water travel through to reach the leaves from the stem?
d) What else is transported in these cells?

Q3) In most plants, the stomata are more open during the day and more closed during the night. In cacti (hot desert plants), the reverse is true.

a) Give a possible reason for this.
b) Explain exactly how the size of the stomata are controlled.

Q4) The table below gives the number of stomata found in five different species of plant. One of these plants is Oat, where the leaves are upright. This means that there is no clear lower and upper leaf surface.

a) i) Which letter represents the oat plant?
   ii) Give one reason for your answer.
b) Give two functions of stomata.
c) i) Name an atmospheric factor that affects one of the functions.
   ii) Explain your answer.

Plant	Average number of stomata (per cm²)	
	Lower Surface	Upper Surface
A	2 300	2 500
B	16 100	5 100
C	46 100	0
D	26 300	6 000
E	1 900	5 900

Q5) The graph below shows what effect the size of the stomata has on the rate of transpiration.

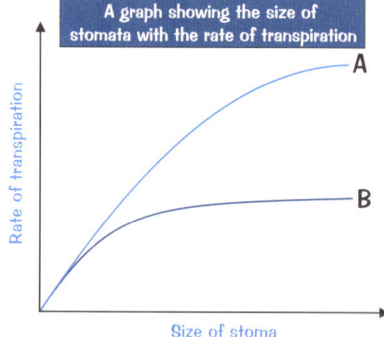

One curve shows what happens in still air and the other in moving air.

a) Which curve represents a plant that is surrounded by still air?
b) How does the difference in air movement affect the rate of transpiration?
c) Which curve resembles more closely what happens on a hot day? Explain your answer.

Section Two — Plants

Transpiration

Q6) A piece of blue cobalt chloride paper was stuck to the upper and lower surfaces of a leaf. Cobalt chloride turns pink as it becomes moist.

a) Which surface will turn the cobalt chloride pink first? Explain your answer.
b) What do we call the process by which water is lost from the leaf?
c) From where did the plant obtain the water that is lost from the leaf?
d) Give one condition that slows down water loss from leaves.

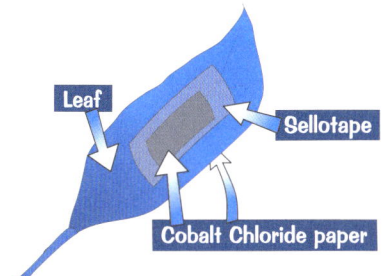

Q7) This experiment shows water being lost from a porous clay pot.

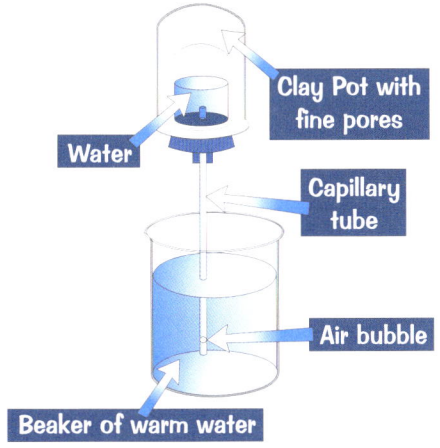

a) What is the name of the process by which the porous pot loses water?
b) State how each of these processes affect the amount of water lost from the porous pot:
   i) Increased humidity.   ii) Greater light intensity.
   iii) Higher temperature.   iv) Less wind.
c) What feature does the pot share with the leaf that allows it to lose water?
d) How does this feature differ between the pot and the leaf?

Q8) Before a "cutting" grows roots, it is common to remove most of its leaves and cover it with a plastic bag.
a) Why are the leaves removed?
b) Why is a plastic bag placed around a cutting?

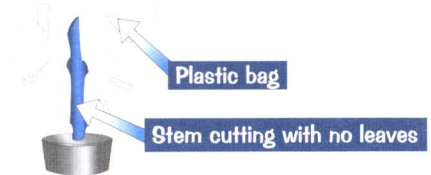

Q9) Complete the blanks with these words.

cuticle   evaporation   greater   guard   leaves   lower   stomata
temperature   thicker   transpiration   xylem   wilt

Plants need to lose water by _____ in order to draw water through the plant. Streams of water travel through the _____ from the roots to the _____. The leaves have pores, called _____. It is through the pores that most water is lost. The size of the pores is controlled by _____ cells. Normally, a plant has more pores on the _____ surface of its leaves. Factors which affect _____ also affect the rate of water loss from the leaves. Factors include light, _____, air movements and the amount of moisture in the air. The drier the air is, the _____ is the loss of water from the leaves. If this loss were allowed to continue, the plant would _____. Leaves are covered by a layer of waxy _____ to prevent too much water being lost. Plants found in drier habitats generally have a _____ waxy layer.

Top Tips: Transpiration isn't the same as evaporation: transpiration is the movement of a whole water column through a plant — it doesn't just happen at a surface. But evaporation draws the water up so they're affected by the same things — make sure you can list them.

Section Two — Plants

Transport Systems in Plants

Q1) On the right is a cross-section of a stem, showing the transport tissue of plants.

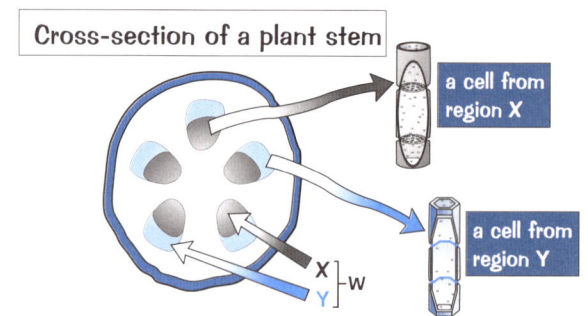

a) i) Give the name for tissue X.
   ii) What is the function of this tissue?
b) i) Give the name for tissue Y.
   ii) What is the function of this tissue?
c) What is the name for W?

Q2) High temperatures kill cells. When a steam jacket is placed around a stem of a tree, that part of the tree is heated to a high temperature. When this was done to a tree, it was noted that sugar no longer moved through the tree, but water did.

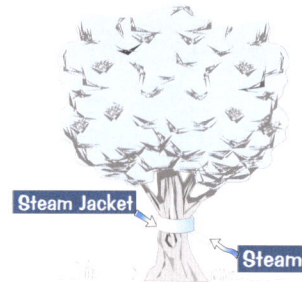

a) What does this tell us about:
  i) the phloem cells?   ii) the xylem cells?

b) In autumn it was found that the area above the steam jacket swelled. Explain why this happened.

c) What time of the year would you expect the area below the steam jacket to swell? Explain your answer.

Q3) The diagram below right shows xylem and phloem cells.

a) Explain why the ends of phloem cells are perforated.
b) Explain why the xylem cells are hollow.
c) Food is made in the leaves. What parts of the plant is it transported to?
d) Give two uses of the transported food.
e) What does the transported food consist of?

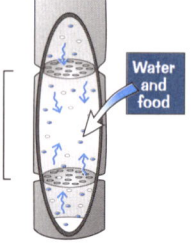
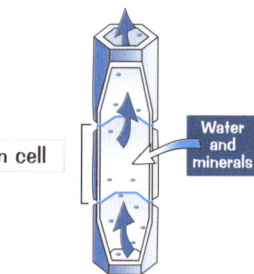

Q4) As grapes mature, they fill up with water and sugar. At the end of their growing season, grapes may lose some of their sugar back into the plant.

The phloem vessels lie just under the bark of the stalk which holds the bunch of grapes. Grape growers sometimes remove the bark and phloem from the stalks holding bunches of grapes. This is done before the end of the growing season.

a) Why is the phloem removed from the stalk?
b) Why is the xylem kept intact?
c) Over-watering can damage the grapes. Explain what might happen.

Q5) The carbon dioxide in the flask shown contains radioactive carbon.

a) What process uses the carbon dioxide?
b) What substance does the radioactive carbon end up in the leaves?
c) What cells in the stem will radioactive material first appear in?
d) Name the substance found in the stem cells that is radioactive.
e) Name one other structure that the radioactive material will appear in.

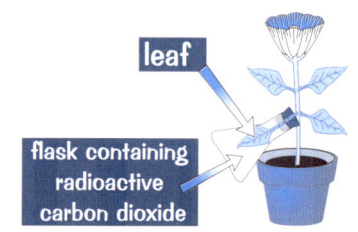

Section Two — Plants

Transport Systems in Plants

Q6) The diagram opposite shows the movement of water through a plant.

a) Name the process involved in moving the water from:
   i) a to b   ii) f to g
b) What carries the water from d to f ?
c) What is the name of the spaces in the leaf that allow water to escape to the atmosphere?
d) What is the name given to the column of water that runs from the roots to the leaves?

Q7) Xylem cells transport water to different parts of a plant. These cells have a substance called lignin in their cell walls. Lignin makes structures waterproof and strong. The insides of xylem cells break down and the cells become empty tubes.

a) How does lignin help xylem cells to carry out their function of transporting water?
b) Give one feature of the xylem cells that enables water to move easily from one cell to the next?
c) What do the xylem cells carry besides water?

Q8) The word xylem comes from the Greek word for wood. Wesley placed one end of a wooden pole he found in his shed in coloured water. He noticed that the colour travelled up the wood.

a) What does this tell us about the movement of water in xylem cells?
b) i) What is the name of the other type of transporting tissue?
   ii) What does this tissue transport?
   Xylem cells are found throughout the plant. All parts of the plant need water. This includes the petals of the flower.
c) What do you think will happen if you cut off a white carnation flower and place the stalk end in red water?

Q9) Aphids use their mouthparts to pierce stems in order to get food.

a) What food substance would you expect the aphid to be feeding off?
b) What cells do the mouthparts pierce to extract the liquid?

Q10) Complete the blanks with the words provided:

cytoplasm, living, minerals, photosynthesis, respiration, starch, stem, stream, sugar, transpiration, vascular, xylem.

Plants have transport systems. The _____ tissue transports water from the roots to the _____ and leaves. The column of water that runs from the roots to the leaves is called the transpiration _____. Water loss from the leaves is called _____ and causes water to be pulled up through the plant. The water contains _____ from the soil. Phloem tissue carries dissolved food, such as _____ from the leaves, where it is made by _____, to the rest of the plant. The food is used for _____, making materials for cells and to produce _____ which is held in storage organs. The xylem and phloem cells are found in the _____ bundles of the plant. Xylem cells are dead and have no _____. Phloem cells on the other hand are _____.

Top Tips: Phloem, sounds like 'flow-'em' — so must transport stuff downhill. Whether it's going up or down the plant tells you what's being transported. And the phloem cells (alive) are nearer the surface of the stem (closer to the oxygen they need) than the dead xylem cells.

Section Two — Plants

Photosynthesis

Q1) The diagram shows what the leaves need to make food.

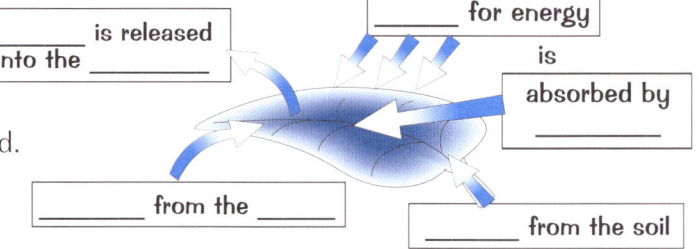

a) Complete the labels on the diagram.
b) Name the process involved in making food.
c) What is the name of the food produced?

Labels on diagram: _____ is released into the _____ ; _____ for energy ; _____ is absorbed by _____ ; _____ from the _____ ; _____ from the soil

Q2) A variegated plant (its leaves have two colours) was placed in a dark cupboard for 48 hours to use up all of its starch. One of its leaves was then covered with a strip of black card across the middle. The plant was placed in the light for 24 hours. The leaf was then tested for starch.

a) Shade in the areas on the unlabelled leaf to show where the starch was found.

b) i) What indicator substance is used to test a leaf for starch?

   ii) What colour does the indicator turn when starch is present?

c) Why was it necessary to get rid of the starch from the leaves?

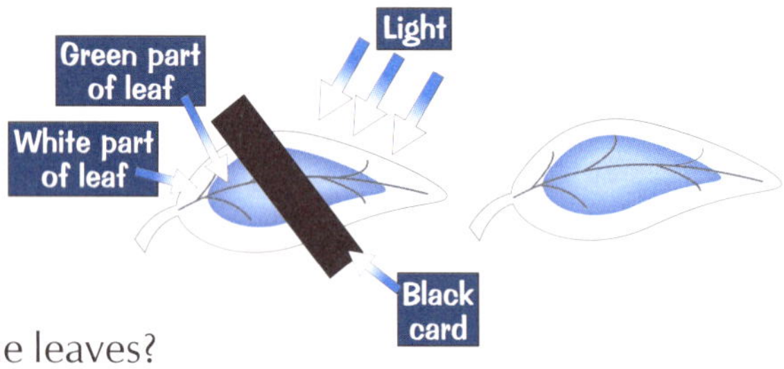

d) Tick or write out the correct conclusion(s) that can be drawn from this experiment.

... carbon dioxide is needed for photosynthesis   ... chlorophyll is needed for photosynthesis
... light is needed for photosynthesis   ... water is needed for photosynthesis

Q3) Complete the table.

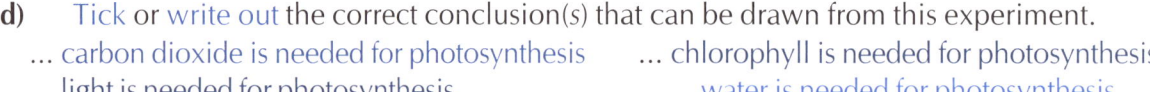

	Photosynthesis	Respiration
Raw materials used		
End products		
Purpose of process		

Q4) The graph shows the exchange of carbon dioxide between a plant and its surroundings.

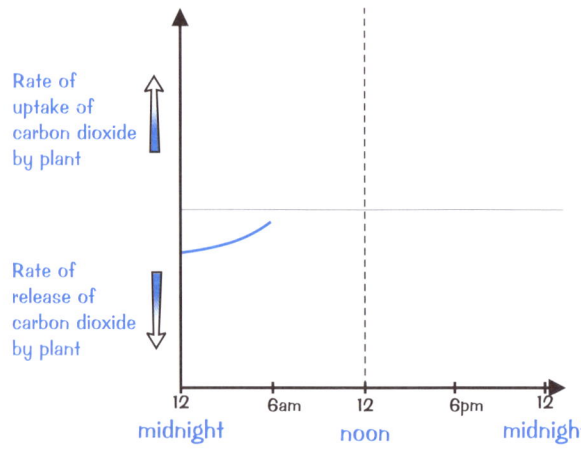

a) Why is the rate of release of carbon dioxide into the atmosphere declining between midnight and 6am?

b) Complete the curve to show what happens between 6am and 6pm.

c) Place an X on the graph to show when the rate of carbon dioxide released is exactly balanced by the rate of carbon dioxide absorbed.

Section Two — Plants

Photosynthesis

Q6) Adam set up a bottle garden. Inside the bottle he grew some plants and placed a butterfly he caught in his garden. He knew the butterfly fed on sugar, so he placed a dish of sugary water inside the bottle. Just before going on a two week holiday to Corfu, Adam caught another butterfly. He placed this butterfly in another bottle, but he did not have time to add the plants. The diagrams show what he saw when he returned from holiday.

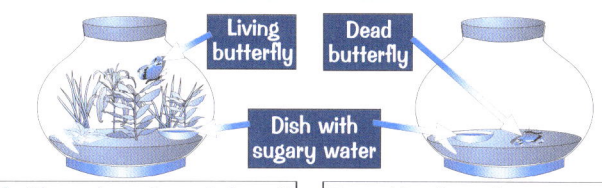

a) Why did the butterfly in the second bottle die?

b) Besides its droppings, what does the first butterfly produce that will help the plants to grow?

Q7) A plant was left in a dark cupboard for 48 hours to make sure it had no starch in its leaves. The plant was then set up in a bell jar as shown in the diagram. The apparatus was then left for 24 hours and the leaves tested with iodine. Place ticks in the correct boxes.

Leaf	Turns blue/black	Has starch
A		
B		
C		
D		

Q8) Complete the following equation for photosynthesis:

a) with words   b) with chemical symbols

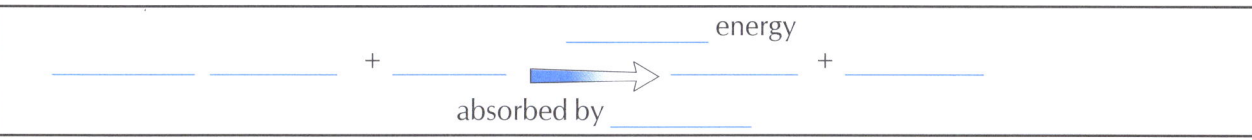

Q9) The graph shows the effect of different conditions on the rate of photosynthesis.

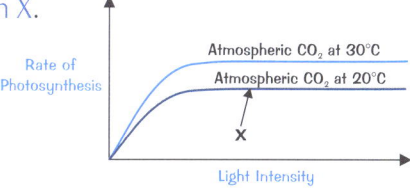

a) Name a factor that limits the rate of photosynthesis at position X.

b) Draw a curve on the graph to show what would happen if the amount of carbon dioxide was increased to a much higher level (at 30°C).

c) What is a limiting factor?

Q10) Four test tubes were set up as shown in the diagram, with hydrogencarbonate added to the tubes as an indicator. The table records the colour of the hydrogencarbonate in each tube after one hour.

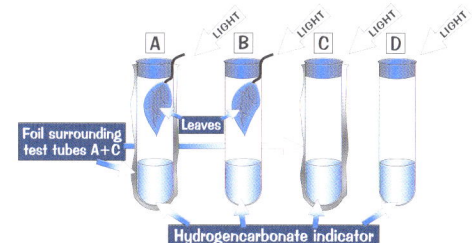

RESULTS

Tube	Colour of hydrogencarbonate indicator after one hour
a	Yellow
b	Purple
c	Orange
d	Orange

a) Which tubes act as controls?

b) i) What substance do you think made the indicator turn yellow in test tube a?

ii) What process produces this substance?

c) i) Why do you think the indicator turned purple in test tube b?

ii) What process is occurring in test tube b that does not occur in test tube a?

Top Tips: Photosynthesis is a basic life process you'll need to know for the Exam — equations and all. Don't forget the differences between photosynthesis and respiration, as this often crops up. Remember the structures in the leaf — and what photosynthesis has to do with transpiration.

Section Two — Plants

Food and Plants

Q1) The diagram on the right shows some of the uses of glucose by plants.

a) i) Name five structures that store food in plants.
  ii) Give the name of the food each structure stores.
b) Why are storage substances insoluble?
c) Fruits are swollen with sugar and water. How does this help the plant?
d) Name the process that makes glucose.
e) Energy can be released from glucose. What is the name of this process?
f) Name two substances that are made from glucose.

Q2) A student has made two models of a cell. One has starch in it, the other contains glucose. Both are placed in test tubes containing pure water.

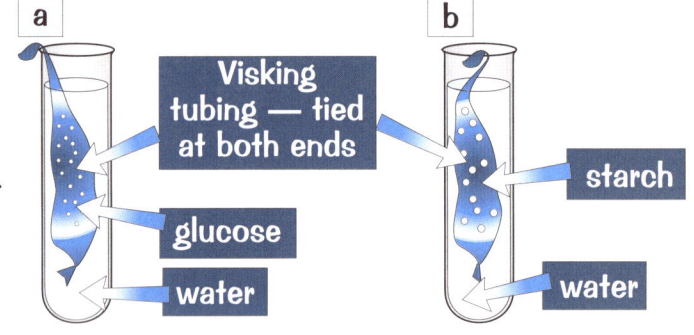

a) Which model becomes swollen?
b) What is the name of the process that causes the 'cell' to swell?
c) Explain why the 'cell' swells.
d) Give one advantage of cells storing starch.
e) Name one other storage substance.
f) Name an organ whose cells could be represented by model 'b'.

Q3) Complete the spaces with these words.

    active   cellulose   glucose   insoluble   larger   lipids
    proteins   respiration   sucrose   starch   stems

When photosynthesis takes place, _____ is produced. Glucose can be converted into the storage substance _____. This substance is _____, therefore stopping cells from swelling with water. Starch is stored in the roots, _____ and leaves. Glucose is changed into _____ before being stored in fruits. In seeds, though, glucose is often made into _____. Amino acids can also be made from this sugar. The amino acids can be joined together to form _____. Glucose can be turned into _____, found in cell walls. This strengthens the walls and helps to give plants support. The release of energy from glucose is called _____. Energy is used to build smaller molecules into _____ molecules. It is also needed for _____ transport. This enables minerals to move into the roots of a plant against a concentration gradient.

Top Tips: Nothing too complicated — just learn all the ways plants use the glucose formed in photosynthesis. Think of the substances it gets converted into, how they are used, and where this happens. The important ones are — starch, sucrose, lipids, cellulose and amino acids.

Hormones in Plants

Q1) Mrs Smith, the science teacher, showed the class a demonstration. Which of the students' ideas correctly explain what happened?

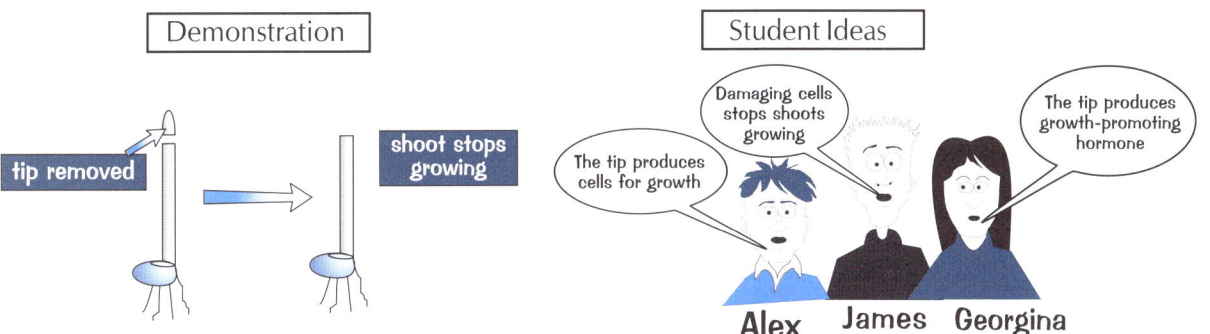

Q2) A young broad bean seedling was placed in the ground sideways.

a) i) In which direction does the root grow?
   ii) What causes the root to grow in this direction?
   iii) What stimuli affect the direction of root growth?

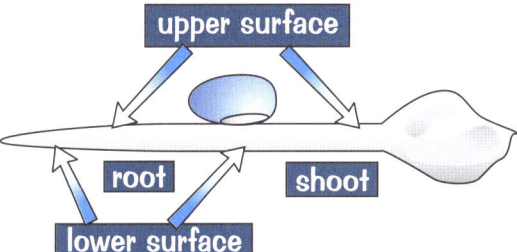

b) i) In which direction does the shoot grow?
   ii) What causes the shoot to grow in this direction?
   iii) What stimuli affect the direction of shoot growth?

c) What name do we give to the main chemical controlling the growth of the shoots and roots?

d) What effect does this chemical have on the cells of the shoot?

Q3) Complete the blanks with these words (words may be used more than once).

auxin   bushier   fruits   gravity   growth
hormones   moisture   roots   seedless   shoots

Plant _____ grow towards the stimulus of light and against the force of _____.
The plant _____ grow towards the stimulus of gravity and _____. Plants produce
chemical _____ to coordinate and control growth. The shoot tip produces the
hormone _____. This hormone causes shoot cells to elongate. When unidirectional
light shines on one side of the plant, the auxin accumulates on the other side.
This promotes uneven _____ in shoots, bending the shoot towards the light.
Rooting powders contain the same hormones. These will promote _____ to grow
on shoot cuttings. Unpollinated flowers can be treated with hormones to produce
_____ fruits, such as grapes. The ripening of _____ can also be regulated with
hormones. Broad-leaved selective weedkillers, such as 2-4 D, also contain hormones.
These work by disrupting the normal _____ of broad-leaved plants. The hormones
produced in the shoot tip inhibit side shoot growth. Removing the tips of shoots encourages
the growth of _____ plants.

Hormones in Plants

Q4) Complete the boxes in the table.

Chemical Involved	How is it used?	What effect does it have?
Rooting hormone		
	Sprayed over broad-leaved weed plants	
		Produces fruit without any pips

Q5) Tony decided that he was going to grow the straightest corn shoots possible.

a) What could he do to corn seedlings to make them grow straight?

b) Two weeks after growing the seedlings, Tony noticed that the shoots were growing to the left.

Give a possible reason for this, and explain how Tony could make the seedlings grow straight again.

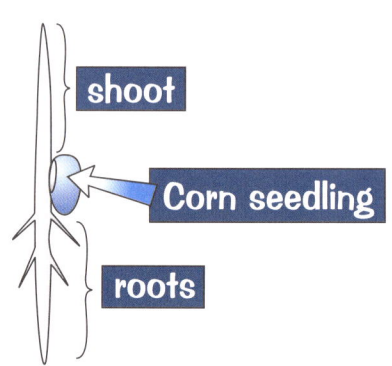

Q6) The diagram shows four boxes. Each of the boxes is placed in the same uniform environment, and has one cress plant placed inside it.

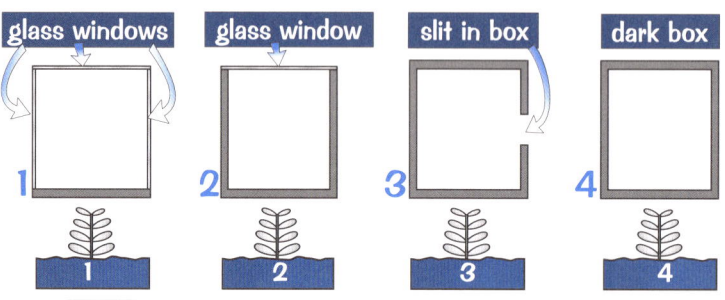

Cress plants before being placed in their respective boxes

a) Redraw the boxes, showing inside each the appearance of the cress plant after a few days.
b) For each box explain the pattern of growth you have drawn.

Q7) Complete these sentences by choosing the correct word or words from inside the brackets:

a) If growth hormones are applied to (pollinated /unpollinated) flowers, seedless fruits are produced.
b) Selective weedkillers act on plants by (disrupting /stopping) the growth of the plant.
c) Cutting the tips of plants makes them grow (bushier /taller).
d) Fruits can be (made to ripen /made to stay unripe) when they are sprayed with hormones.

Top Tips: Shoots and roots grow in response to **light** and **gravity**, pretty obvious — but you must be able to **name** the responses and how **hormone levels** cause them. Remember growth hormones are used **commercially** — for questions on the **applications** of science.

Section Three — Human Biology Part One

The Digestive System

Q1) One of the purposes of the digestive system is to break down food.

Where is food first broken down?

Describe how is it broken down. What else happens to food here?

Q2) The diagrams below show the major parts of the digestive system.

D shows the mouth, salivary glands and the oesophagus.
Identify the other labelled parts, and write down their letter and name.

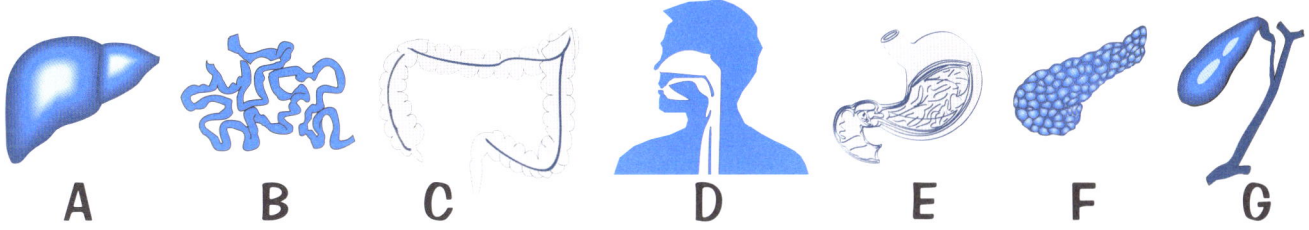

A B C D E F G

Q3) These are the parts of the digestive system that food actually goes through.

Match each part to its correct function:

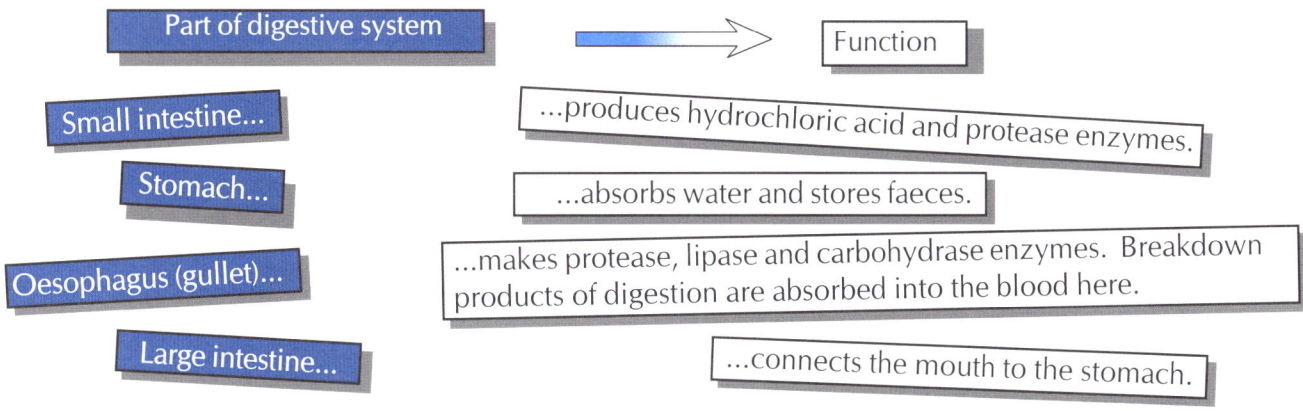

Part of digestive system → Function

- Small intestine...
- Stomach...
- Oesophagus (gullet)...
- Large intestine...

...produces hydrochloric acid and protease enzymes.

...absorbs water and stores faeces.

...makes protease, lipase and carbohydrase enzymes. Breakdown products of digestion are absorbed into the blood here.

...connects the mouth to the stomach.

Write down the parts of the digestive system with their function in the order they would work to digest some food.

Q4) Identify these parts of the of the digestive system:

a) Which parts of the digestive system does food *not* pass through?
b) Which parts of the digestive system are *muscular*?

The Digestive System

Q5) Sometimes when we eat, the food "goes down the wrong way", and we end up coughing.

What is the "wrong way"? What is the "right way"? What makes food go down the "right way"?

Q6) Look at the diagram below. It shows food moving through the inside of the oesophagus.

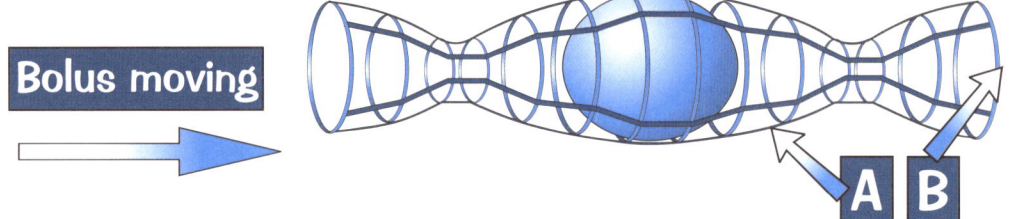

a) The labels A and B point to two types of muscle. Name A and B.

b) What is the name given to the muscular process that forces food through the oesophagus and intestines?

c) Explain how the mechanism named in **b)** works. Mention muscles in your answer.

Q7) The stomach produces hydrochloric acid and protease enzymes.

What else does the stomach do to help digest food?

Q8) The internal surface of the small intestine has around five million finger-like projections, each about 1mm long.

a) What are these "fingers" called?
b) *The diagram on the right shows one of these "fingers".* Copy the diagram and name the parts labelled A, B and C.
c) What is the advantage of not having a smooth internal surface in the small intestine?
d) In adults, the small intestine can be up to 6m long, and the large intestine 1.5m long. How do they fit inside the body and why are they so long?

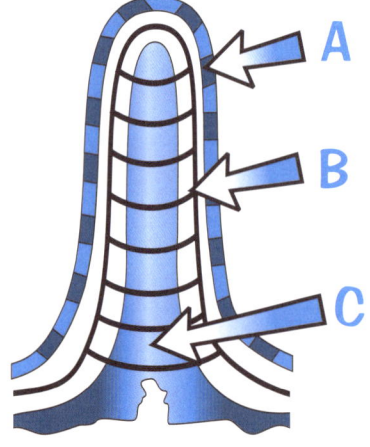

Top Tips:
You may be asked to label a diagram of the digestive system in the exam, so you do need to know the whole thing. Remember how the structures of the parts help them do their jobs efficiently. If you can answer all these questions you're well on your way to good marks, if not, try, try and try again. As for enzymes, read on...

Section Three — Human Biology Part One

Digestive Enzymes

Q1) What is a catalyst? What is an enzyme?

Q2) What is digestion? What are digestive enzymes?

Q3) You need to know about three types of digestive enzymes. In the table below, the names of these enzymes, the substances they digest and the products that are made have all been muddled up. Write down the correct sentence for each enzyme.

carbohydrase		protein		fatty acids and glycerol
protease	catalyses the breakdown of	fat	into	sugar (maltose)
lipase		starch		amino acids

Q4) Gastric juice is added to food when it reaches the stomach. This juice contains an acid.

a) Name the acid secreted by the stomach.
b) Estimate the pH of the stomach contents, and give a reason for your answer.
c) Give two reasons why the stomach secretes this acid.

Q5) Use the diagram below to answer the following questions.

| salivary glands | oesophagus | stomach | small intestine | liver | pancreas | gall bladder | large intestine |

a) Which parts of the digestive system listed above produce carbohydrase enzymes?
b) Where in the digestive system is starch digested by carbohydrase enzymes?
c) What is likely to prevent digestion of starch by carbohydrase enzymes in the stomach?
d) Which parts of the digestive system produce protease enzymes?
e) Where in the digestive system is protein digested by protease enzymes?
f) Which parts of the digestive system produce lipase enzymes?
g) Where in the digestive system is fat digested by lipase enzymes?

Q6) It is difficult for lipase to digest fat. Enzymes work in solution, but fat does not dissolve in water. If fat can be broken up into smaller droplets, lipase can digest the fat more effectively.

a) Bile emulsifies fat. What does emulsify mean?
b) What happens to the surface area of fat when it is emulsified?
c) Explain why bile allows lipase to digest fats more effectively.

Q7) The diagram to the right is a flow chart for digestion.

Copy the diagram. Use your answers to Question **Q5) a)** to **g)** to complete it.

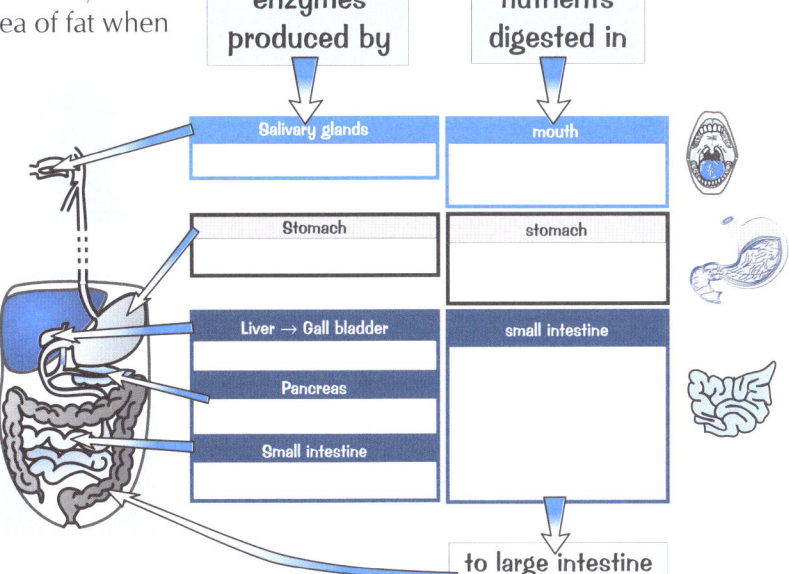

Your finished flow chart should show where each digestive enzyme is produced, and where each nutrient is digested.

Q8) Describe in words what happens to food after it enters the body. Mention where the nutrients are being digested, the names of the nutrients, the names of the digestive enzymes and where they are produced, and the products of digestion.

Top Tips: There's a lot to learn on these pages, including some strange long names. But don't be tempted to cut corners, because you really need to learn all this stuff. Go through bit by bit, and remember all the enzymes, where they come from and what they do.

Absorption of Food

Q1) Match each nutrient to its correct form when digested:

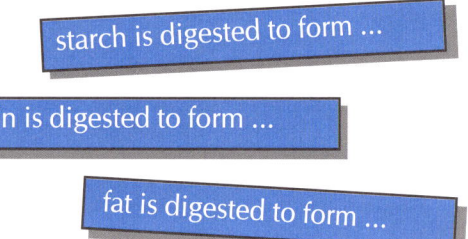

- starch is digested to form ...
- protein is digested to form ...
- fat is digested to form ...

- ... smaller molecules called fatty acids and glycerol
- ... smaller molecules called sugars
- ... smaller molecules called amino acids

Q2) A student was given a mixture of sand and sugar in a beaker. He was asked to separate the sand from the sugar. He decided to use the method shown in the diagrams below.

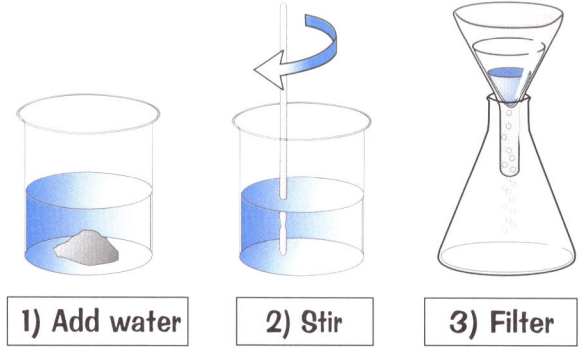

1) Add water   2) Stir   3) Filter

- **a)** What happens to the sand when the mixture is stirred?
- **b)** What happens to the sugar when the mixture is stirred?
- **c)** What happens to the sand when the mixture is filtered?
- **d)** What happens to the sugar when the mixture is filtered?
- **e)** Look at your answers so far. Explain what we mean by filtration — what kind of substances can be filtered and what kind cannot?

Q3) Make a table like the one below.

soluble	insoluble

- **a)** Put the substances in the box below into the correct columns in the table:

    amino acids   fat   protein   glycerol
    starch   sugar   fatty acids

- **b)** Which of these substances could be separated from water using filter paper? Explain your answer.
- **c)** What is wrong with the idea that the products of digestion are "filtered into the blood"?

Section Three — Human Biology Part One

Absorption of Food

Q4) A student did an experiment to show the movement of nutrients through the walls of a model intestine.

She made a watertight bag using Visking tubing, which is partially permeable. She put a mixture of starch suspension and sugar solution into the bag, and put the bag into a test tube containing distilled water (see diagram). At the beginning of the experiment she tested the contents of the bag and the water for starch and sugar. She did this again after 30 minutes.

Her results are shown in the table.

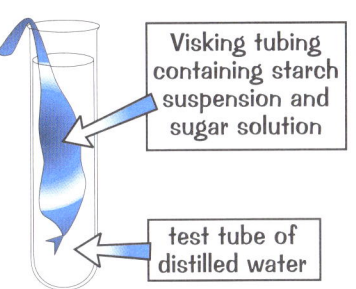

time (minutes)	contents of bag		water	
	starch	sugar	starch	sugar
0	✔	✔	✘	✘
30	✔	✔	✘	✔

a) How did sugar get into the tube of water during the experiment?
b) Why was there no starch in the water at the end of the experiment?
c) Suggest three ways that the student could speed up the process described in your answer to part **a)**

Q5) The products of digestion are absorbed into the bloodstream.

a) In which part of the digestive system does this happen?
b) Is dietary fibre absorbed?
c) The various digestive juices add greatly to the volume of water taken in by eating and drinking. In which part of the digestive system is excess water absorbed?
d) What other function does this part of the digestive system have?
e) What do you think will happen if too much water is absorbed?
f) What will happen if too little water is absorbed?

Q6) The following passage is about diffusion.

a) Choose the correct words from the underlined pairs and copy it out:

"Diffusion is the active / passive movement of particles up / down a concentration gradient from a high / low concentration to a high / low concentration. Diffusion through membranes is faster / slower when the membrane is thin and has a small / large surface area."

b) Explain how the structure of the small intestine allows for the efficient movement of the products of digestion through its wall. Include the words "villi" and "epithelium" in your answer. A labelled diagram may help.

c) Explain how the structure of the small intestine allows for the rapid absorption of the products of digestion into the bloodstream. Include the word capillaries in your answer.

Top Tips: Get easy extra marks by using the word "absorb". Protein is digested into amino acids so don't write, "protein is filtered into the blood". Write, "in the small intestine amino acids are absorbed into the bloodstream".

Food Tests

Q1) Iodine occurs as a shiny black solid at room temperature which can easily turn into a purple vapour. When dissolved in water with a little potassium iodide, iodine forms a brown solution.

   a) What type of nutrient can be detected using iodine solution?
   b) What colour change happens when iodine solution is added to this type of nutrient?

Q2) Iqbal wanted to see if the amylase in his saliva could digest starch to sugar. His teacher wasn't keen on the class spitting, even in the name of science, and supplied some ready-made amylase instead. He set up the experiment shown on the right.

   a) What should Iqbal see when he tests a sample of the starting mixture with iodine solution? Explain why he should get this result.

   b) After 20 minutes, Iqbal tested the mixture with Benedict's reagent. It turned red. What does this result mean?

   c) Iqbal's teacher wasn't sure that the experiment showed that starch had been digested to sugar. Two important tests had been missed out. What were these missing tests? What results would you expect to see if the starch had been digested to sugar?

   d) Iqbal repeated the experiment, and included the two missing tests. Unfortunately, his teacher was not convinced that the experiment showed that amylase was needed to digest starch. What control experiment should have been set up?

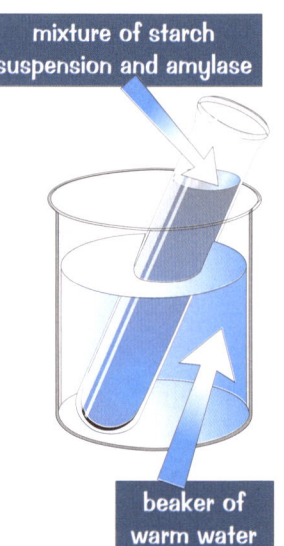

Q3) John has lost his instructions for the biuret food test. He can remember bits of it, but isn't sure of the details. He has written down as much as he can remember, but there are gaps. Copy John's instructions (below), replacing the dodgy splodges with the correct words.

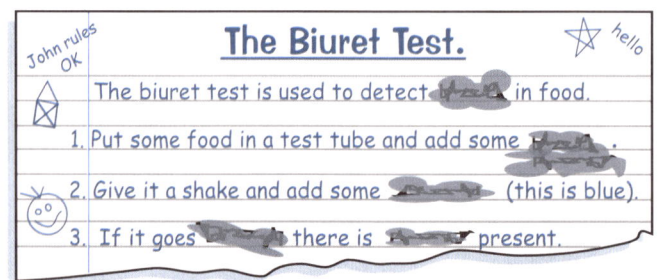

Top Tips: You do need to know the chemicals and conditions needed — and the expected results — for the four food tests on these pages. It's easy to guess the reaction is a colour change, but you've got to write down the start colour and the end colour.

Section Three — Human Biology Part One

Circulatory System

Q1) There are two main components of the circulatory system which maintain a continuous flow of blood around the body. What are they?

Q2) What are the main functions of the circulatory system? Why is it called the circulatory system?

Q3) The diagram below represents the main features of the circulatory system. Deoxygenated blood is represented by black lines, and oxygenated blood by white lines. The arrows show the direction of movement.
Using your knowledge and the clues in the diagram below, match the blood vessels labelled 1 — 3 and the organs labelled A — D to their correct names in the table.

Blood vessels	Number	Organs	Letter
Pulmonary vein		Intestines	
Aorta		Kidneys	
Vena cava		Liver	
		Lungs	

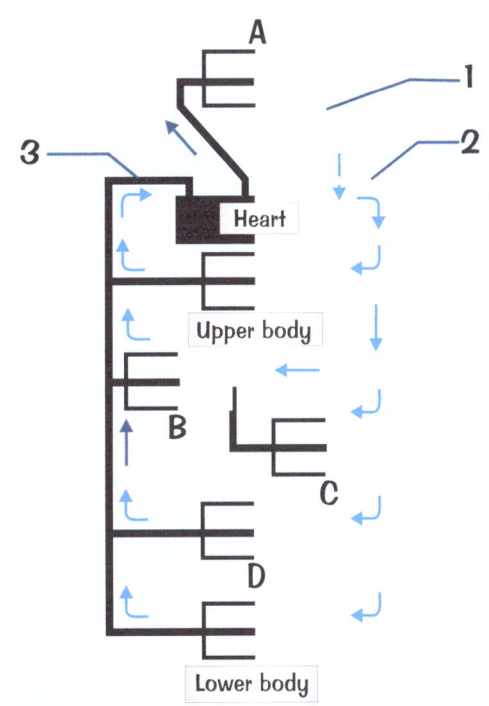

Q4) After the pulmonary artery leaves the heart, it branches into two (although this is not shown in the diagram). Why does it do this?

Q5) From the evidence in the diagram, and from what you have learnt so far what is the difference between an artery and a vein?
Name the vein which doesn't go directly back to the heart.

Q6) The smooth muscle in the walls of the arteries can contract, especially when you are under stress.
a) What is the effect on the diameter of the arteries when these smooth muscles contract?
b) Is this process called vasodilation or vasoconstriction?
c) Suggest the likely effects on the circulatory system as a result of prolonged stress.

Q7) Mr Spanner's car broke down, and he had to push it. The table shows what happened to his heart when he did this exercise.

	At rest	Pushing Car
Heart rate (beats per minute)	60	150
Stroke volume (cm^3)	100	120
Cardiac Output (cm^3 per minute)	6000	18000

a) What is the effect of exercise on the heart rate and stroke volume (volume pumped in one beat)?
b) Study the table carefully. What cardiac output would you expect if Mr Spanner had a heart rate of 100 beats per minute and a stroke volume of 110cm^3? Show your working out clearly.
c) Why do we need an increased cardiac output when we exercise?
d) Fit athletes often have very low resting heart rates. Suggest a reason why.

Top Tips: Plenty of facts on these pages, and you need to learn them all to get to grips with what the circulation system does. You must be prepared to name the blood vessels in diagrams — there's only one way, learn those odd names.

The Heart

Q1) The diagram on the right shows the human heart as a simple engineering drawing viewed from the front, rather than as a cross-section of a real heart.

Black arrows show the movement of deoxygenated blood, and the white arrows show the movement of oxygenated blood. Valves are shaded in grey.

a) How many chambers are there in the heart?
b) What are the upper chambers called?
c) What are the lower chambers called?
d) To which side of the heart does deoxygenated blood return from the body?
e) To which side of the heart does oxygenated blood return from the lungs?
f) There are four valves in the heart. What is their function?
g) The heart forms two pumps. What does each pump do?

Q2) You may be asked to label the components of the heart.

The diagram on the right represents a cross-section of the human heart drawn from the front. Identify each of the parts labelled A — D. (Your answers to question 1 should help you to do this.) Make a table to show your answers.

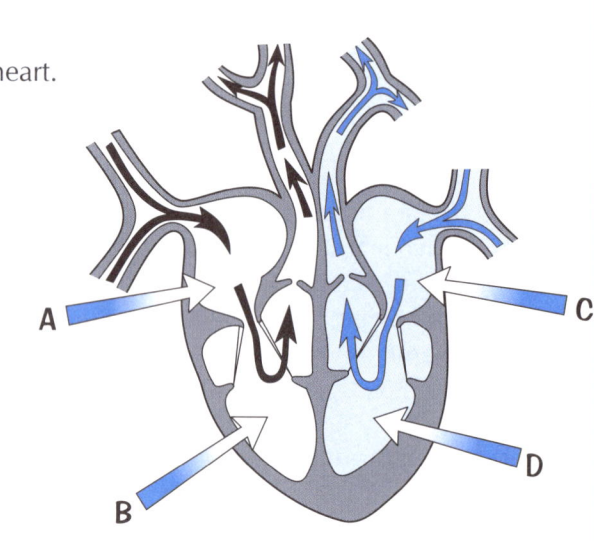

label	part of heart

Q3) You may also be asked to label the blood vessels going into and out of the heart.

The diagram on the right represents a cross-section of the human heart drawn from the front. Identify each of the blood vessels labelled 1 — 4.
Make a table to show your answers.

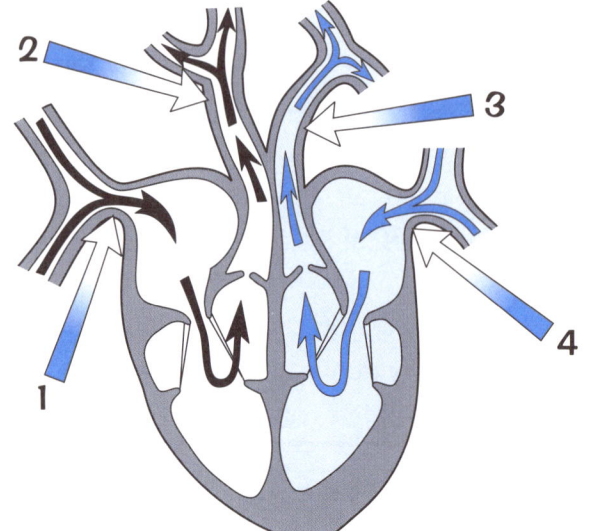

label	blood vessel

The Heart

Q4) Match each blood vessel to its correct function:

- the vena cava...
- the pulmonary vein...
- the pulmonary artery...
- the aorta...

- ...carries oxygenated blood to the rest of the body
- ...carries deoxygenated blood to the lungs
- ...carries oxygenated blood away from the lungs
- ...carries deoxygenated blood to the heart

Q5) The walls of the left side of the heart are generally thicker than those of the right side of the heart, and the walls of the ventricles are thicker than those of the atria.

a) Suggest reasons for these differences.

b) What type of tissue are the walls of the heart made from? Explain how you could work this out from your knowledge of the action of the heart.

c) Explain what could happen to the heart if a clot or a fatty plaque blocked a coronary artery.

d) Some babies are born with an abnormal opening joining their two ventricles. This is often called "blue baby syndrome" because their skin has a bluish tinge. Suggest a reason why their skin looks this colour.

Q6) Look at the sentences below. They all describe the way in which the right side of the heart pumps blood received from the body to the lungs. To make things tricky, they are muddled up.

- The atrium contracts to finish filling the ventricle with blood.
- The semi-lunar valves stop blood flowing backwards into the ventricle.
- The tricuspid valve shuts to stop blood going back into the atrium.
- The walls of the ventricle push the blood out of the heart through the pulmonary artery.
- The ventricle contracts, squeezing the blood inside.
- The vena cava brings blood from the body to the heart.
- While the right ventricle is relaxed, blood flows into it through the open tricuspid valve.
- Blood pours into the right atrium.

a) Write down the sentences in the correct order, starting with "The vena cava brings blood from the body to the heart" and finishing with "The semi-lunar valves stop blood flowing backwards into the ventricle".

b) Work out what must happen when the left side of the heart pumps blood received from the lungs to the rest of the body. Write down your answer with the same amount of detail as part **a)**.

c) Look at your answers to parts **a)** and **b)**. What events are common to the working of both sides of the heart? Draw a flow chart to show these common events in the correct order.

Top Tips: The heart is a **double pump**, and you need to remember why. You've got to learn the diagram of the heart, because **you're bound** to be asked to label one in the Exam — don't forget, it's drawn from the front, so the right side is on the left of the page.

Section Three — Human Biology Part One

Blood Vessels

Q1) Two sentences can be made from the one below by choosing the correct words from the pairs. Find them both:

"Arteries /veins carry blood to /from the heart at low /high pressure"

Q2) The diagrams below show cross-sections of arteries and veins. They are not drawn to scale.

a) Copy the diagrams and fill in the missing labels.

b) Describe the similarities and differences between the cross-sections of arteries and veins.

c) Explain how each blood vessel is adapted for its function. Your correct answer to question **Q1)** should help you.

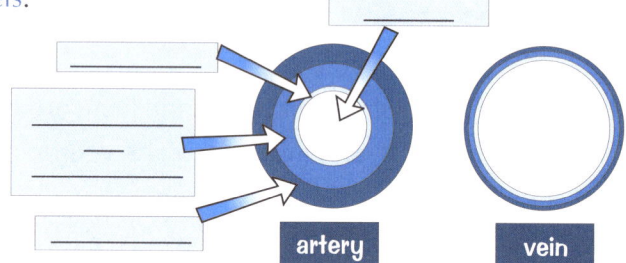

Q3) The diagrams on the right show pieces of artery and vein sliced along their length. They are not drawn to scale.

a) Copy the diagrams with the correct names of the blood vessels.
b) What is the name of the extra structure in diagram A?
c) What is the function of this structure?
d) Where else in the circulatory system can these structures be found?
e) Work out which way the blood must be flowing in vessel A and add an arrow to your diagram to show the direction of blood flow. Explain how you worked this out.
f) What keeps the blood moving in vessel A?
g) What keeps the blood moving in vessel B?
h) Look at your answers to parts **f)** and **g)**. What type of tissue is common to both answers?

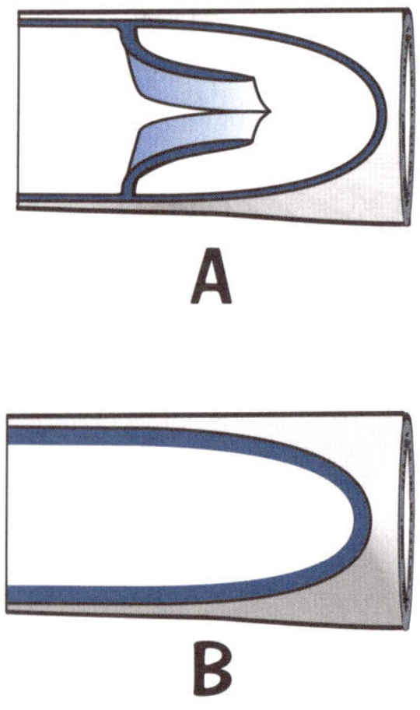

Q4) Arteries divide into narrower arterioles, which then divide into even smaller vessels, called capillaries (see diagram). These form dense networks between cells in tissues and organs.

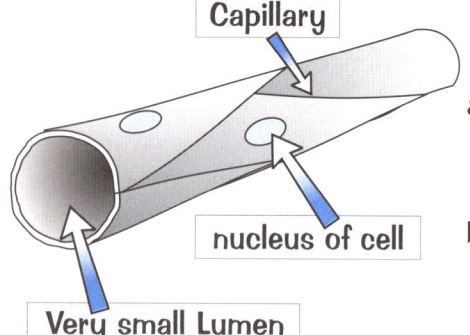

a) Although capillaries join arteries and veins together this is not their main function. What is their main function?

b) How does the structure of the capillary wall allow it to carry out this function effectively?

Section Three — Human Biology Part One

The Blood

Q1) The main components of blood are red cells, platelets, white cells and plasma. There are about 5 litres of blood in an average adult. We can take a test tube of blood, and put it in a centrifuge.
A centrifuge works a bit like a spin drier, and pulls the contents of the blood down towards the bottom of the test tube. The diagram on the right shows the sort of results you get if you do this.

a) Layer A is a straw-coloured liquid. What is its name?

b) What cells are found in layer B and C? What else will be found in layer B?

c) Looking at the diagram, estimate what proportion of blood is made up of cells.

Q2) There are about five million red blood cells in each 1mm^3 of blood. That's a lot!

a) What is the function of red blood cells?

b) Red blood cells have a shape called a biconcave disc (see diagram on the right). Explain how this shape helps a red blood cell to carry out its function.

c) Name the substance contained in red blood cells which allows them to carry oxygen. How does it work?

d) Red blood cells in humans and most other mammals have no nucleus. How does this feature help a red blood cell carry out its function effectively?

Q3) If a gas fire burns without enough ventilation, a colourless, odourless gas called carbon monoxide is formed due to a shortage of oxygen. This combines more strongly with haemoglobin than oxygen does, and is difficult to split from it.

Explain why carbon monoxide is so dangerous, and why gas fires should be checked regularly.

Q4) Platelets are small fragments of cells. Like red cells, they do not have a nucleus, but they are only about a third of the size of a red cell. There is one platelet to every 12 red cells in the blood. That's a lot too. What is the function of platelets?

Q5) There is one white cell to every 600 red cells in the blood. That's still quite a lot! White cells are involved in protecting the body against infection, and don't just occur in the blood.

a) Copy the diagram of a white cell. Complete the labels.

b) Give three ways in which white cells protect us against infection.

c) Where else in the body might you find white cells?

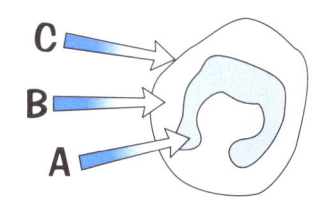

Q6) Plasma is important because the red cells, platelets and white cells are suspended in it.

One other important function of plasma is transport. What substances does plasma transport? Choose from the list below.

| of digestion | hormones | antitoxins | oxygen | water |
| urea | products | dissolved mineral salts | carbon dioxide | antibodies |

Q7) Draw a summary table to show the functions of each of the four components of blood.

Top Tips: Remember — **arteries** carry blood **from** the heart, **veins** carry blood **towards** the heart — whether the blood is blue or red. You need to know the **four** main components of blood on this page — what they **look like**, and what they **do**.

Section Three — Human Biology Part One

Lungs and Breathing

Q1) Copy and complete the passage below about the breathing system, choosing the correct words from the underlined pairs:

"The breathing system takes air /oxygen into and out of the body. This allows carbon dioxide /oxygen to pass from the air into the bloodstream, and carbon dioxide /oxygen to pass out of the bloodstream into the air".

Q2) The diagram to the right represents the thorax.

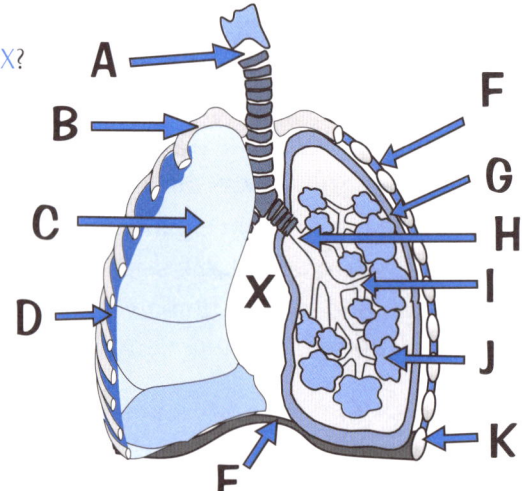

a) Which organ would normally be found in the space at X?
b) Match up the letters A — K with the correct labels given below:
- alveoli
- bronchiole
- bronchus
- diaphragm
- intercostal muscles
- lung
- pleural membranes
- rib
- trachea

Q3) a) What feature of the thorax protects the lungs from external damage?
  b) What feature of the thorax separates the lungs from the abdomen (lower part of the body)?
  c) What is the function of the pleural membranes?

Q4) When air is breathed in through the nose or mouth, it passes through parts of the breathing system to the alveoli.

Write down these parts of the breathing system in the correct order :

bronchioles   trachea   bronchi   alveoli

Q5) Answer these questions about air passages:

a) Give another name for the trachea.
b) The trachea has rings of cartilage around it. What is the purpose of these?
c) The trachea splits into smaller air passages called bronchi (one on its own is called a bronchus). How many bronchi are there in each lung?
d) What is a bronchiole?
e) What is an alveolus?

Lungs and Breathing

Q6) Look at the sentences below. They are all to do with movements of the thorax and diaphragm when we breathe in, but to make things tricky they have been muddled up.

- The pressure inside the thorax gets less than atmospheric pressure.
- Air is pushed into the lungs from outside to make the pressures equal.
- This pulls the ribcage upwards.
- The pressure inside the thorax goes down.
- This causes the diaphragm to flatten.
- The diaphragm muscles contract.
- The muscles between the ribs contract.
- The volume of the thorax increases.

a) Write down the sentences in the correct order, starting with "The muscles between the ribs contract" and finishing with "Air is pushed into the lungs from outside to make the pressures equal".

b) Work out what must happen when we breathe out.
Write down your answer with the same amount of detail as your answer to part a).

Q7) If you hiccup for more than 48 hours, you ought to see your doctor. Apparently, Charles Osbourne did a hiccup every 1½ seconds for nearly 70 years until February 1969, when he suddenly stopped! When you hiccup, air is inhaled very quickly.

What must your diaphragm be doing when you hiccup?

Q8) We each have over 300 million alveoli in the lungs. This ensures that we can pass enough oxygen into our bloodstream and remove the waste carbon dioxide from it by diffusion.

Explain how the structure of the alveoli allows this gas exchange between air and blood to happen quickly.

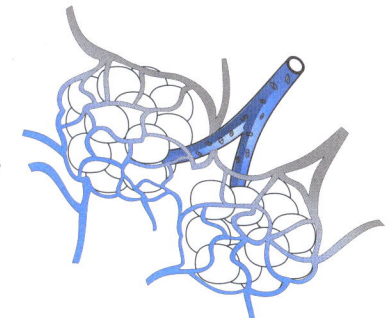

Q9) The table opposite should show the approximate percentages of oxygen, carbon dioxide and nitrogen in a person's inhaled and exhaled air.

Copy and complete the table placing the muddled percentages provided in their correct places.
The percentages are 0.04, 21, 78, 16, 4 and 78.

GAS	% in inhaled air	% in exhaled air
oxygen		
carbon dioxide		
nitrogen		

Q10) Breathing is sometimes called ventilation — not quite the same thing as leaving the window open! Remember that in science, respiration is not the same thing as breathing, either.

The questions above are all about the lungs and breathing but, for practice, write down the equation for respiration.

Top Tips: Once again, there's a diagram that you have to be able to label. You need to know **how** the air gets in — remember, it's to do with **pressure** inside and outside, **not** sucking. Remember what alveoli do — their size, number and structure help them to do it.

Section Three — Human Biology Part One

Respiration

Q1) What is the correct function of respiration — is it to get air in and out of the lungs, or is to release energy from cells? Do plants respire?

Q2) Answer these questions about both aerobic and anaerobic respiration:

> glucose + _____ → _____ + water (+ energy transferred)

a) Copy and complete the word equation for aerobic respiration.

b) The chemical symbol for glucose is $C_6H_{12}O_6$. Copy and complete the symbol equation for aerobic respiration.

c) What substances are needed for respiration? How does each substance travel to where 1it is used in the body. Where do these substances come from?

d) What substances are produced by respiration? How do these substances leave the body?

e) What else is produced by respiration?

Q3) The word equation below shows the process of anaerobic respiration in animal cells.

> glucose → lactic acid (+ energy released)

a) Using your knowledge of the word equation for aerobic respiration, describe the similarities and differences between aerobic respiration and anaerobic respiration.

b) Why are the two types of respiration named aerobic and anaerobic?

c) It is possible to measure the amount of energy released by the two processes. Aerobic respiration releases 16kJ from 1g of glucose, and anaerobic respiration releases 833J from 1g of glucose. Which process releases the most energy from glucose? How many times more energy does this process release?

d) Adenosine triphosphate, or ATP, is a chemical made by cells using energy from respiration. ATP acts as a temporary store of energy that can be used to drive the chemical reactions in cells. One molecule of glucose produces 38 molecules of ATP by aerobic respiration, but only 2 molecules of ATP by anaerobic respiration. Suggest a reason for this difference.

Respiration

Q4) David does a simple experiment to investigate respiration and muscle activity. He rapidly clenches and unclenches his fist, counting how many times he can do this before his hand feels like it's going to fall off. His results are shown in the table on the right.

Number of clenches	
hand lowered	hand raised
68	19

a) Why are David's muscles unable to keep on contracting? What chemical causes the pain he feels?

b) Why is David able to keep his muscles working much longer with his hand lowered?

Q5) The word enzyme means "in yeast".
Suggest why enzymes have been named in this way.

Q6) Kathryn has entered a running race. The graph on the right shows the amount of lactic acid in her blood and her rate of oxygen uptake during the race. The race takes place between the times marked A and B on the graph.

a) What type of respiration is most likely to be occurring when Kathryn is resting before the race?

b) Why does her rate of oxygen uptake increase when she begins to run?

c) Why does Kathryn's rate of oxygen uptake reach a maximum during the race? Why can't she take up any more oxygen than this?

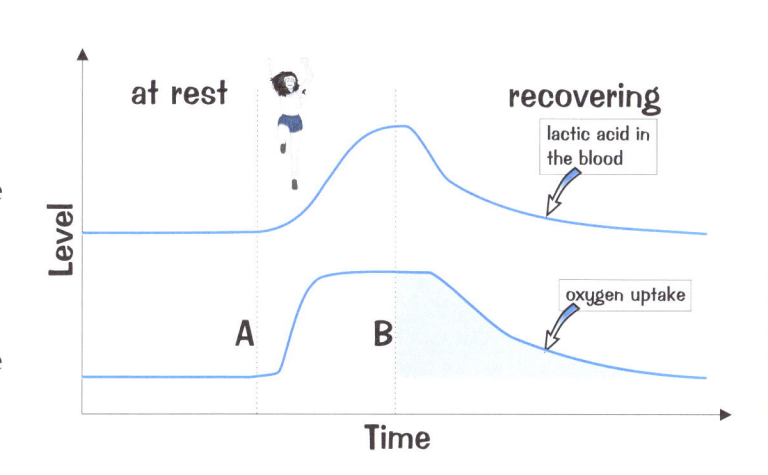

d) Why does the concentration of lactic acid in her blood increase during the race?

e) Why do the concentration of lactic acid in Kathryn's blood and her rate of oxygen uptake take time to return to the resting levels after the race?

f) The shaded area on the graph is known as the oxygen debt. What does this mean?

Section Three — Human Biology Part One

The Nervous System

Q1) One of the functions of the nervous system is to allow us to react to changes in our surroundings.

a) What do we call the changes in the environment to which we respond?
b) What do we call the cells that detect these changes in the environment?
c) Suggest some advantages of being able to detect and respond to changes in the environment.

Q2) You need to know about five sense organs — the nose, the tongue, the ears, the eyes and the skin.

a) Match these sense organs to the following senses (some organs have more than one sense):

| balance   hearing   sight   smell   taste   temperature   touch |

b) The senses work because each sense organ contains cells that are able to detect certain stimuli. For example, the sense of balance arises from the appropriate sense organ being able to detect the position of the body. Match the senses in part **a)** to the following stimuli (some stimuli may produce more than one sense):

| chemicals   light   position   sound   pressure   temperature change |

c) Draw up a table with the headings shown on the right. Put your answers to parts **a)** and **b)** together to complete your table. It should show which stimuli are detected in each sense organ, and the sense produced as a result.

Sense organ	Stimulus	Sense

Q3) The receptor cells in sense organs are able to convert or transduce the energy from a stimulus into a nerve impulse.

What is a nerve impulse?
How many directions can a nerve impulse travel in?

Q4) If you touch a hot object with your finger, you quickly move your finger away without having to think about it. This is a reflex action.

a) What is the stimulus in this reflex action?
b) What is the response in this reflex action?
c) What is the effector that causes this response?

The diagram on the right represents a reflex arc.

d) Copy the diagram. Label the sensory neurone, the connector (relay) neurone, and the motor neurone. Label the receptor and the effector in the appropriate circle or box. Add arrows to show the direction of the nerve impulses.
e) What is the role of the neurones in this reflex action?
f) Use your answers to rearrange these features of a reflex arc into the correct order:

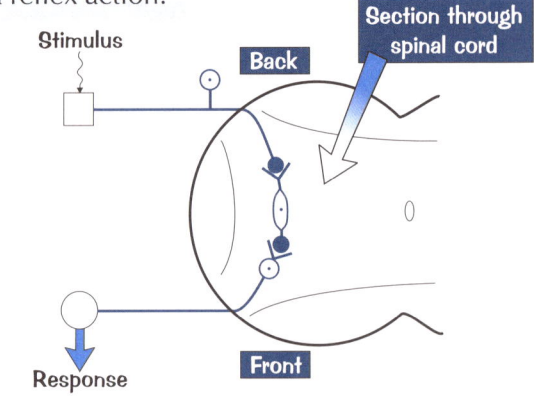

| neurones (coordinator) → effector → receptor → response → stimulus |

g) Use the reflex arc to explain why reflex actions are such fast responses.

Q5) Describe the reflex arcs that are undergone when you are hit just below the knee-cap, and when you get a speck of grit in your eye.

The Nervous System

Q6) The two diagrams on the right show a sensory neurone and a motor neurone.

a) Describe what a sensory neurone and a motor neurone do.

b) Which diagram, A or B, represents a sensory neurone? Explain how you know this.

c) Copy the diagrams. Add an arrow to each to show the direction of the nerve impulse. Label as many features as you can in each diagram.

d) Each neurone is making connections with other nerves or tissues at the part marked X. Label each diagram to show what X is connected to.

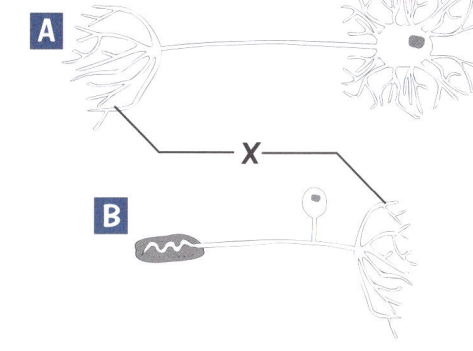

e) Explain how the structures of neurones are adapted to their function.

Q7) Copy these sentences about reflex actions, choosing the correct words from each underlined pair:

"A reflex action is an conscious /automatic response to a stimulus /receptor. It happens very quickly /slowly and involves /does not involve the brian /brain. Reflex actions allow us to co-ordinate body activity by remote control /nervous control."

Q8) Look at the diagram on the right:

a) Identify the parts of the nervous system labelled X, Y and Z.

b) What is the collective name given to the parts represented by X and Y?

c) In which direction can nerve impulses travel in the part labelled Y?

d) Give two functions of the part labelled X. Is X involved in reflex actions?

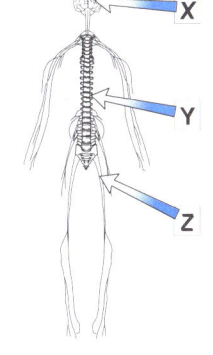

Q9) The diagram on the right shows a synapse greatly magnified.

a) Where do you find synapses? What is the function of a synapse?

b) What do the bubbles of chemical crossing the synapse do?

c) There are mitochondria in the diagram. What does this suggest about the working of a synapse?

d) Electrical wires can be joined together using solder, a junction box, or simply by twisting the ends together. Suggest a reason why neurones cannot be connected together directly in this way.

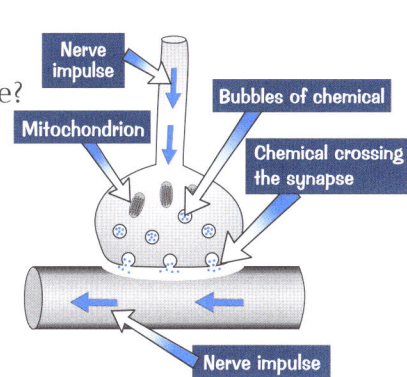

Top Tips: First, you have to be able to recognise sye parts of the nervous system and say what they do. Remember that the whole point about a **reflex** is that it allows a **rapid response** to a stimulus. The brain comes in **later** to allow us to feel the pain.

Section Three — Human Biology Part One

The Eye

Q1) Look at the diagram on the right. It shows a section through an eye.

a) Match the names below to the parts of the eye labelled A — H. Make a table for your answers.

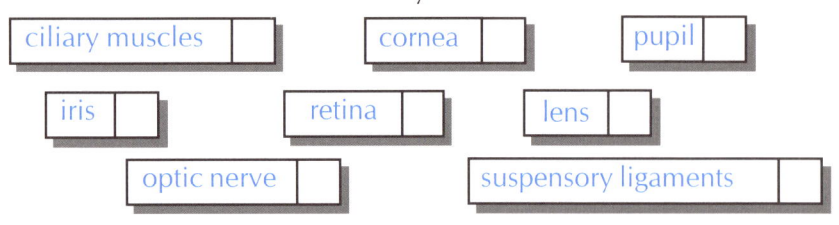

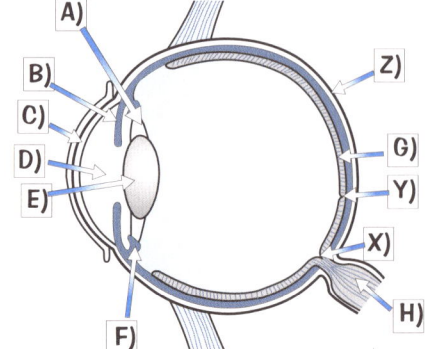

- ciliary muscles
- cornea
- pupil
- iris
- retina
- lens
- optic nerve
- suspensory ligaments

b) You may also be asked to identify the sclera, the blind spot and the fovea. Match these parts to the labels X, Y and Z, and add these to your table.

Q2) Make sure you know what all the parts of the eye do, by matching the part to its function:

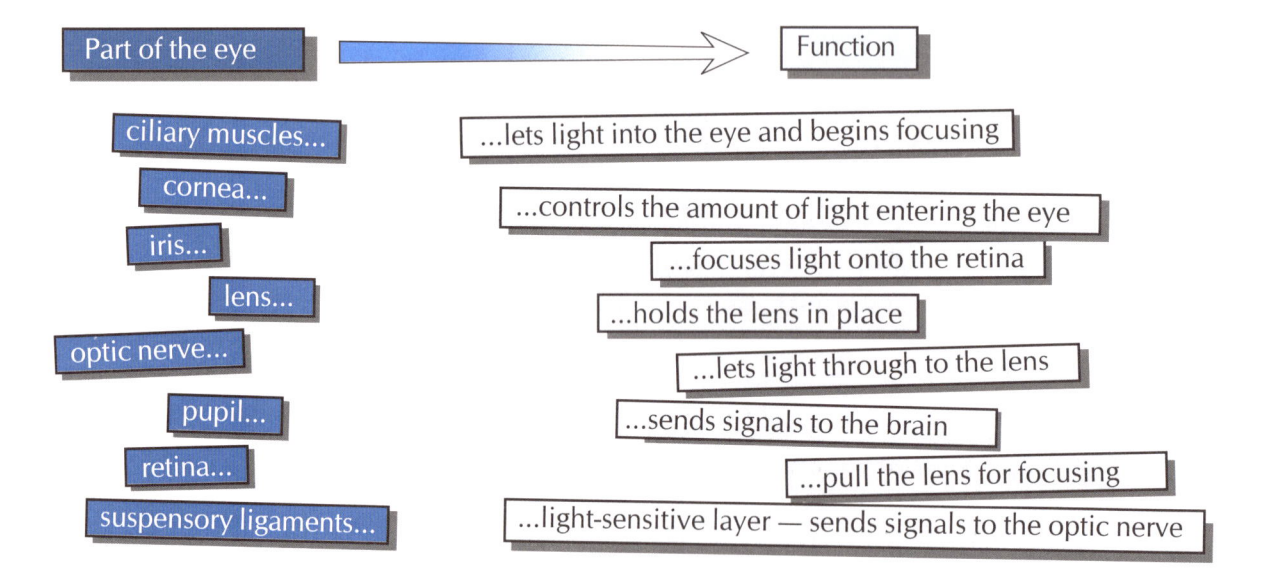

Part of the eye → Function

- ciliary muscles...
- cornea...
- iris...
- lens...
- optic nerve...
- pupil...
- retina...
- suspensory ligaments...

- ...lets light into the eye and begins focusing
- ...controls the amount of light entering the eye
- ...focuses light onto the retina
- ...holds the lens in place
- ...lets light through to the lens
- ...sends signals to the brain
- ...pull the lens for focusing
- ...light-sensitive layer — sends signals to the optic nerve

Q3) When light enters the eye, it travels through some parts of the eye but not others.

a) Which parts of the eye does light travel through? Write them down in order.

b) Which parts of the eye does light hit, but cannot travel through?

Q4) The iris contains circular and radial muscles. These muscles control the diameter of the pupil. The diagrams on the right show the iris in two different light conditions.

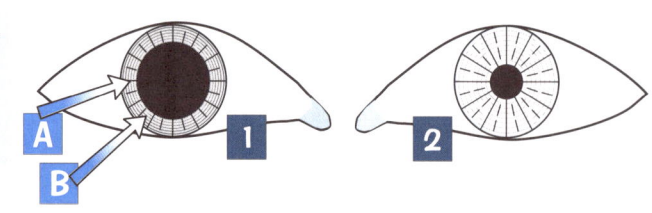

a) What is the black circle in the centre?

b) Identify the two muscle types, A and B.

c) Which diagram, 1 or 2, shows the eye in bright light? Explain why you chose this diagram.

d) In diagram 1, which type of muscle is relaxed and which is contracted?

e) In diagram 2, which type of muscle is relaxed and which has contracted?

f) Use your answers so far to explain how the iris controls the amount of light entering the eye.

g) What other muscles are involved with the eye? What is their function?

The Eye

Q5) The diagrams below show rays of light coming from an object on the left and going through a thick and a thin lens.

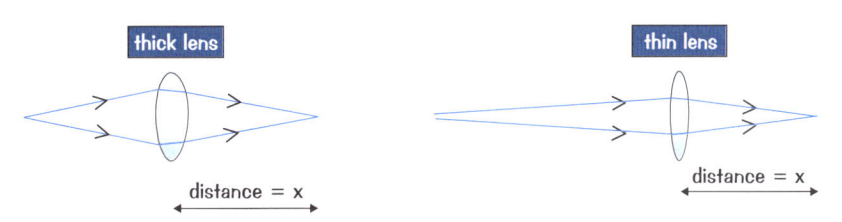

thick lens **thin lens**
distance = x   distance = x

If a screen were placed where the rays come together on the right of the lens, an image of the object would be seen on the screen — the light from the image would be focused onto the screen.

a) What sort of lens is needed to focus the light from a distant object and from a nearby object?

b) From which diagram are the light rays bent most to come together on the right?

Q6) For light to be focused onto the retina, it must change direction in the eye.

a) Which parts of the eye can do this?

b) The lens of our eye is different from the lens of a magnifying glass — it can change its shape from fat to thin. What is the advantage of doing this?

Q7) The diagram on the right shows the lens of the eye focusing a nearby object onto the retina.

a) Why must the lens be thick here?

b) The suspensory ligaments are slack. What does that tell you about the natural shape of the lens?

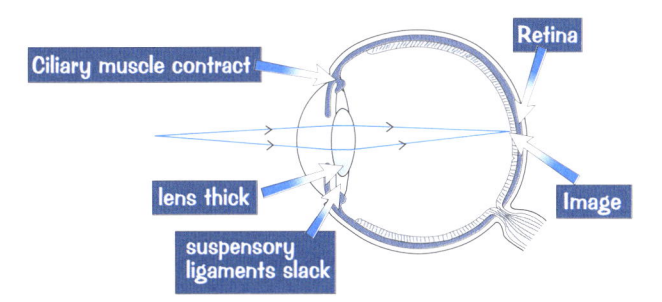

c) The ciliary muscles in the diagram are in a ring around the lens. If the ciliary muscles relax, what will happen to the suspensory ligaments? What will happen to the lens?

d) If the lens changes as in part **c)**, what sort of object will be focused onto the retina?

e) Draw a diagram, similar to the one in this question, to show how light from a distant object can be focused onto the retina. Make sure you label your diagram clearly.

Top Tips: Another diagram to label and learn.
You've got to understand **how** the eye focuses images of near and distant objects on the retina and how the **iris** makes the pupil get bigger and smaller to vary the amount of light.

Section Three — Human Biology Part One

Hormones

Q1) Copy and complete the following sentences by adding the most suitable words from the box:

receptors　　　　hormones　　　　systems　　　　glands
　　　nervous system　　　　bloodstream　　　　chemicals

Many processes within the body are coordinated by _____ called _____. These substances are produced by _____ and transported to their target organs by the _____.

Q2) Copy and complete the following table.

AQA only {

Name of hormone	Gland	Function
a) Insulin		turns glucose to glycogen
b)	Pancreas	turns glycogen to glucose
c) Oestrogen		develops female sexual characteristics
d) Follicle Stimulating Hormone (FSH)		causes eggs to mature and ovaries to produce oestrogen
e) LH (Luteinising Hormone)	Pituitary	

Q3) The diagram opposite shows the system that controls the body's blood-sugar level.

Hepatic vein carries blood with a normal glucose level.

Hepatic artery carries insulin hormone made in the pancreas.

Liver turns glucose into glycogen when insulin is present, and stores glycogen.

Hepatic portal vein carries blood rich in glucose to the liver from the intestines.

a) If a meal rich in carbohydrate was eaten, what substance would be found to excess in the blood?

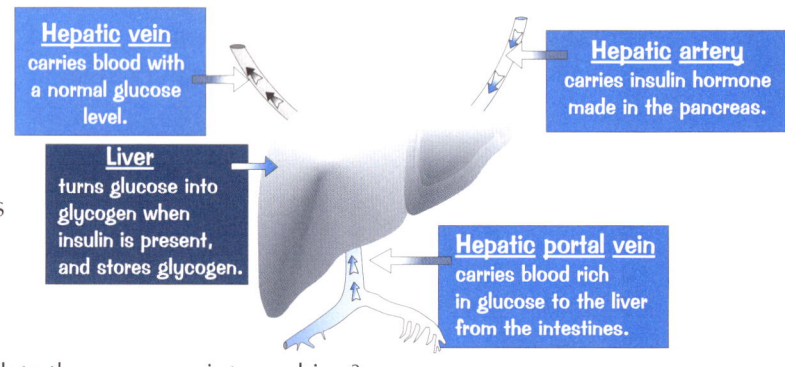

b) Which hormone would this stimulate the pancreas into making?

This hormone initiates the changing of the excess glucose to a form in which it can be stored.

c) Which organ does this and in what form does it store it?

d) Complete the flow diagram opposite to show how the blood-sugar level is returned to normal after a meal rich in carbohydrates.

Hepatic artery blood rich in carbohydrates → .... → .... → Glucose turned to glycogen → Normal blood sugar level

Pancreas

e) (AQA only) After a work-out in the gym the blood-sugar level falls below normal. Explain how it would be returned to normal.

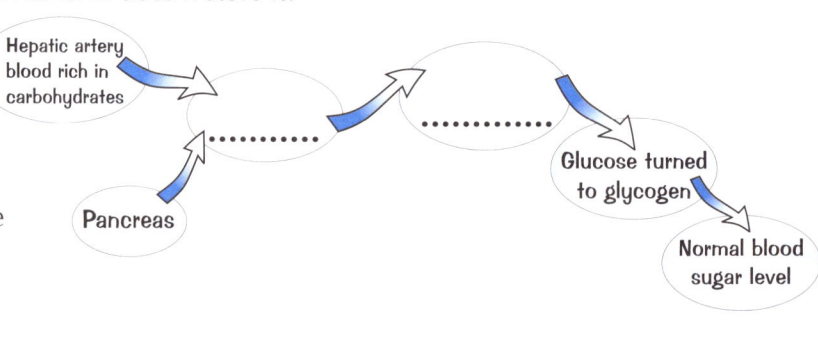

The Use of Hormones

Q4) The hormones and treatments below are given by doctors to control various body functions. Match each with the correct description.

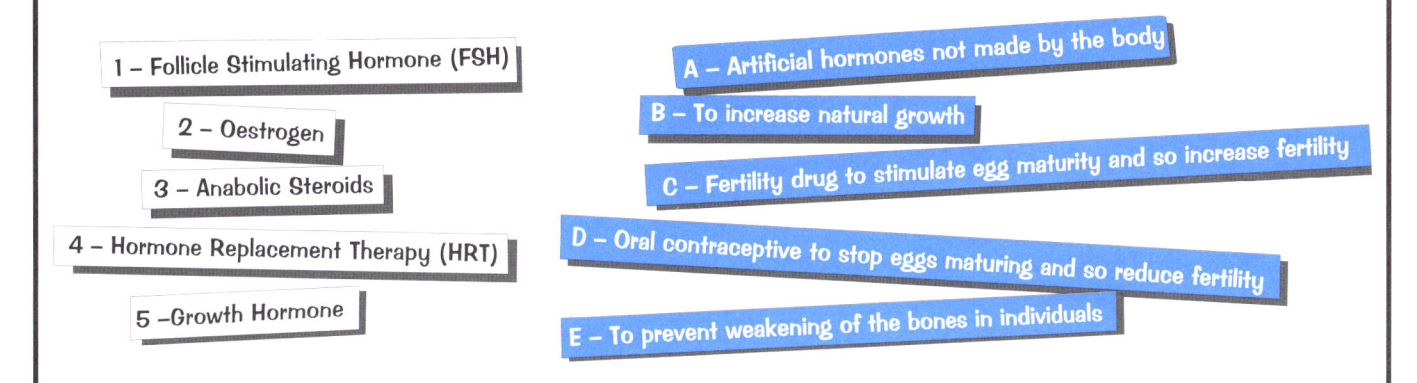

1 – Follicle Stimulating Hormone (FSH)
2 – Oestrogen
3 – Anabolic Steroids
4 – Hormone Replacement Therapy (HRT)
5 – Growth Hormone

A – Artificial hormones not made by the body
B – To increase natural growth
C – Fertility drug to stimulate egg maturity and so increase fertility
D – Oral contraceptive to stop eggs maturing and so reduce fertility
E – To prevent weakening of the bones in individuals

Q5) Write a sentence to explain each of the following terms:

hormone, glands, insulin, glucagon, FSH, oestrogen,

AQA only

Q6) Explain in a sentence the meaning or function of each of the following terms:

glucose, glycogen, pancreas, liver, ovaries, pituitary.

Q7) The bloodstream provides the method of transport that enables hormones to reach their target organ.

a) Using the labels below, copy and complete the diagram opposite showing the production and action of hormones in the body.

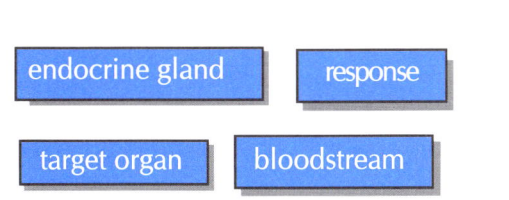

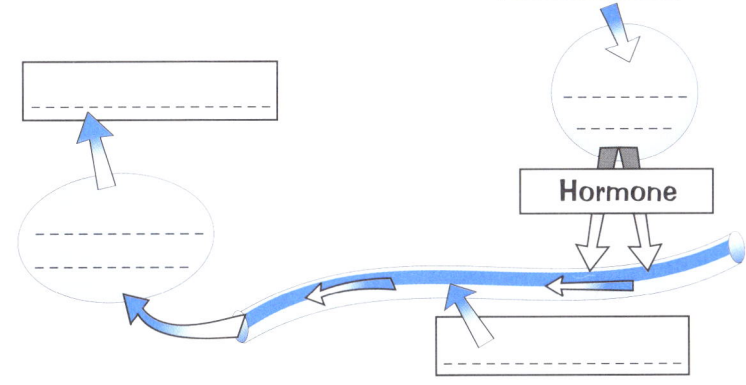

endocrine gland   response
target organ   bloodstream

Stimulus
Hormone

b) There are two types of messenger in the body — chemical ones (hormones) and nervous ones. Name four differences between the two types. (Think about the speed of the message and the way they act).

Top Tips: Any hormone released into the blood will go to all organs — but it's only the target organs that respond to it. Exam questions ask you to compare the endocrine system with, say, the nervous system — so think how they're different — and how they work together.

Section Four — Human Biology Part Two

Insulin Diabetes

Q1) The diagram opposite shows a number of bodily organs with glands coloured black.

Label the pancreas on a copy of the diagram.

Q2) a) Name the hormone produced by the pancreas that controls the level of blood-sugar.

b) How is production of one of these hormones different in someone with diabetes?

c) How do you think this would affect the levels of glucose in the bloodstream?

Q3) State two ways in which a diabetic person might cope with this problem.

Q4) Name a problem a diabetic person could face when:

i) the blood-sugar level becomes too low.

ii) the blood-sugar level becomes too high.

Q5) How much glycogen would you expect there to be in the liver of a diabetic person?

Explain your answer.

Q6) The work of the hormone insulin is an example of a negative feedback mechanism because the release of insulin tends to result in a situation where less insulin is required.

a) Explain how the blood-glucose level in a non-diabetic is lowered if it is too high.

b) Explain how the blood-glucose level in a non-diabetic is increased if it is too low.

AQA only {

Q7) Glucagon secretion is a response controlled by the blood-sugar level.

a) Give an example of when the blood-sugar level could be rapidly reduced.

b) In this case, what would happen to glucagon production and how would this return blood-sugar level back to normal?

Q8) Could insulin injections be changed easily to oral medicine and so make it more attractive to diabetics? Explain your answer.

Q9) Name any enzymes that could digest insulin.

Q10) A person was thought to have diabetes and so was asked by the doctor to produce a sample of urine to test at the pathology laboratories.

a) What substance would be tested for in the urine?

b) Describe briefly how you would test a liquid for the presence of this substance.

Q11) Unscramble the following key words linked with this section. There is a clue to help you.

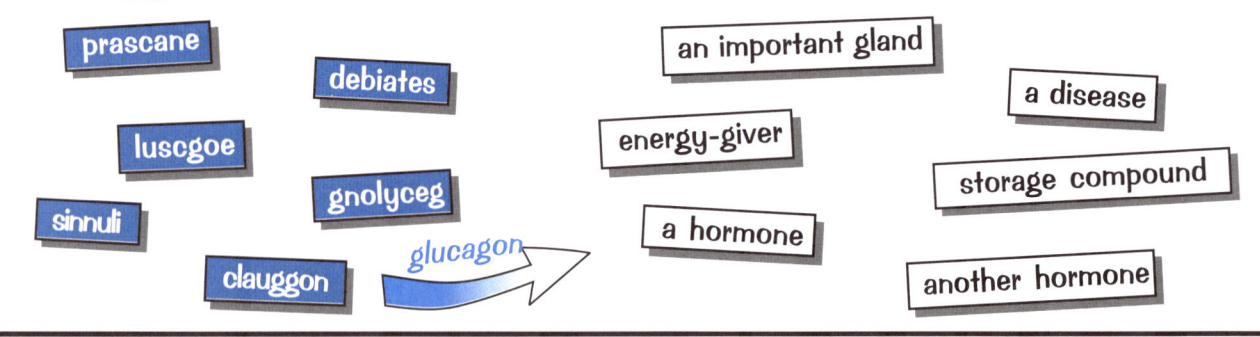

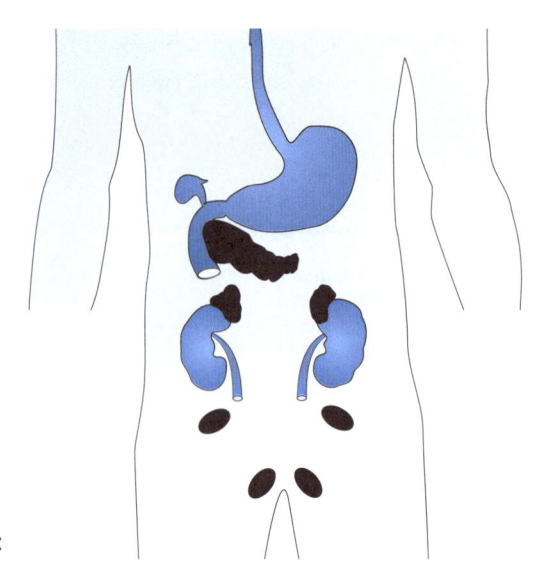

- prascane — an important gland
- debiates — a disease
- luscgoe — energy-giver
- sinnuli — a hormone
- gnolyceg — storage compound
- clauggon → glucagon — another hormone

Section Four — Human Biology Part Two

The Menstrual Cycle

Q1) If fertilisation has not taken place, the lining of the uterus breaks down. What is the name given to this process?

Q2) What name is given to the release of an egg from the ovary?

Q3) The female reproductive cycle can be seen as the journey undertaken by the egg and its development during that time.

a) What is the *process* of preparation, egg release and breakdown in the uterus of a woman called?

b) In what *two* ways could the process continue after ovulation?

Q4) How many eggs are generally released every month?

Q5) Fill in the gaps in the sentences below to describe what happens to the uterus during the menstrual cycle.

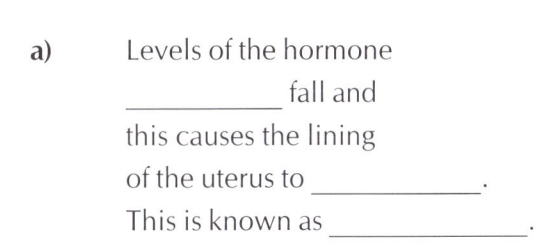

a) Levels of the hormone _____ fall and this causes the lining of the uterus to _____. This is known as _____.

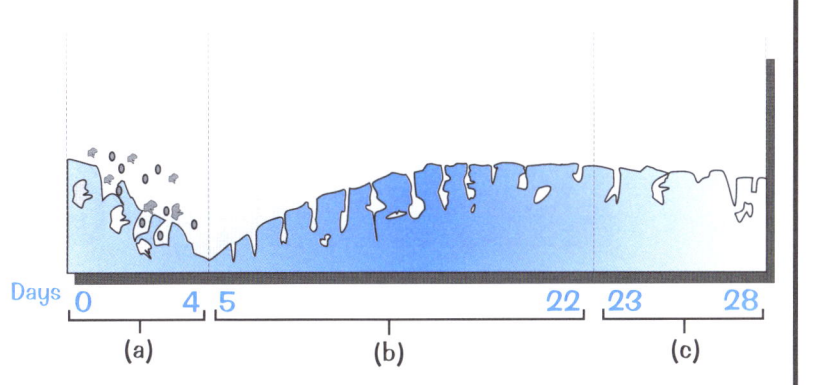

Days 0   4 5   22 23   28
     (a)   (b)   (c)

b) Levels of the hormone _____ increase, and this causes the lining of the uterus to _____ with _____ _____ ready to receive a _____ _____.

c) An increase in the production of _____ maintains the _____ _____ until around day ___. If no _____ _____ has landed there by then, the spongy lining begins to break down and the cycle begins again.

Q6) Do both ovaries contain immature eggs?

Q7) Approximately how long into the menstrual cycle is the mature egg released from the ovary?

Q8) Why are there only a few days in each menstrual cycle when fertilisation is likely to occur?

Q9) A healthy woman produces approximately 400-500 eggs in her lifetime. Are all of the eggs *mature*? If not, *when* do they become mature?

Section Four — Human Biology Part Two

The Menstrual Cycle

Answer these questions about ovulation:

Q1) What is the period of time between successive ovulations called?

Q2) What happens to the uterus between each ovulation?

Q3) How many eggs are likely to be fertilised at once?

Q4) The diagram below shows what happens in the ovary during the menstrual cycle.

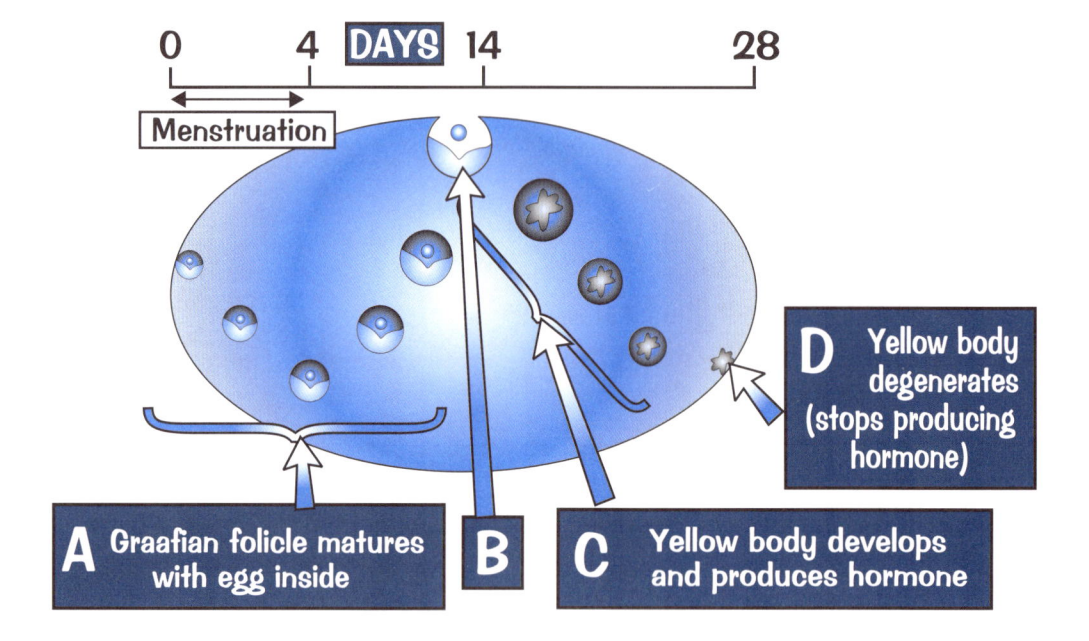

A Graafian follicle matures with egg inside
B
C Yellow body develops and produces hormone
D Yellow body degenerates (stops producing hormone)

Days: 0, 4, 14, 28
Menstruation: 0–4

a) What is occurring at B?

b) What hormone is produced during period C?

c) At D, this hormone is no longer produced. What do we call the period which follows this?

Q5) Explain the meaning of the following terms:

ova, ovary, puberty, ovulation, Fallopian tube, uterus, cervix, vagina, menstruation, menstrual cycle.

Top Tips: Lots more interacting hormones and glands to learn. But if you can draw and label a **diagram** with all the bits of the female **reproductive system**, and if you can say **what's happening** at all the **stages** of the **menstrual cycle** — then you'll have pretty much got it.

Section Four — Human Biology Part Two

Hormones in the Menstrual Cycle

Q1) What type of tissue produces hormones?

Q2) Which part of the body carries these hormones?

Q3) In total, four hormones control menstruation. Name the two places where they are produced.

Q4) Copy the table opposite and fill in the parts labelled i) to iv).

Hormone Name	Source	Function
FSH (Follicle Stimulating Hormone)	Pituitary	i)
Oestrogen	Ovaries	ii)
iii)	Pituitary	Stimulates the release of an egg
Progesterone	iv)	Causes uterus lining to become thicker and full of blood vessels

Q5) The diagram opposite shows the order in which the glands and hormones are involved in the menstrual cycle.

    a) Fill in the missing hormones (i), (ii) and (iii).
    b) What is the name of the gland which produces hormones (i) and (iii)?
    c) Which other hormone is produced by the ovaries to maintain the lining of the uterus?

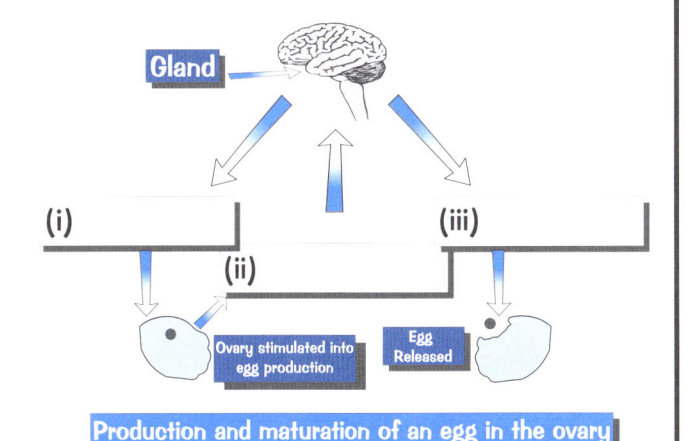

Q6) Copy and complete the diagram below to show what happens at different stages of the menstrual cycle and during pregnancy.

Q7) With the help of the diagram, answer the following questions:

    a) Name the hormone that brings about the repair and thickening of the uterus lining.

    b) Name the hormone that maintains the uterus lining and prepares the body for pregnancy.

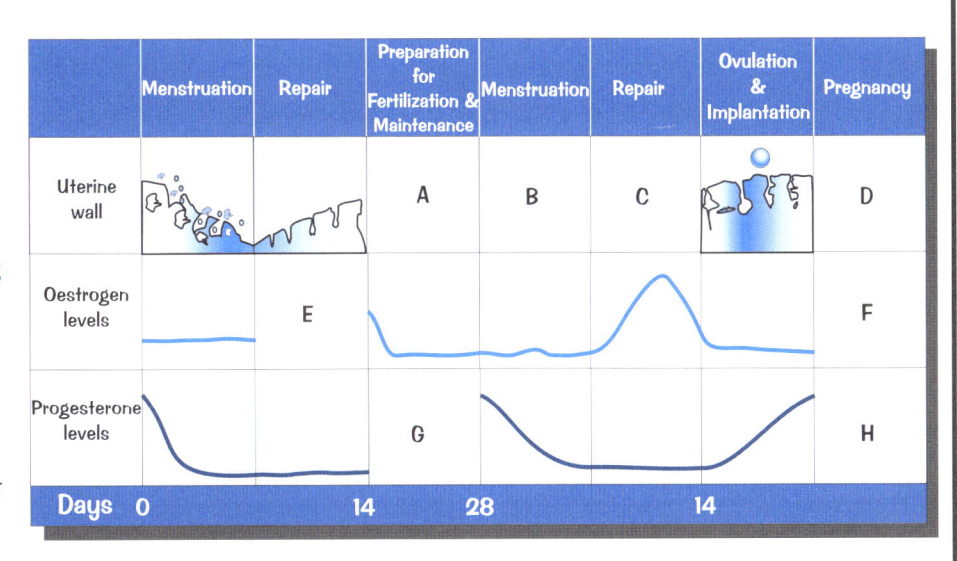

Q8) What do you understand by a "target organ" in the menstrual cycle?

Section Four — Human Biology Part Two

Hormones in the Menstrual Cycle

Q9) Copy and complete the diagram, filling in the hormones 1 & 2, and the missing effects A & B.

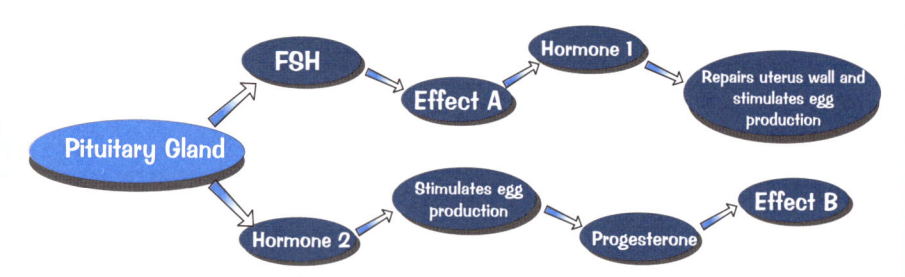

Q10) "The Pill" is a contraceptive taken by women that works by controlling egg production.
   a) Which *two* hormones does the pill contain?
   b) What do you think the effect of taking the pill *regularly* would be on the level of oestrogen in the body?

   Maintaining oestrogen at this level inhibits production of FSH.

   c) After a period of time, what effect would this have on *egg production*?
   d) Would you expect the egg production of someone on the pill to *return to normal* after they stopped taking it? Why?

Q11) Are the effects of taking the pill an example of a feedback mechanism? Explain your answer.

Q12) Women's fertility can be altered with the introduction of a particular hormone.
   a) Which hormone would be given to *increase* the fertility of a woman?
   b) *Explain* how this hormone has the required effect.

Q13) The period of pregnancy also stimulates the production of a particular hormone.
   a) Which hormone *remains* in production throughout pregnancy?
   b) *Explain* why this needs to happen

Q14) Using the normal menstrual cycle as an example, state two ways in which one hormone has a "feedback control" on another hormone.

Q15) Fertility treatment can be used by couples who are having problems conceiving. Part of this treatment can involve stimulating egg production.
   a) Which hormone would be taken to stimulate *egg development*?
   b) Which hormone is then produced by the ovaries to stimulate *egg release*?
   c) Give *two* examples of problems with this treatment.

Top Tips:
Hormones can be pretty tricky but you've got to know it — for *each hormones* you must know *what controls it* and *what it controls*. Drawing a *graph* of all the hormone levels should fix the details in your brain — and it's the sort of graph that tends to appear in the Exams.

Section Four — Human Biology Part Two

Disease in Humans

Q1) Answer these microbe questions:
 a) Name the two different types of microbe.
 b) In what conditions do most everyday microbes tend to live and multiply well?
 c) What effects can microbes have in our bodies?

Q2) Name the two different types of microbes shown opposite.

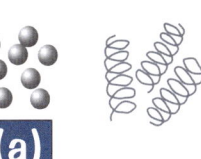

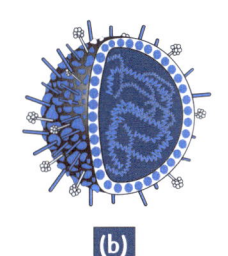

Q3) Copy and complete the following table below by deciding whether each property in the box applies to bacteria, viruses or both.

about 1/10,000mm, about 1/100,000mm, can produce toxins, cell wall, slime capsule, always contain DNA, coat of protein, cytoplasm, can reproduce rapidly.

	Bacteria	Viruses
1		
2		
3		
4		
5		
6		
7		
8		

Q4) Bacteria are extremely tiny (about 1/100th the size of most body cells), which enables them to enter the human body very easily.
 a) What process of gaseous exchange does their small size allow bacteria to use?
 b) Name the substance used to kill bacteria in swimming pools.

Q5) Name two situations that allow large numbers of microbes to enter the body.

Q6) State three conditions in the body that make the it an ideal place for microbes to grow.

Q7) What does the word "pathogen" mean?

Q8) What are the three main groups of pathogens?

Q9) Which one of the main groups of pathogens only occasionally produces a disease?

Section Four — Human Biology Part Two

Disease in Humans

Q10) Copy and complete the table below, stating the type of microbe that causes the disease and how the disease then spreads.

Disease	Type of microbe (bacteria, virus, fungus) that causes it	How it is spread (air droplets, infected water, food contamination)
Common cold		
Measles		
Cholera		
Polio		
Whooping cough		

Q11) Explain how a cold-sufferer could pass on their cold to another person by sneezing.

Q12) Name four ways in which microbes can spread and so pass on a disease.

Q13) Answer these bacteria questions:

a) What type of conditions are bad for bacterial growth?

b) How do bacteria protect themselves from these types of conditions?

Q14) Both viruses and bacteria can develop from just a few into a large colony very quickly. This can be difficult for the body to deal with.

If the infection was bacterial, how might you help your body get rid of the infection? And if it was viral?

Q15) Give three ways in which you could stop microbes developing and spreading in your home.

Top Tips: You need to know your **bacterium** and **virus** inside out — so you'd better be able to **draw** them (and **label** the bits). Exam questions will often tell you how **fast** a bacterium **divides**, and then ask you how many there'll be a day or so later. Don't forget the things that affect their numbers — like **competition**, **food supply**, **temperature** and **toxins**.

Section Four — Human Biology Part Two

Fighting Disease

Q1) The body has many natural defence systems to prevent infection and disease.
List three of these natural defences.

Q2) Match the correct name below to each of the blood cells **a)**-**c)**.

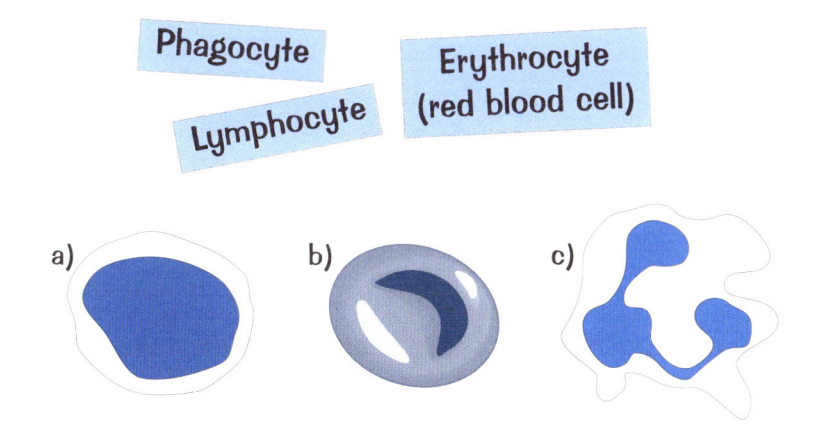

Phagocyte   Erythrocyte (red blood cell)   Lymphocyte

a)   b)   c)

Q3) Which of these blood cells carries oxygen by changing haemoglobin to oxyhaemoglobin?

Q4) Which of the blood cells produces antibodies?

Q5) If bacteria enter the body, special blood cells respond automatically.

Which type of blood cell engulfs bacteria?
Explain how the bacteria are then destroyed.

Q6) The human body is protected by a versatile tough outer layer. This is of course the skin.

a) What is the outer layer of the skin called?
b) What features of this outer layer prevent the entry of pathogens?
c) Under what circumstances do you think a pathogen could enter the body through the skin?

Q7) Clotting is an important defence mechanism of the body.

a) Which two parts of the blood are involved in clotting a wound?
b) Give two reasons why blood clotting is important

Section Four — Human Biology Part Two

Drugs

Q1) Drugs are classified as chemicals which can affect human behaviour.
Name three of the main groups of drugs.

Q2) What does it mean to say that a drug is:
a) obtained from living things?
b) man-made?

Q3) Copy and complete the table opposite, showing the effects of different types of drugs on the nervous system.

Drug type	Effect on brain and rest of nervous system	Examples of drug type
Sedatives	(a) --------------------------	Valium / barbiturates
(b) ------------	Speed up the brain and increase alertness	Ecstasy / cocaine milder drug (c) --------------
(d) ------------	Reduce sense of pain	Paracetamol / heroin

Q4) Give two reasons why drugs are dangerous.

Q5) What do the following words mean in relation to drugs?
a) addiction
b) withdrawal

Q6) Drugs come in all shapes and forms — not just tablets and pills. This is evident with solvents.
a) What are solvents?
b) Why do we often refer to solvent abuse as "glue-sniffing"?
c) What are the four main organs that glue-sniffing affects?
d) What symptoms may a glue-sniffer display?

Q7) Answer these questions about painkillers:
a) Name two examples of painkillers.
b) Heroin is a particularly dangerous form of painkiller because it is very addictive. What problems can this drug cause?

Q8) Copy and complete the table below for the spaces labelled **a) — h)**.

Drug Group	Highs	Lows	Long-term effects
Stimulants	a)_____	Anxiety, Irritability	b)_____
c)_____	Distorts the senses	d)_____	Causes breathing disorders if smoked
e)_____	Total relaxation kills pain	Sickness, apathy, self-neglect	f)_____

Drugs

Q9) The boxes to the right show a number of drugs and their effects. Match each drug A-F with the correct effect 1-6.

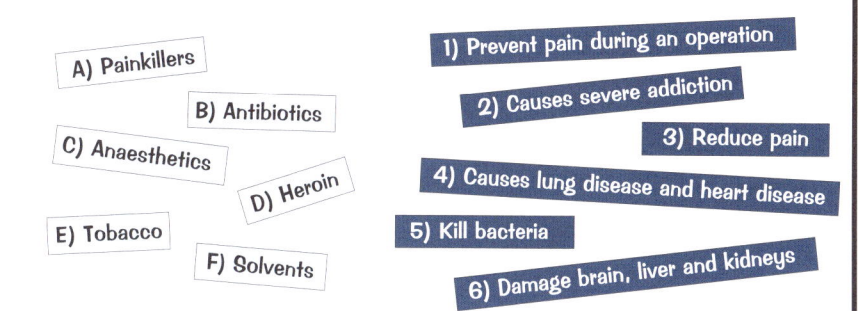

A) Painkillers
B) Antibiotics
C) Anaesthetics
D) Heroin
E) Tobacco
F) Solvents

1) Prevent pain during an operation
2) Causes severe addiction
3) Reduce pain
4) Causes lung disease and heart disease
5) Kill bacteria
6) Damage brain, liver and kidneys

Q10) a) Identify organs Q1) to Q5) in the illustration below.

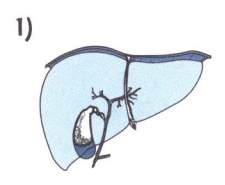

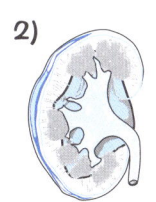

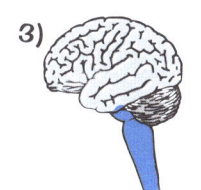

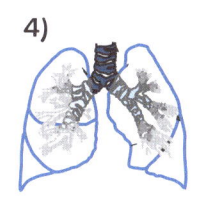

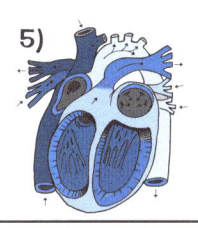

1) 2) 3) 4) 5)

| A) Solvent | B) Alcohol | C) Tobacco | D) Stimulants | E) Sedatives |

b) For each drug A – E in the box above, list which of the organs it affects (it might be more than one).

Q11) If a person is dependent on a drug they are said to be addicted to that drug.
  a) Name the two different types of addiction.
  b) Give three examples of physical symptoms that withdrawal from a drug might cause.

Q12) Complete the following sentences on a number of common drugs.

> Stimulants affect the _____ system and give a person a feeling of increased energy. _____, found in tea, coffee and some soft drinks, is a m_____ stimulant and fairly harmless, though people will often suffer from h_____ after reducing their intake. On the other hand, stronger stimulants, such as a_____, are very dangerous. Prolonged use can lead to h_____ and p_____ c_____, and coming off them results in severe d_____. Ecstasy (a h_____) in smaller doses has a similar effect and gives a feeling of boundless _____ which can put a person at risk of o_____ and d_____.
> Painkillers are another class of drug. The stronger ones such as h_____ are hugely addictive. Its expense often means that users turn to c_____ as a way of financing their habit, and the severe w_____ symptoms make it difficult to give up. It is also easy to o_____.
> Solvents are easily available drugs and are contained in such things as p_____ and g_____. Their effects are wide-ranging and include b_____ problems and damage to many vital organs such as the _____, _____, _____ and _____.

Top Tips: You need to know how the main types of drugs affect the body. Remember that painkillers, tranquillisers and sleeping pills help ill people, but are often abused. When the body has got used to the effects of a drug, painful and unpleasant withdrawal symptoms happen when the person tries to stop taking the drug — which creates physical addiction.

Section Four — Human Biology Part Two

Alcohol

Q1) Quite apart from its effect on a person's behaviour, alcohol consumption can severely affect the body's ability to function properly.
  a) What system in the body is most affected by alcohol in the short term?
  b) What are the short-term effects of moderate alcohol consumption?

Q2) Which two organs in the body are most prone to damage by long-term excessive alcohol consumption?

Q3) Look at these two diagrams, then answer the questions that follow:

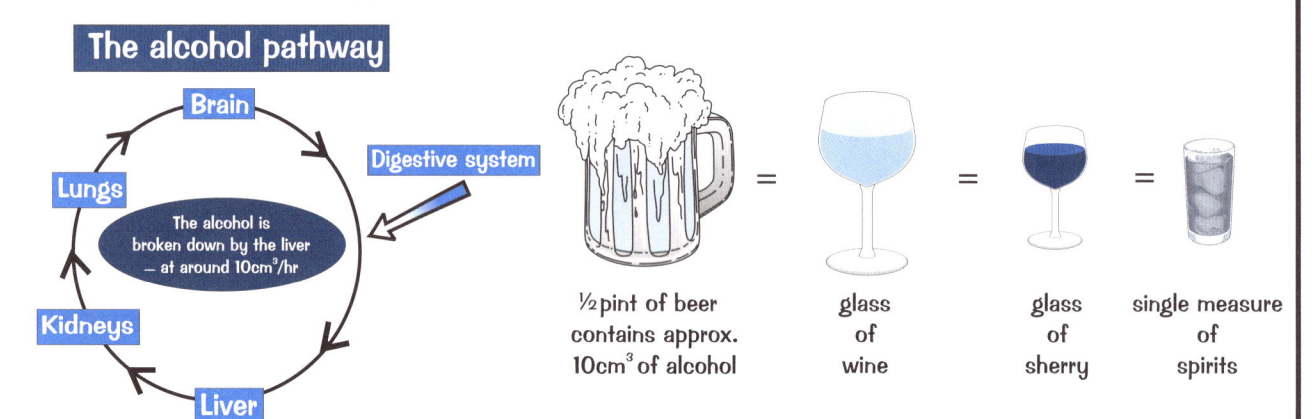

The alcohol pathway

Brain → Digestive system → Liver → Kidneys → Lungs → Brain

The alcohol is broken down by the liver — at around 10cm³/hr

½ pint of beer contains approx. 10cm³ of alcohol = glass of wine = glass of sherry = single measure of spirits

  a) A person at an office party has 2 double whiskies, 3 glasses of wine and a pint of beer. Approximately how much alcohol have they consumed? (Show your working.)

  b) What is the earliest time that the person in the question above would have their body free from alcohol if they drank from midday to 3pm? (Show your working.)

Answer these questions about the effects of alcohol:

Q4) Why would it be dangerous to give a person suffering from hypothermia a drink of brandy or whisky?

Q5) Why is taking a drop of alcohol before competing in a very important sporting event not recommended?

Q6) Cirrhosis is a disease most commonly caused by long-term alcoholism. Which organ does this disease affect in alcoholics?

Q7) What is an alcoholic?

Q8) Why do alcoholics often suffer from deficiency diseases?

Q9) Why is drinking and driving a stupid combination?

Q10) Give a reason why the same amount of alcohol would be likely to have a greater effect on a small person than on a large person.

Q11) State three of the long-term effects of constant heavy drinking.

Q12) Complete the following sentences on the uses and effects of alcohol.

> Alcohol is usually used for r_____ or to relieve s_____. It s_____ down the brain and can make you feel less i_____. However, excessive drinking can lead to both l_____ disease and a drop in _____ function. Recovering alcoholics often suffer from d_____ and sickness.

Section Four — Human Biology Part Two

Tobacco

Answer these questions:

Q1) Name the main addictive substance found in tobacco.

Q2) Name two harmful substances that are produced when tobacco is burnt.

Q3) What is the name of the most serious lung problem caused by tobacco smoke?

Q4) Name two other lung diseases caused by tobacco smoke.

Q5) Carbon monoxide produced by smoking has a serious effect on red blood cells. Explain why this gas is so dangerous.

Q6) How can smoking affect the blood vessels?

Q7) What is "smoker's cough" and how is it caused?

Q8) What is "passive smoking"?

Q9) State four effects of passive smoking on a person's health.

Q10) Why are pregnant women who smoke strongly advised to give up?

Q11) The diagrams to the right show the alveoli of a normal lung and that of someone suffering from emphysema.

Which diagram is which? Explain your answer.

Q12) Lung cancer is linked with smoking.

a) Tar in cigarette smoke affects the cells in the lungs. How could this cause lung cancer?
b) Why is painful lung action a common symptom of lung cancer?

Q13) Complete the following sentences on the effects of tobacco.

> Nicotine makes up a very small part of tobacco, but it is a_____. Many severe long-term effects of smoking are caused by the tar in tobacco smoke. This c_____ the insides of the l_____, preventing the efficient removal of f_____ bodies, including b_____. This can lead to e_____, b_____ and l___ c_____. And as if that wasn't enough, it also causes diseases of the h_____ and b_____ v_____, leading to heart attacks and strokes. People trying to stop smoking often suffer headaches, d_____ and problems with their appetite.

Top Tips: Alcohol and tobacco are legal, but can still harm the body. Alcohol damages the liver and brain, and can be addictive. It **slows down** reactions big-style, which makes driving **horribly dangerous**. In tobacco smoke, **nicotine** is the **addictive** substance, and **tar** damages the lungs. Emphysema, lung cancer, heart disease and strokes are all effects of smoking.

Section Four — Human Biology Part Two

Homeostasis

Q1) What does the word homeostasis mean?

Q2) What group of substances coordinates homeostasis?

Q3) The body produces two main waste substances that it needs to get rid of.

  a) Name these two substances.

  b) For each, say which process produces them and which organ excretes them from the body.

Q4) The diagram opposite shows some of the body's main organs.

  a) Name each of the organs A – H in the diagram.

  A homeostatic organ is one that helps to actually remove substances from the body, rather than just controlling the levels of substances indirectly.

  b) Which of the organs A - H are homeostatic organs?

  c) Which organ continually checks all the homeostatic conditions?

Q5) Name four internal conditions that the body's homeostatic controls try to maintain at optimal levels.

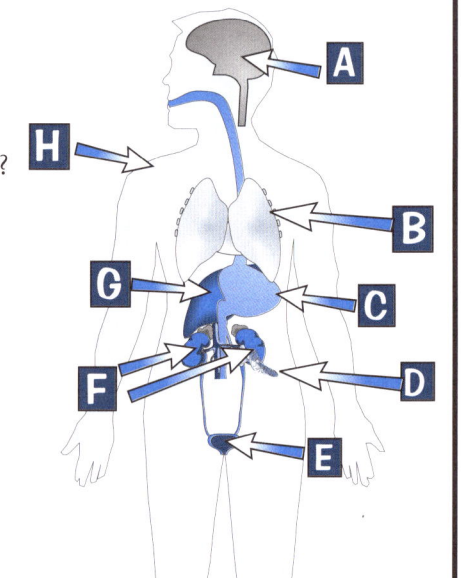

Q6) Humans are warm-blooded — that is our body temperature is controlled internally.

  a) What system controls the body's temperature?

  The part of the brain which monitors and adjusts temperature is called the Thermoregulatory Centre.

  b) If the core temperature of a human is above 37°C what two measures could this system use to lose heat? Describe how each measure takes heat away from the body.

  One of these heat-loss systems involves losing water.

  c) What else is lost in the water at the same time?

  d) In what two ways does the thermoregulatory system increase the temperature of the body if it dropped below 37°C?

Homeostasis and the Kidneys

Q7) Controlling the blood-sugar level is part of homeostasis too.

   a) Which two organs are involved in controlling blood-sugar level?
   b) Name the two hormones which serve as messengers between these two organs.

The hormones use a feedback mechanism to keep the blood-sugar level fairly constant.

   c) What do we mean by a feedback mechanism of hormones?
   d) Briefly describe how the feedback mechanism for maintaining blood-sugar level works.

Q8) Water is a major component of the blood.

   a) Name the hormone that controls the water content of the blood.
   b) What gland produces this hormone?
   c) What part of the brain monitors the blood's water content?
   d) Copy and complete the flow diagram below for the two cases when
      (i) the blood is too dilute and **(ii)** the blood is too concentrated, by filling in the missing words.

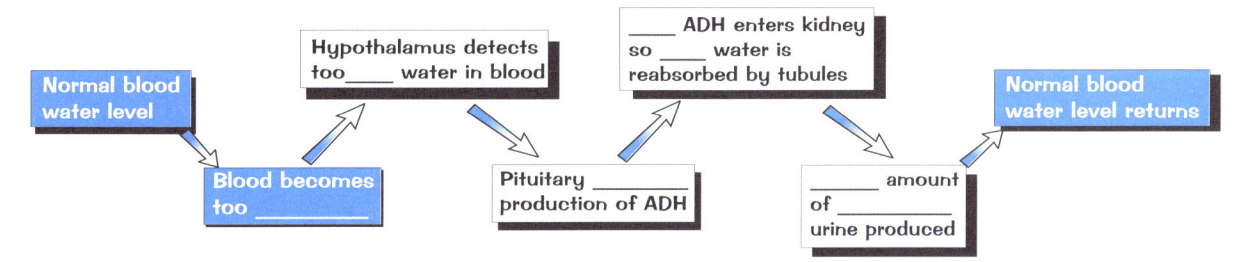

Normal blood water level → Blood becomes too ____ → Hypothalamus detects too ____ water in blood → Pituitary ____ production of ADH → ____ ADH enters kidney so ____ water is reabsorbed by tubules → ____ amount of ____ urine produced → Normal blood water level returns

Q9) The flow chart opposite shows the homeostatic process of regulating the amount of water and other substances in the blood. It is carried out by the kidneys.

   a) What is (Q1) – the process that removes liquid from the blood?
   b) The kidney tubules adjust the amounts of water and three other substances in the blood. Name the three substances (**Q2**), (**Q3**) and (**Q4**).
   c) What do we call (**Q5**)? One of the substances named in (b) is taken back fully into the bloodstream. Which one?
   d) What is the waste liquid eventually produced by the kidney? What three things does it contain?

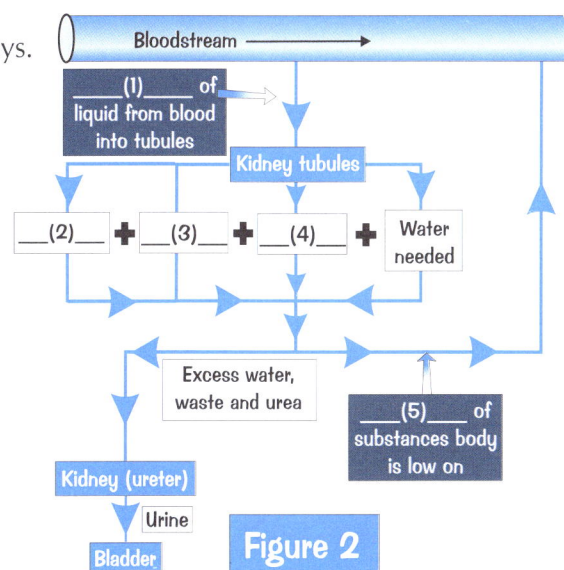

Figure 2

Top Tips: Homeostasis — another long word to learn — but it's just the maintenance of a constant internal environment in the body. We have to get rid of waste, and keep ion, water, sugar content and temperature at the right levels. Homeostasis happens automatically — controlled by the hypothalamus and the pituitary gland in the brain.

Section Four — Human Biology Part Two

Kidneys

Q1) The kidneys are the body's filters. They adjust the levels of various substances in the blood and remove ones we don't need.

   a) What are the three main roles of the kidneys?
   b) What does the word excretion mean?

Q2) The diagram opposite shows part of the system involving the kidneys.

   a) Name the parts of the system A – F.
   b) How does the blood travelling through parts B and C differ?

Q3) There are approximately a million tube systems in a kidney.

   a) What is the name given to these tube systems.

   b) What surrounds each of them?

   c) Below is a diagram of a single tube system. The table opposite contains a description of each part.

      Match the labels (**a**) — (**h**) with their correct description 1 — 10.

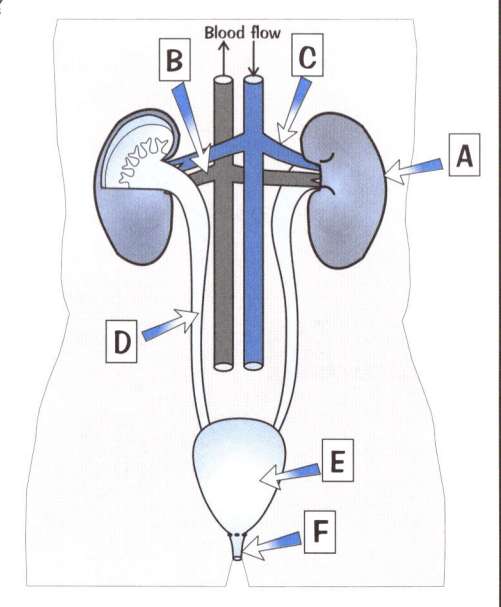

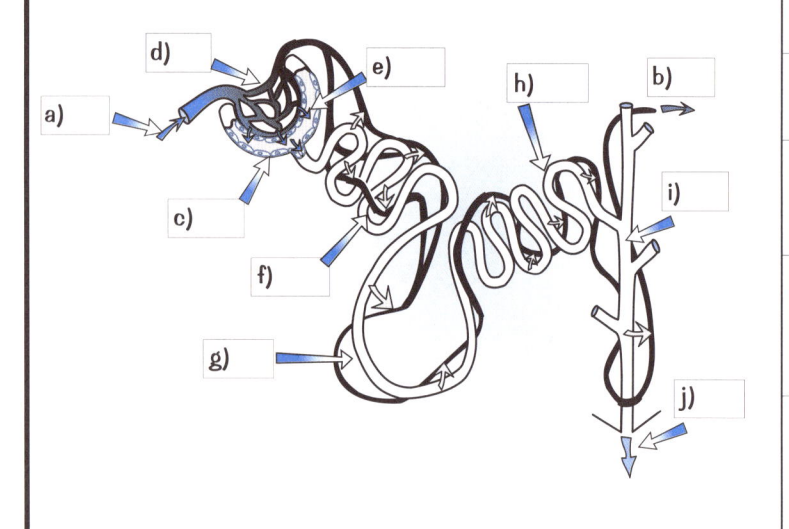

1. Branch of the renal artery — blood here requires "cleaning".	6. Glomerulus — a knot of capillaries that increases the blood pressure.
2. Glomerular filtrate — produced by the process of ultrafiltration.	7. Branch of renal vein taking away filtered blood.
3. First coiled tubule — glucose and amino acids reabsorbed back into blood here.	8. Second coiled tubule — selective reabsorption occurs here to prevent the loss of water and salts.
4. The Loop of Henlé — ion exchange allows sufficient water to be reabsorbed – depends on level of ADH in liquid.	9. Collecting duct — carries away waste liquid after reabsorption.
5. Bowman's Capsule — water, urea, ions and glucose are squeezed into here. Also supports knot of capillaries and leads to tubule.	10. Tubes leading to the bladder — carry away urine, the waste liquid consisting of urea and excess ions and water.

Section Four — Human Biology Part Two

Section Five — Genetics and Evolution

Variation in Plants and Animals

Q1) When Alex looked at the ivy plant growing up the oak tree in his back garden, he was surprised how much the size and colour of the leaves varied.

  a) What kind of variation is this?

  b) What can affect the size and colour of ivy leaves?

  c) Ivy plants have a very distinctive shape to their leaves. All mature leaves have the same shape. Is this genetically or environmentally determined?

Q2) The jumbled list below shows different human characteristics.

Mass   Eye Colour   Fitness (measured by resting pulse)   Hair Colour   Intelligence   Height

  a) Which of these characteristics show:
    i) continuous variation?
    ii) discontinuous variation?

  b) Which of the features are:
    i) affected by the environment?
    ii) not affected by the environment?

  c) Give the characteristic least affected by inheritance.

  d) Choose any one feature and explain how it is affected by the environment.

Q3) Identical twins have the same genes, so they are genetically identical. The table shows four people, identified by the letters a, b, c and d.

Characteristic	Person a	Person b	Person c	Person d
Have a sun tan	✓	✓		
They are male	✓	✓	✓	
They are female				✓
Can tongue roll	✓		✓	
Normal hair colour is brown	✓	✓	✓	✓
Have bleached white hair			✓	✓
Have brown eyes	✓	✓	✓	

  a) i) Use the information in the table to identify which two people are identical twins.
    ii) Explain your answer.

  b) From the table, give one characteristic which shows:
    i) continuous variation.
    ii) discontinuous variation.

Q4) Place ticks in the table below to give the correct information for each of the human characteristics.

Characteristic (human)	Type of Variation Continuous	Type of Variation Discontinuous	Affected by Environment Yes	Affected by Environment No
Birth weight				
Skin colour				
Blood group				
Hand span				
Eye colour				
Haemophilia				

Q5) People belong to one of these four blood groups: A, B, AB and O. Use the words from the list to fill in the spaces.

discontinuous   environmental   inherited   range

Blood groups show _____ variation. Here, there is not a wide _____ of characteristics. Our blood group is _____ and is not altered by _____ conditions.

Genetics

Q1) Complete the crossword by answering these questions.

Across
- 3 - A male gamete. (5,4)
- 6 - Sex of child when an ovum joins with a Y carrying sperm cell. (4)
- 8 - A sex cell. (6)
- 11 - Contains genes. (10)
- 12 - The genes that are present. (8)
- 14 - The allele that is masked when a dominant gene is present. (9)

Down
- 1 - Has a nucleus, cytoplasm and a membrane. (4)
- 2 - One of two genes that control a particular characteristic. (6)
- 4 - The bases in DNA aren't single they're.... (6)
- 5 - Genetically identical individual. (5)
- 7 - The condition when the two alleles are different. (12)
- 8 - A section of DNA that controls a particular characteristic. (4)
- 9 - Produced when a sperm joins with an egg. (6)
- 10 - Cell division which produces sex cells. (7)
- 13 - Egg cells. (3)

Q2) In humans, the haploid number is 23.

a) Are sperm haploid or diploid?
b) What is the process that joins the sperm and egg cell called?
c) How many chromosomes are there in the zygote of a human?
d) How many chromosomes are there in the zygote of a crayfish whose diploid number is 112?
e) What type of cell division produces the sperm and egg cells?
f) What type of cell division is used for growth?
g) What is a gamete?

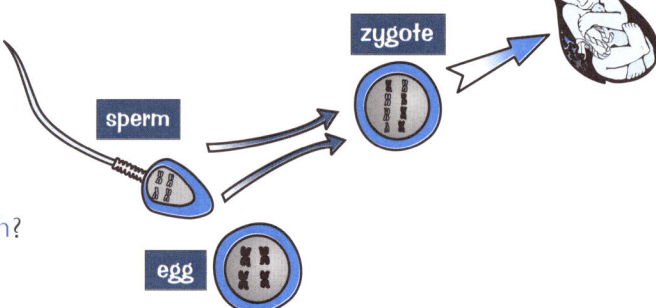

Q3) The diagram shows the arrangement of four genes on a pair of chromosomes.

a) Give the letters of two genes that are alleles.
b) State which of the alleles are:
   i) dominant,
   ii) recessive.
c) "B" determines brown eye colour and "b" blue eye colour. What colour eyes would the person with the arrangement in the diagram have? Explain your answer.

Section Five — Genetics and Evolution

Genetics

Q4) Complete the sentences by choosing the correct word from inside the brackets.

a) The allele that determines a characteristic in the heterozygous state is (dominant / recessive).
b) Another name for a sex cell is a (gamete / zygote).
c) The genes a person has is called his (genotype / phenotype).
d) Chromosomes are made up of (carbohydrates / DNA).
e) In humans, a cell that has all 46 chromosomes is said to be (diploid / haploid).
f) Our bodies use (meiosis / mitosis) to produce cells for growth.
g) The (heterozygous / homozygous) condition is when two alleles are the same.
h) An egg cell is an example of a (gamete / zygote).
i) Genetically identical organisms are (clones / mutations) of each other.
j) Random combination of chromosomes in meiosis creates (mutation / variation).

Q5) Match up the dark boxes with the correct pale boxes, on the right. An example has been done for you.

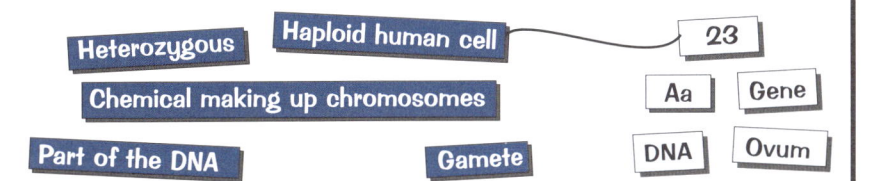

Dark boxes: Heterozygous | Haploid human cell | Chemical making up chromosomes | Part of the DNA | Gamete

Pale boxes: 23 | Aa | Gene | DNA | Ovum

(Haploid human cell — 23)

Q6) On the right is a genetic diagram showing how two pea plants could share their genes by cross fertilisation.

a) What do we mean by:
 i) phenotype?
 ii) genotype?
b) What do we mean by "F1 generation"?
c) What is the ratio of their:
 i) genotypes?
 ii) phenotypes?
d) Give all the possible genotypes from the alleles T and t.
e) What are the possible phenotypes from these alleles?

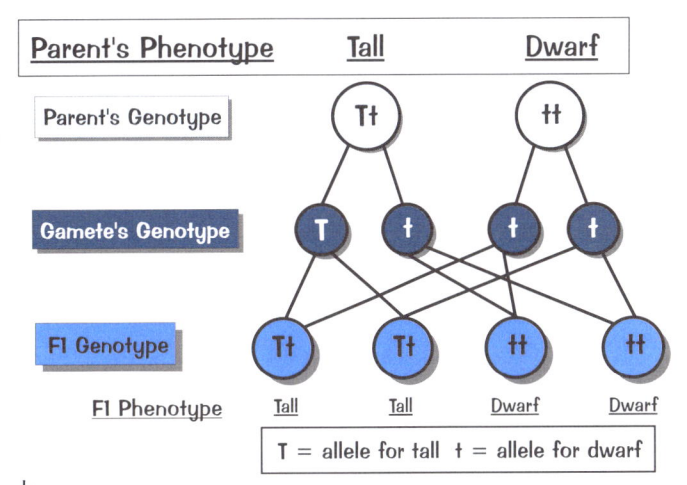

Parent's Phenotype: Tall — Dwarf
Parent's Genotype: Tt — tt
Gamete's Genotype: T, t, t, t
F1 Genotype: Tt, Tt, tt, tt
F1 Phenotype: Tall, Tall, Dwarf, Dwarf

T = allele for tall   t = allele for dwarf

Q7) Fill in the blanks with the following words.

alleles   centromere   chromatids   DNA   dominant
gene   heterozygous   homozygous   recessive

Chromosomes are made of _____. They are made up of separate arms called _____. The middle part of chromosomes, connecting the chromatids is called the _____. A _____ is a section of DNA. Different versions of the same gene are called _____. The allele which determines the characteristic is said to be _____. The one whose characteristic is masked is _____. When both alleles are the same, we say the individual is _____. Whereas, when they are different the individual is said to be _____.

Top Tips: The really important thing here is to learn the words. If you don't know what they mean, you won't be able to understand the rest of this topic. In Question 4, there are a lot of words that look similar but mean very different things.

Section Five — Genetics and Evolution

Genes, Chromosomes and DNA

Q1) This is a typical animal cell.

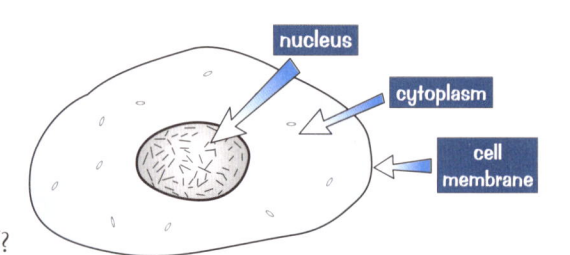

a) What part of the cell are chromosomes found in?

b) If this was a human cheek cell, how many chromosomes would there be inside it?

c) What is the chemical that chromosomes are made of?

Q2) Complete the blanks using the following words.

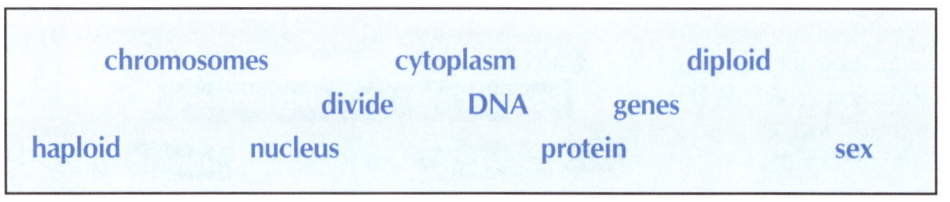

> chromosomes   cytoplasm   diploid
> divide   DNA   genes
> haploid   nucleus   protein   sex

The _____ contains the chromosomes that carry the genes. Every species has its own number of _____. In humans, it is 23 pairs (46 chromosomes). This is called the _____ number. Every cell in the body of living things has the diploid number, except the _____ cells. These cells have the _____ number which in humans is 23 chromosomes. The _____ on the chromosomes control the characteristics of organisms. Chromosomes are made up of a double helix of _____. A gene is a portion of DNA that acts as a code for the production of a particular _____. Proteins are assembled in the _____ of a cell. When cells _____ the DNA has to be copied accurately.

Q3) The diagram shows the connection between DNA and several characteristics.

a) i) Where is the DNA found in cells?
   ii) Where are proteins made in the cell?

b) Fill in the spaces to complete the diagram.

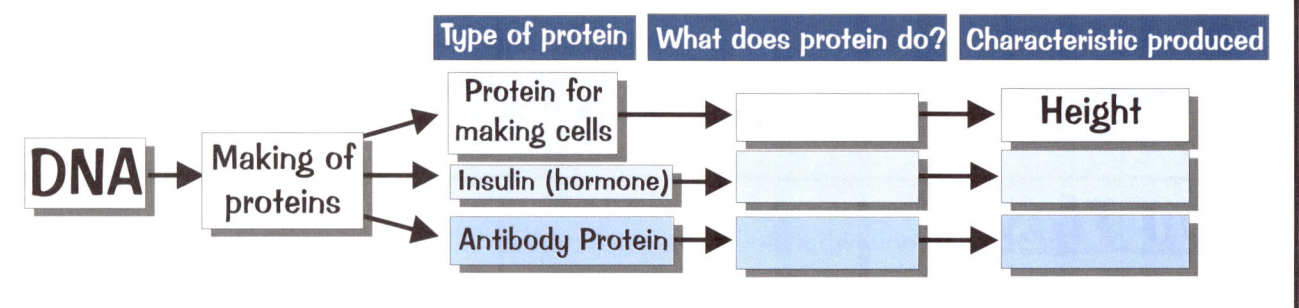

	Type of protein	What does protein do?	Characteristic produced
DNA → Making of proteins →	Protein for making cells		Height
	Insulin (hormone)		
	Antibody Protein		

Section Five — Genetics and Evolution

Genes, Chromosomes and DNA

c) What happens to the characteristics if the DNA is changed (mutated)? Explain your answer.

d) Milk has proteins in it. The proteins contained in milk vary for different mammals. Why is this?

Q4) The figures below show the chromosomes of a human male and female.

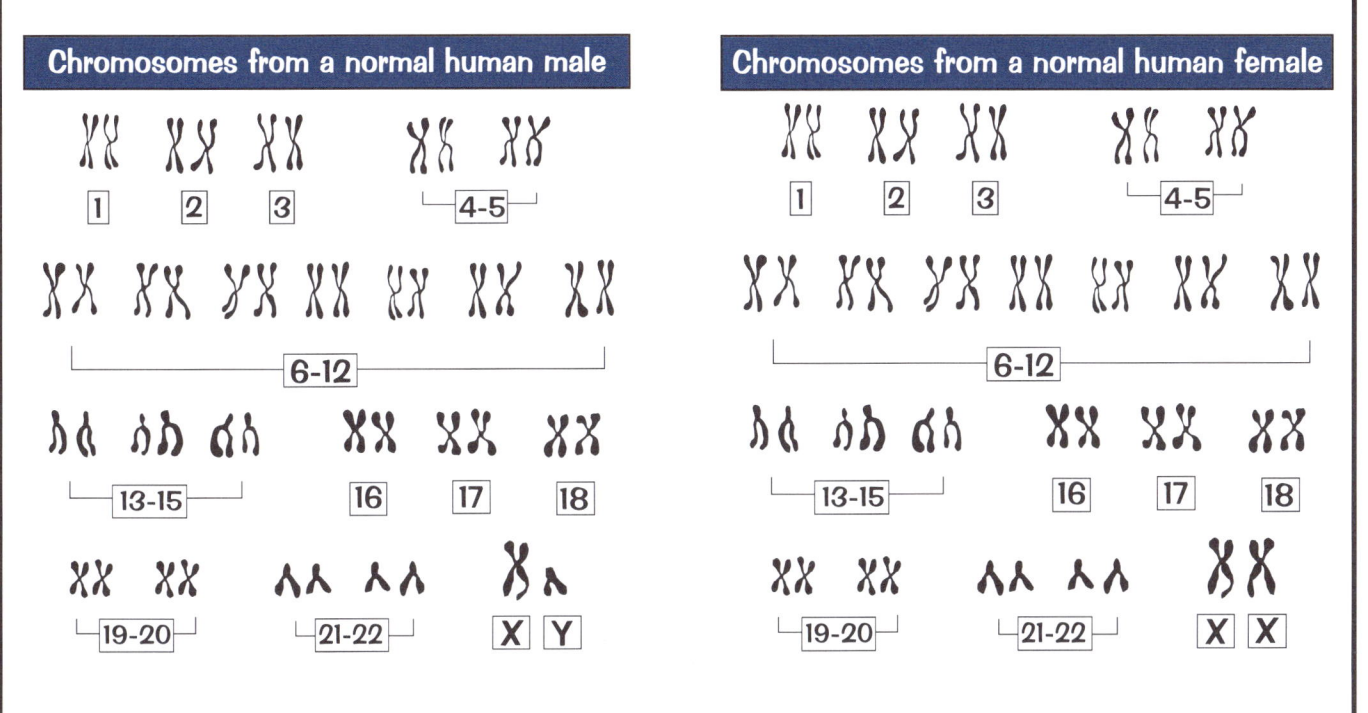

Chromosomes from a normal human male

1, 2, 3, 4-5, 6-12, 13-15, 16, 17, 18, 19-20, 21-22, X Y

Chromosomes from a normal human female

1, 2, 3, 4-5, 6-12, 13-15, 16, 17, 18, 19-20, 21-22, X X

a) What is the difference between the two sets of chromosomes?

b) Why do we talk in terms of pairs of chromosomes?

c) i) How many chromosomes do we have in each body cell?
   ii) Where in the cell are the chromosomes found?

d) i) What is the name of the chemical that makes up chromosomes?
   ii) How is this chemical arranged?
   iii) What do we call sections of this chemical?

Top Tips: You need to know what a chromosome is, where in the cell it's found and what a gene is, what it's made of and what it does. Remember that portions of DNA that have the code for one protein are called genes. We have pairs of chromosomes, one from each parent.

Section Five — Genetics and Evolution

Mitosis and Meiosis

Q1) Use the following words to complete the blanks.

| asexual | exact | gametes | parent | reduction | two |

Mitosis is a process used during growth and _____ reproduction. Each chromosome in the original cell makes an _____ copy of itself. When this type of division is complete, _____ daughter cells are produced, each having the same chromosome number as the _____ cell. Meiosis is a _____ division — this means that the number of chromosomes in the original cell is reduced (halved). This process is used in the production of male and female _____. Meiosis involves some jumbling of genetic material, so producing variation.

Q2) State whether the following statements apply to meiosis or mitosis.

a) Produces *haploid* cells.

b) Produces identical cells to *parent* cell.

c) At the end of division, two *daughter* cells are produced.

d) Used in *sexual* reproduction.

e) Used in a*sexual* reproduction.

Q3) The diagram opposite shows the difference between the two types of cell division.

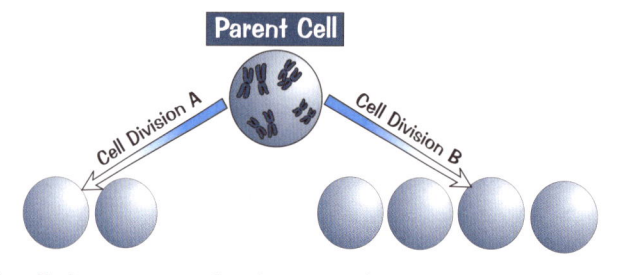

Parent Cell

Cell Division A   Cell Division B

a) Name the type of cell division involved in A and B.

b) Where does A take place in the human body?

c) Where does B take place:
   i) in a plant?   ii) in the human body?

d) If the diagram represents cell division in the human body, how many chromosomes are there in one of the cells produced from:
   i) division A?   ii) division B?

Section Five — Genetics and Evolution

Mitosis and Meiosis

Q4) Complete the information in the spaces in the table.

Organism	Number of chromosomes in a body cell	Number of pairs of chromosomes	Number of chromosomes in each gamete	Haploid number	Diploid number
Fruit Fly	8				
Kangaroo	12				
Rye Plant	20				
Chicken	36				
Mouse	40				
Humans	46				
Crayfish	200				

Q5) Diagram A shows the stages involved in cell reproduction by mitosis.
Diagram B shows the stages involved in cell reproduction by meiosis.

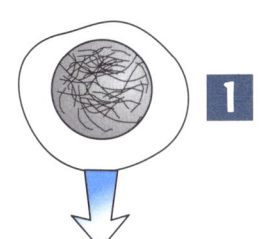

For each diagram, describe in your own words what is happening at each of the numbered stages.

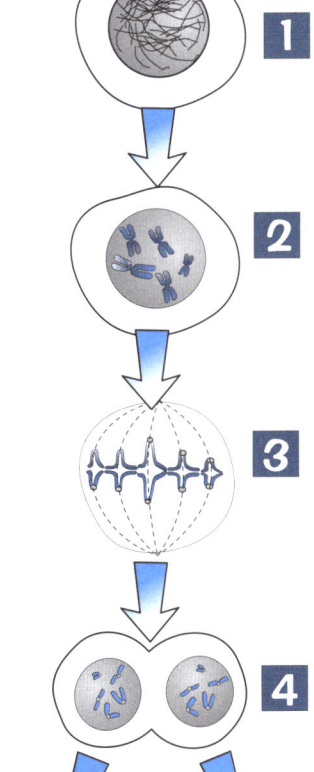

Diagram A

Diagram B

Top Tips:
The big thing is remembering the difference between mitosis and meiosis.
Mitosis gives you **two identical diploid cells** — it's used for growth, repair and asexual reproduction. **Meiosis** gives **four different haploid cells** and is **only** used for the production of sex cells.

Section Five — Genetics and Evolution

Fertilisation

Q1) The diagram shows the progress from sex cells to a baby.

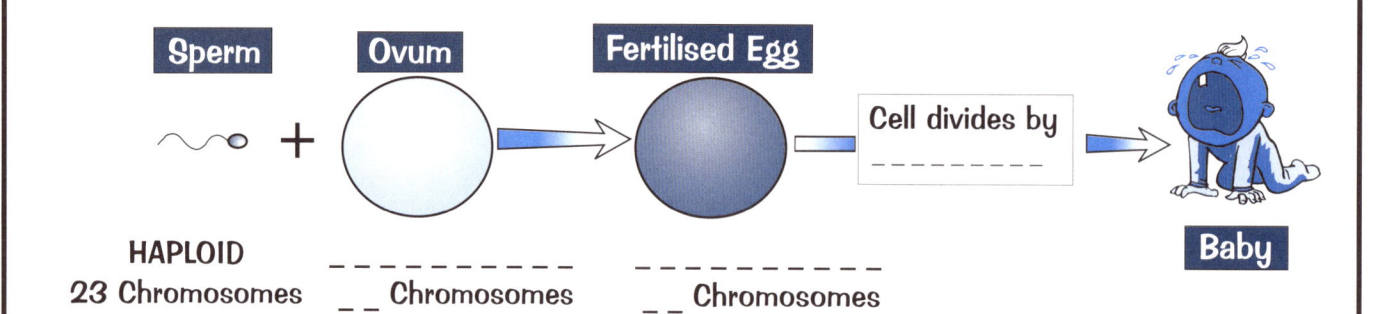

Sperm + **Ovum** → **Fertilised Egg** → Cell divides by _____ → **Baby**

HAPLOID
23 Chromosomes   _ _ Chromosomes   _ _ Chromosomes

a) Complete the five spaces in the diagram above.
b) Name the reproductive organs that produce:
 i) sperm cells.
 ii) ova.
c) What word also means sperm and egg cells?
d) What is another name for a fertilised egg?
e) What do we call the process where sperm and egg cells join together?
f) Where does fertilisation take place in the body of the human female?

Q2) Gametes are haploid, that is to say, they carry only one chromosome from each pair found in their parent cells.

a) Complete the diagram below by drawing how the chromosomes in the fertilised egg would appear after the joining of the sperm and ovum.

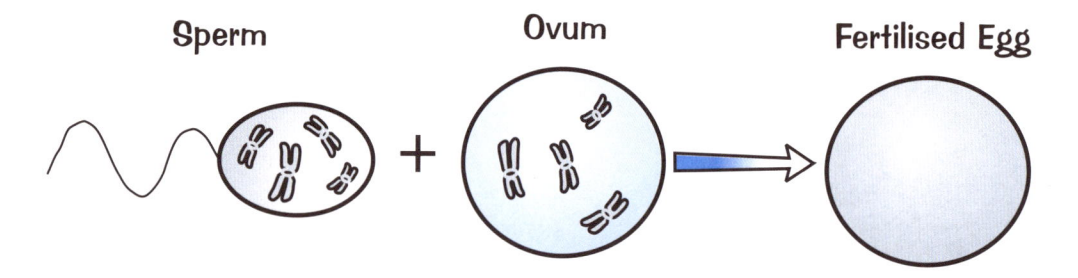

Sperm + **Ovum** → **Fertilised Egg**

b) i) Where are sperm cells produced?
 ii) Where are egg cells produced?
c) How is information carried from:
 i) the father to the child?
 ii) the mother to the child?
d) Chromosomes appear in pairs.
 i) What word describes a matching pair of chromosomes?
 ii) How many pairs of chromosomes do we have in our body cells?

Section Five — Genetics and Evolution

Fertilisation

Q3) Use the following words to complete the blanks.

| children   chromosome   diploid   egg   fertilisation   gametes |
| meiosis   ova   ovaries   sperm   testes   variation |

Sexual reproduction involves the production of _____, followed by _____. Random combination of chromosomes in _____ creates genetic _____ amongst the sperm and _____ cells produced. The random fusion of gametes gives rise to variation in the _____. The male gametes are the _____ cells and the female gametes are the egg cells (also called _____). Male gametes are produced in the _____ and female gametes are produced in the _____. The gametes contain one _____ from each homologous pair. When fertilisation occurs, these chromosomes come together to produce the correct _____ number, which in humans is 46.

Q4) Define the following words.

diploid   fertilisation   gamete   haploid   ova   ovaries   zygote

Q5) Match the appropriate descriptions on the left to the terms on the right.

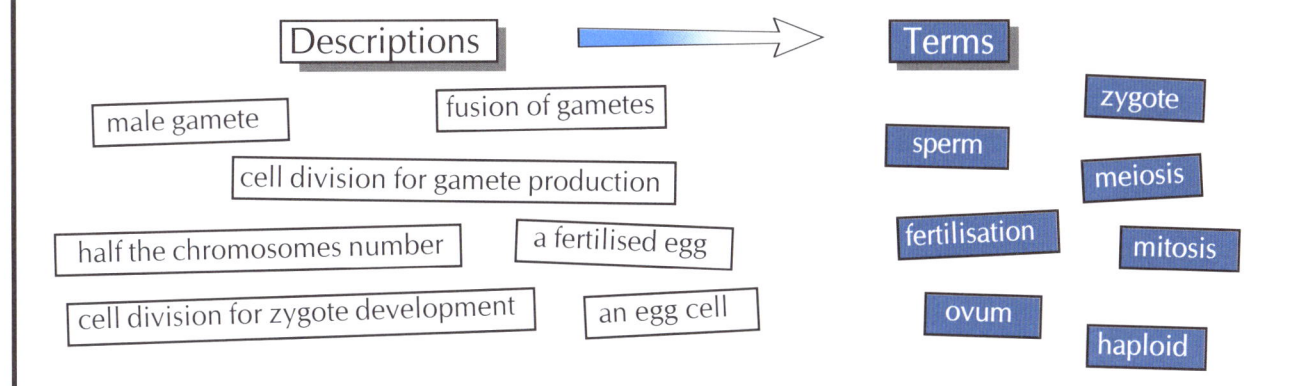

Descriptions →   Terms

- male gamete
- fusion of gametes
- cell division for gamete production
- half the chromosomes number
- a fertilised egg
- cell division for zygote development
- an egg cell

Terms: zygote, sperm, meiosis, fertilisation, mitosis, ovum, haploid

Q6) Complete the sentences below by choosing a word from inside the brackets.

a) Gametes are produced by (meiosis / mitosis).

b) Another name for sex cells is (gametes / zygotes).

c) Chromosomes occur in (homologous / homozygous) pairs.

d) Gametes are (diploid / haploid) cells.

e) Another name for an egg cell is an (ovary / ovum).

Top Tips: You know the basic point that fertilisation is when a sperm and an egg cell fuse together, but remember that two **haploid** cells are fusing together to form a **diploid** cell. Don't forget that **after** fertilisation, this cell is called a **zygote** — a funny name, but you need to know it.

Section Five — Genetics and Evolution

Mutations

Q1) Cells A and B are taken from two different Drosophila flies (fruit flies). One cell is normal, the other has a mutation which gives the fly misshapen eyes. Cell A has the mutant gene.

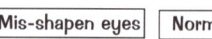

a) What is a gene?
b) How can mutations like this one arise?
c) i) Is there any chance that this fly's offspring will have the mutation?
   ii) Explain your answer.

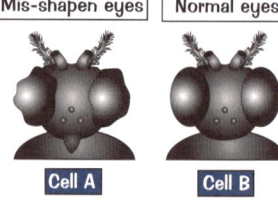

Q2) Complete the blanks by using the following words.

antibiotics	beneficial	carcinogens	divide
genetic	sex	harmful	
ionising	mitosis	mutagens	mutations
	naturally	neutral	
chromosome	nucleus	replication	

A mutation is a change in a gene or a _____. Different genes can result from such a change. Mutations can occur _____ when DNA is incorrectly copied during _____. Gene mutations may start in a single _____ of one cell. As the cells _____ to produce more cells, the number of cells carrying the new form increase. The chance of _____ occurring can be increased by exposure to _____ radiation, X-rays, ultra-violet light and also certain chemicals. The greater the dose, the greater the chance of mutations occurring. Chemicals that cause mutations are called _____ and include substances found in cigarette smoke. Such substances are called _____ because they can increase the chance of people having cancer. Most mutations are _____. If mutations occur in _____ cells, the children may develop abnormally. This can result in early death. Mutations that occur in body cells can cause uncontrollable cell division (_____), resulting in cancer. Some mutations are _____ in their effects, causing no apparent harm or benefit to the individual. On rare occasions, a mutation can be _____, increasing an organism's chances of survival. Bacteria mutating has definitely benefited them by giving them resistance to the _____ we use against them. Mutation is the source of _____ variation. Changing by acquiring new forms of old genes is how living things have evolved by natural selection.

Q3) Answer these questions about mutations:

a) Mutations can be both beneficial and harmful. Give one example of each.

b) The blue colour in budgies appeared as a mutation in green budgies. This does not affect the survival of budgies in any way. What does this tell us about some mutations?

Section Five — Genetics and Evolution

X and Y Chromosomes

Q1) The graph on the right shows the relationship between the amount of ionising radiation and the number of recessive, lethal (deadly) alleles induced in the sperm cells of a mouse.

  a) What does the graph show us?
  b) i) What does ionising radiation do to genes?
     ii) What is an allele?
  c) Besides ionising radiation, what else can cause similar effects?

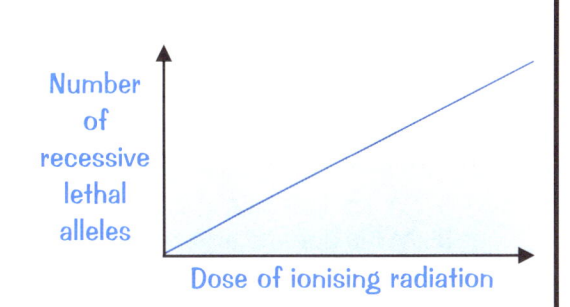

Q2) Cells A and B are male and female reproductive cells.

  a) Label the two sex chromosomes in cells A and B. Which cell is male and which female?
  b) Where are cells A and B found in the body?
  c) What are male gametes and female gametes called?

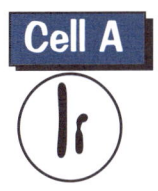

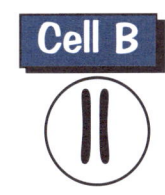

Q3) Answer these questions:

  a) Copy and complete the diagram which shows how sex is inherited.

Parents' Phenotype:	————	————
Parents' Genotype:	X X	X _
Gametes' Genotype:	X X	X _
Childrens' Genotype:	_ _ X Y	X X _ _
Childrens' Phenotype:	—— ——	—— ——

  b) Work out from the diagram the ratio of boys to girls.
  c) A couple have one child, Janet. The couple are convinced that their next child will be a boy because they already have a daughter. Is this true? Explain your answer.
  d) Genotypes of offspring can also be worked out with a checkerboard type diagram (sometimes called a Punnett Square) Complete the diagram to the right.

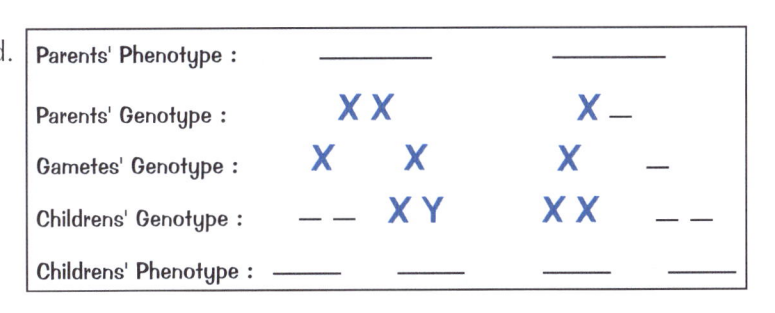

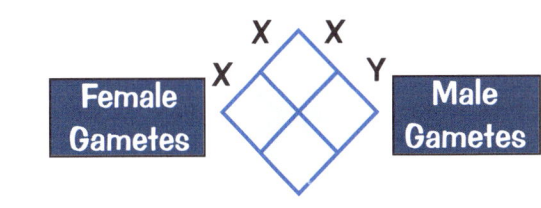

Q4) In the old days, kings have been known to behead their wives for not giving them sons.

  a) What sex chromosomes do sperm cells have?
  b) What sex chromosomes do egg cells have?
  c) i) Is it the man's or woman's gametes that determine the sex of the child?
     ii) Explain your answer.

Section Five — Genetics and Evolution

Monohybrid Crosses

Q1) The diagram shows a cross between a black male mouse and a brown female mouse.

a) What does homozygous mean?

b) Why are some genes represented by "B" and others by "b"?

c) Explain why B and b are alleles.

d) The F1 are all heterozygous black.
  i) What does F1 stand for?
  ii) What does heterozygous mean?

e) i) Which allele is dominant?
  ii) Explain what dominant means.

f) i) What does genotype mean?
  ii) What does phenotype mean?

Parents' Phenotype:	Homozygous Black Male	Homozygous Brown Female
Parents' Genotype:	BB	bb
Gametes' Genotype:	B B	b b
Offsprings' Genotype:	Bb Bb	Bb Bb
Offsprings' Phenotype:	All Heterozygous Black	

g) Two individuals from the F1, a male and a female, are taken and mated.
  i) Use a checkerboard type diagram to show the cross.
  ii) What are the phenotypes and genotypes of the offspring?
  iii) What is the ratio of the phenotypes of the offspring?
  iv) What do we call this generation?

Q2) A brown eyed man married a blue eyed woman. The allele for brown eyes is dominant and that for blue eyes is recessive. (The father is heterozygous for the gene)

a) What letters would you use for the brown and blue alleles?

b) On the diagram, complete the cross by filling in the spaces.

c) Which individuals are homozygous?

Parents' Phenotype:	Blue eyed mother	Brown eyed father
Parents' Genotype:	___	___
Gametes' Genotype:	___ ___	___ ___
Offsprings' Genotype:	___ ___	___ ___
Offsprings' Phenotype:	___ ___	___ ___

d) How is it possible for two brown eyed individuals to have a blue eyed baby?

Q3) Complete the blanks with these words.

alleles   F1   F2   genotype   height   heterozygous
homozygous   monohybrid   phenotype   recessive

In _____ crosses, we only cross for one characteristic, such as _____ in pea plants or colour in mice. Each gene has two different forms — these are called _____. The allele whose characteristic is masked in the presence of a dominant gene is _____. If two alleles are the same, we say they are _____ and if they are different, they are _____. The word _____ refers to the appearance or the physical characteristic that results, whereas _____ refers to the alleles present. In genetic crosses, we talk about different generations. The _____ represents the children and the _____ the grandchildren.

Q4) The Stewarts are a Scottish family from Glasgow. Margarite Stewart is a dark haired woman who has an auburn haired son called Cameron. Margarite's mum has auburn hair. Half of Margarite's brothers and sisters have dark hair, the other half have auburn hair.
Auburn hair is recessive to dark hair.

a) What letters would you use to represent the two alleles?

b) What genotypes do the following have:
i) Margarite? ii) Cameron? iii) Margarite's two parents? iv) Margarite's dark haired brother?
v) Margarite's auburn haired sister?

Section Five — Genetics and Evolution

Monohybrid Crosses

Q5) This is a pedigree chart showing how the ability to taste the chemical PTC is inherited. PTC is a chemical that tastes bitter to some people but is tasteless to others. The ability to taste this substance is determined by a dominant allele.

a) i) Is person 9 a male or female?
   ii) Is this person a taster or non-taster?

b) i) What letters would you use to represent the two alleles?
   ii) What is the genotype of person 2?
   iii) How did you work this out?

c) i) What is the genotype of 4?
   ii) What is the evidence for this?

d) Give one example of a person who must be
   i) homozygous.
   ii) heterozygous.

e) Draw two genetic diagrams to show the possible genotypes for offspring of 1 and 2.

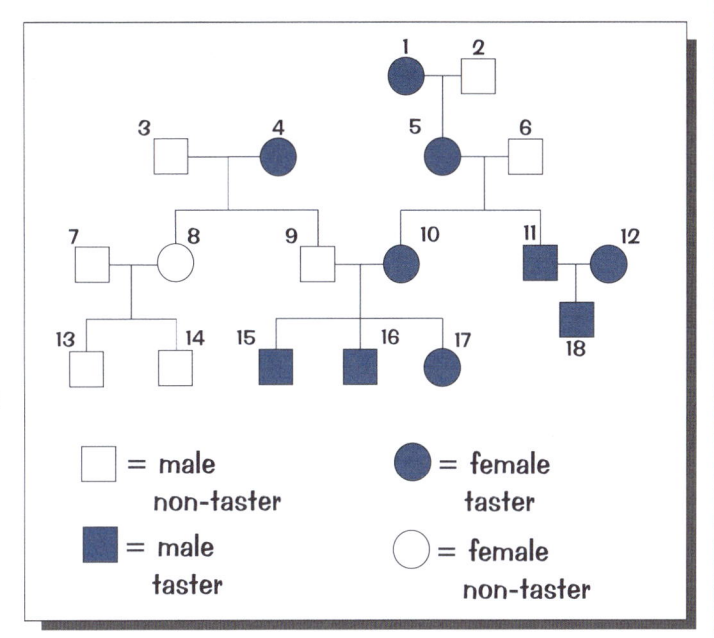

☐ = male non-taster
■ = male taster
● = female taster
○ = female non-taster

Q6) Gregor Mendel was an Austrian monk. He trained in mathematics and natural history at the University of Vienna. On his garden plot at the monastery, Mendel noted how characteristics in plants were passed on from one generation to the next. The diagrams show two of the crosses that Mendel carried out.

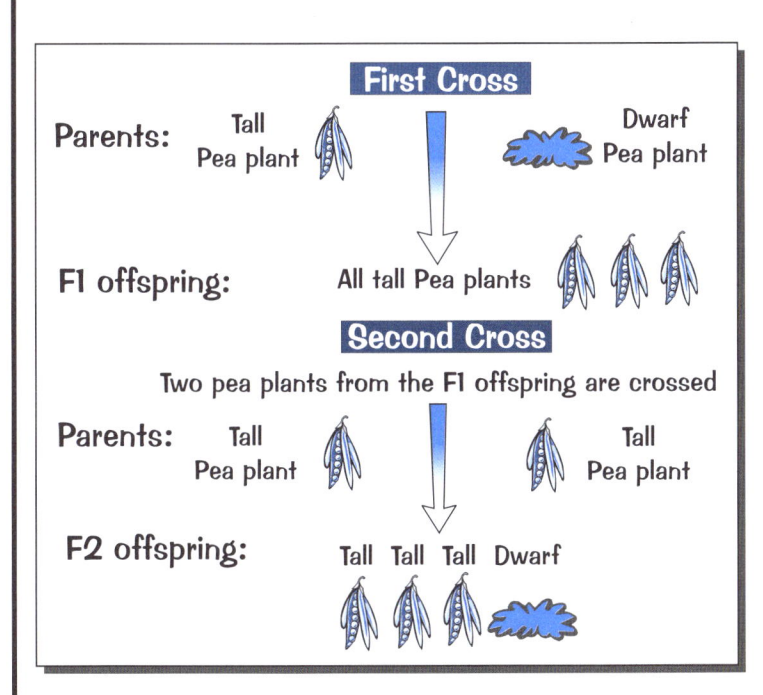

First Cross
Parents: Tall Pea plant × Dwarf Pea plant
F1 offspring: All tall Pea plants

Second Cross
Two pea plants from the F1 offspring are crossed
Parents: Tall Pea plant × Tall Pea plant
F2 offspring: Tall Tall Tall Dwarf

From the first cross:
a) i) Give the genotypes of the dwarf and the tall parents.
   ii) Give the genotypes of the F1 offspring.

From the second cross:
b) i) What is the ratio of genotypes of the F2 offspring?
   ii) What is the ratio of genotypes of the F2 offspring?
   iii) Which individuals are homozygous?
   iv) Which individuals are heterozygous?

c) What other characteristics in a pea plant could Mendel have experimented with?

Top Tips: Enough already with the confusing words. A **monohybrid cross** means you're crossing for just **one** characteristic. Remember that a **heterozygous** individual displays the **dominant** characteristic, **not** something in between dominant and recessive.

Section Five — Genetics and Evolution

Cystic Fibrosis

Q1) Use these words to complete the blanks.

| allele | both | carriers | digestive | genetic |
| lungs | membranes | mucus | recessive | |

Cystic fibrosis is a _____ disease. One in twenty people in this country carry the recessive allele. Sufferers must have two _____ alleles. Cystic fibrosis is a disorder of cell _____. In the lungs, the membranes produce thick sticky _____ which makes breathing more difficult and causes more infections to the _____. Infections are treated with antibiotics. The mucus can be removed by regular physiotherapy and massage. Excess mucus is also produced in the pancreas, causing _____ problems. Sufferers have a shortened life. Since the disease is caused by a recessive _____, it must be inherited from _____ parents. Parents who have the recessive allele are _____ of the disorder. Carriers have no ill-effects themselves.

Q2) Match the genotypes with the correct description.

normal   carrier   sufferer   CC   cc   Cc

Q3) The diagram below shows a cross between two unaffected people.

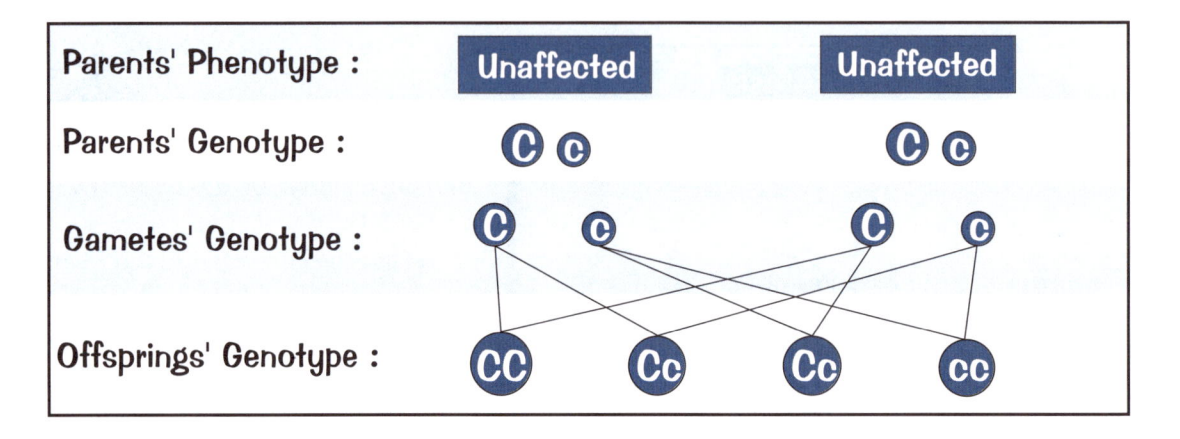

Parents' Phenotype :	Unaffected	Unaffected
Parents' Genotype :	C c	C c
Gametes' Genotype :	C c	C c
Offsprings' Genotype :	CC Cc Cc cc	

a) From the diagram, which individuals are:

i) carriers?
ii) sufferers?
iii) homozygous?
iv) heterozygous?

b) What do we mean by carriers?

c) Draw this diagram in the form of a checkerboard.

Section Five — Genetics and Evolution

Cystic Fibrosis

Q4) Complete the sentences by selecting the correct word or words from inside the brackets.

a) Cystic fibrosis is an (infectious / inherited) disease.
b) Cystic fibrosis is caused by a (dominant / recessive) allele.
c) Children can inherit the cystic fibrosis disease when (both/one) of their parents have the recessive allele.
d) Sufferers of cystic fibrosis have breathing problems due to (small lungs / the excessive production of mucus).
e) The allele for cystic fibrosis is found (equally in men and women / only in men).

Q5) The diagram shows a family who have been tested for the cystic fibrosis allele.

a) Using appropriate letters, give the genotypes of the mother and father.
b) Will any of the children be sufferers?
c) i) Can you say which children will carry a recessive allele?
   ii) Explain your answer.
d) What is the chance of Beth being a carrier?
e) What proportion of their children are likely to be normal?
f) i) From the diagram, can we tell whether both of the father's parents were carriers?
   ii) Explain your answer.

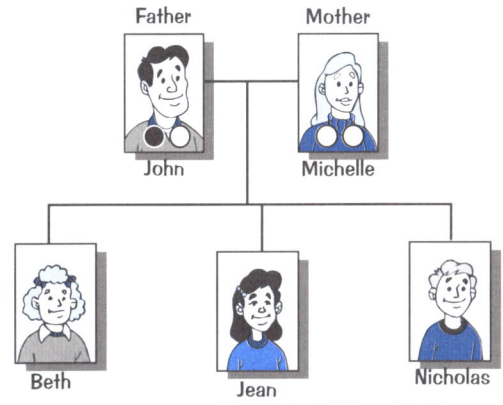

Q6) If two carriers have children, there is a 1 in 4 chance of each child having the disease.

a) Show how this ratio is derived with a genetic diagram.
b) Can children suffer from the disease if only one parent has a recessive allele?
c) One in twenty people carry the allele for cystic fibrosis in this country. What do we mean by "carrying" the allele?

Q7) Match up the statements on the left with the correct answers from the right. There may be more than one correct answer.

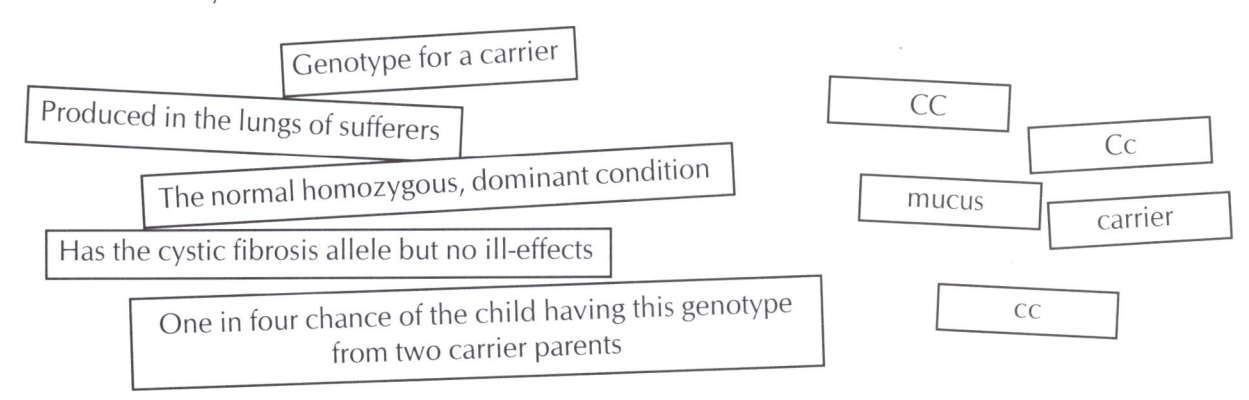

Left:
- Genotype for a carrier
- Produced in the lungs of sufferers
- The normal homozygous, dominant condition
- Has the cystic fibrosis allele but no ill-effects
- One in four chance of the child having this genotype from two carrier parents

Right:
- CC
- Cc
- mucus
- carrier
- cc

Top Tips: This is a good example of a genetic disease that's caused by having **one** faulty gene. This means you can work out a **monohybrid cross**, as in question 3. Remember, you're expected to know about the **symptoms** as well as the genetics behind the disease.

Genetic Diseases

Q1) Use the following words to complete the blanks:

alleles	blood	carrier	malaria	oxygen	protected	recessive	red

Sickle cell anaemia is a disorder of _____ blood cells. It is caused by a _____ allele. Being a _____ of this disorder can be an advantage in countries where _____ is prevalent. Carriers are _____ from malaria. The disease gets its name from the shape of the red _____ cells. Children who inherit two recessive _____ from their parents have red cells which are less efficient at carrying oxygen. The red blood cells also stick together in the blood capillaries. This deprives the body cells of _____ .

Q2) Map A shows the distribution of the sickle cell allele in Africa.
Map B shows the distribution of malaria in the same geographical region.

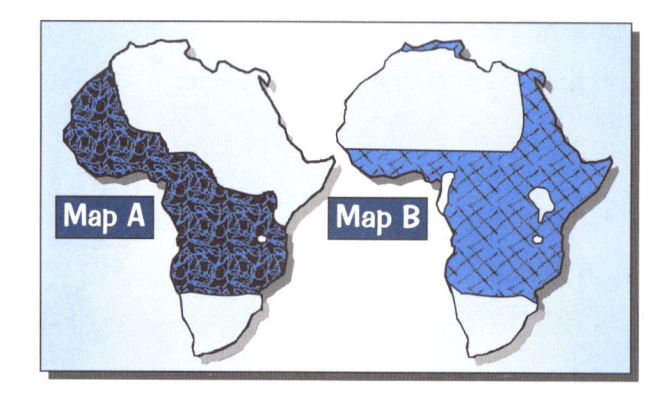

a) Why are the distributions so similar?
b) Sickle cell anaemia is a killer disease.
  i) What is an advantage for people who are carriers of the disease?
  ii) What is a disadvantage for people who are carriers of the disease?

Q3) Two carriers marry and have three children.

a) Complete the spaces in the diagram.

Parents' Phenotype : _____ _____
Parents' Genotype : _____ _____
Gametes' Genotype : ___ ___   ___ ___
Offsprings' Genotype : ___ ___ ___ ___
Offsprings' Phenotype : ___ ___ ___ ___

b) i) What is the chance of one of the children being a sickle cell sufferer?
  ii) What problems do sufferers of sickle cell anaemia experience?
c) Carriers can enjoy good health, except that they can be anaemic.
  i) What is anaemia?
  ii) What is the advantage of being a carrier?

Section Five — Genetics and Evolution

Genetic Diseases

Q4) Use the following words to complete the blanks.

| allele | disease | dominant | mental | nervous | one |

Huntington's Chorea is caused by a _____ allele. This means that _____ parent can pass on the disorder. A child has a 50% chance of inheriting the condition from one parent with a single dominant _____. This disease affects the _____ system. Symptoms often develop when the person who has inherited the allele is over 35-40 years of age. The _____ causes involuntary movements and _____ deterioration. There is no cure and the condition progressively worsens.

Q5) Answer these questions:

a) A man who is heterozygous for the condition marries a normal woman. What is the chance of their first child having the disease?

b) Diseases caused by a dominant allele are often expected to disappear.
   i) Explain why.   ii) Why is Huntington's Chorea not disappearing?

Q6) The table shows the prevalence of Huntington's Chorea in a number of places. Tasmania with the highest number of cases has a small community.

Suggest a possible reason why the number of cases of Huntington's Chorea is highest in Tasmania.

The prevalence of Huntington's Disease (per million of the population)	
Cornwall	50
Tasmania	170
Victoria	45
USA	50

Q7) Use the diagram on the right to answer these questions on Huntington's Chorea:

a) Complete the spaces to show a cross between a heterozygous man and a woman who is homozygous recessive.

b) What proportion of offspring from this cross are sufferers?

Parents' Phenotype : _____ Father   Mother _____
Parents' Genotype : _____   _____
Gametes' Genotype : ___ ___   ___ ___
Offspring's Genotype : ___ ___ ___ ___
Offspring's Phenotype : ___ ___ ___ ___

Top Tips: Remember, two recessive alleles are needed for someone to suffer from sickle cell anaemia, but the carriers are protected from malaria. The important thing about Huntington's Chorea is that it's caused by a dominant allele.

Section Five — Genetics and Evolution

Selective Breeding

Q1) Use the following words to complete the blanks:

    alleles   breed   characteristics   colours   ears
    milk   people   selective   variety   varieties

Artificial selection is when _____ choose what characteristics to breed into living things. This can be used to produce new _____ and breeds of organisms. We choose the individuals which have _____ which are useful to us. We then _____ from these individuals. We choose individuals from the offspring which have the features useful to us, and breed from them. We repeat this over and over again. This is called _____ breeding. A use for selective breeding in agriculture is the production of varieties of plants and breeds of animals that produce greater yields or other desired characteristics. Examples of selective breeding in animals include the Fresian cow that produces greater _____ yields and dogs like the Basset hound that has droopy _____. Plants like wheat have been bred to grow bigger 'ears' with more grain. Also, new varieties of roses now exist with a wide range of flower _____ and shapes. Selective breeding, though, greatly reduces the number of _____ in a population (the gene pool) and therefore reduces _____.

Q2) People have produced new breeds of dogs to achieve either a particular look or temperament in the dog. Some of the features we have bred in dogs, though, are not advantageous to the dog.

Shar-pei   Basset hound   Bedlington   Bulldog

  a) All dogs have been bred from wolf ancestors. Give two features of wolves that are no longer found in some modern breeds of dogs.
  b) Why are mongrels (random crossbreeds) healthier than pedigree dogs?
  c) Some features bred into dogs are not only of no advantage to the dog, they are harmful to their well being (the price we pay for beauty!). Suggest features of the dog breeds above which could lead to health problems in the dogs.
  d) Bulldogs have narrow hips. Often, these dogs can only give birth if they are assisted by people. What would happen to this breed of dog if people stopped assisting them to give birth?

Q3) Choose the correct word from inside the brackets to complete the sentence.
  a) The process where people breed animals with the best characteristics is called (artificial / natural) selection.
  b) Selective breeding (increases / decreases) the number of alleles in a population.
  c) Farmers often selectively breed to (decrease / increase) yields of food produced.
  d) Selective breeding involves (asexual / sexual) reproduction.
  e) Breeding characteristics like floppy ears into dogs is (advantageous / disadvantageous) to the dog.

Top Tips: This is when people **select** the characteristics they want to breed into plants and animals — it's very useful. You'll need to know **examples** of plants and animals that have been selectively bred. Don't forget the **disadvantages**, too.

Section Five — Genetics and Evolution

Cloning

Q1) This country exports date palms to Iran and oil palms to Malaysia. The reason we can do this is because Britain has advanced technology in tissue culturing. The diagram shows how tissue culturing works.

a) What type of reproduction is this?

b) i) Why are all the plants produced identical?
   ii) What name is given to identical offspring?

c) i) What are the advantages of using tissue cultures?
   ii) What are the disadvantages of using tissue cultures?

d) What other technique produces identical plants?

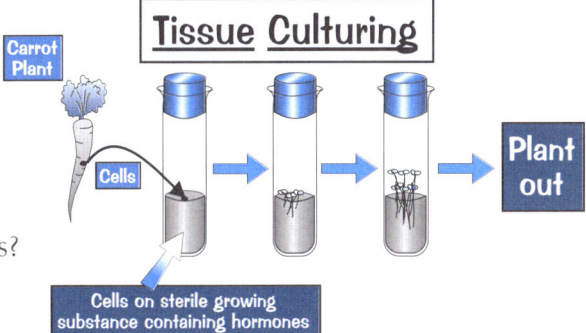

Q2) When we grow parts of plants into new plants, we call these cuttings.

a) What type of reproduction is demonstrated here?

b) How do the plants on the right of the diagram compare genetically with the plants that the cuttings were taken from?

c) How do seeds from these plants compare genetically with the parent plants?

d) i) What is the advantage of taking cuttings?
   ii) What is the disadvantage of taking cuttings?

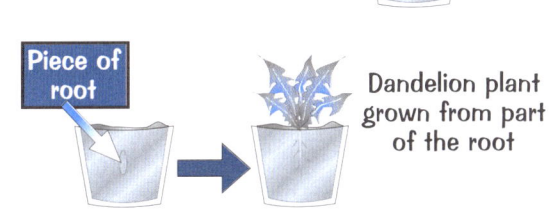

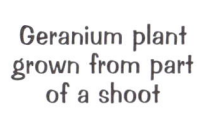

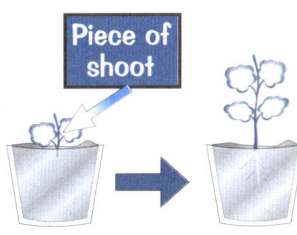

Q3) Choose the correct word from inside the brackets to complete the sentences.

a) Plants produced from cuttings grow into new plants by (meiotic / mitotic) cell division.

b) Tissue cultures are a useful way of producing large numbers of (different / identical) plants from a small number of cells.

c) Genetically identical plants are produced by (asexual / sexual) reproduction.

d) Growing plants from tissue cultures (decreases / increases) the gene pool.

e) Cloning techniques are also used in producing identical animals by splitting embryo cells (after / before) they specialise.

Section Five — Genetics and Evolution

Cloning

Q4) Use the following words to complete the blanks.

*asexual   cells   cuttings   embryo   genetically   host
identical   mitosis   naturally   splitting   tissue*

Clones are _____ identical organisms. These are produced in plants during _____ reproduction when _____ takes place. In plants, examples include reproduction by bulbs, stem tubers and runners, as well as _____. Using _____ cultures also results in genetically _____ offspring, plants or clones. This technique involves growing new plants from small groups of _____ from part of a plant. Cloning techniques are also used in producing identical cells in agriculture. This is done by _____ embryo cells (before they become specialised) from a developing animal _____ and then transplanting the identical embryos into a _____ mother. Clones are also produced _____ as in the case of identical twins.

Q5) The diagram shows how animal clones, like cattle, are produced in agriculture. (This isn't how the famous Dolly the sheep was produced, by the way)

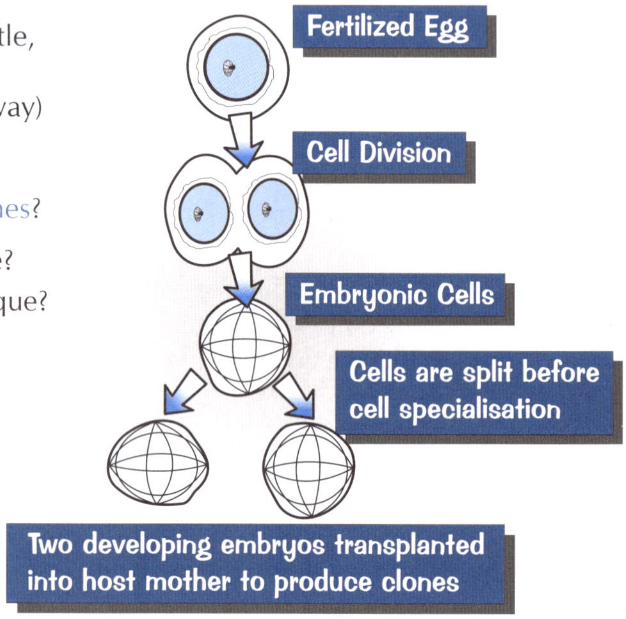

a) By what process does the fertilised egg divide?

b) Why are the two offspring produced called clones?

c) i) What are the advantages of using this technique?
   ii) What are the disadvantages of using this technique?

d) A farmer has a sheep with an excellent coat for making wool. The farmer wants to increase the number of sheep like this he has.
   i) Would you advise him to use breeding or cloning techniques?
   ii) Give a reason for your answer.

Q6) Match the definition with the correct word.

- cell division which produces identical cells
- genetically identical individuals
- reproduction which produces variation in plants
- reproduction which produces identical plants
- cell division producing variation in daughter cells

sexual   clones   asexual   mitosis   meiosis

Top Tips: A scary sci-fi topic if ever I saw one — but clones are just **genetically identical** organisms. You need to be able to describe how **plants** are cloned naturally **and** artificially and the advantages and disadvantages of producing crops and livestock that are clones.

Section Five — Genetics and Evolution

Fossils

Q1) Fossils in good condition are nearly always found in sedimentary rocks.

a) Common places where fossils are found are quarries, rocky beaches and where rocks are cut for road building.
Give a reason why these are good places to find fossils.

b) Fossils of sea creatures can be found in rocks at the top of mountains. Explain how this happens.

c) Most of the fossils found are those of sea animals. Why is this?

d) Most fossils of sea animals only show the shell. The soft parts of the animal are not present. Explain why this is.

Q2) The diagrams below show the four stages that an animal with a shell would undergo to become fossilised.

a) Complete the flow diagram to show how a shell fish is fossilised.

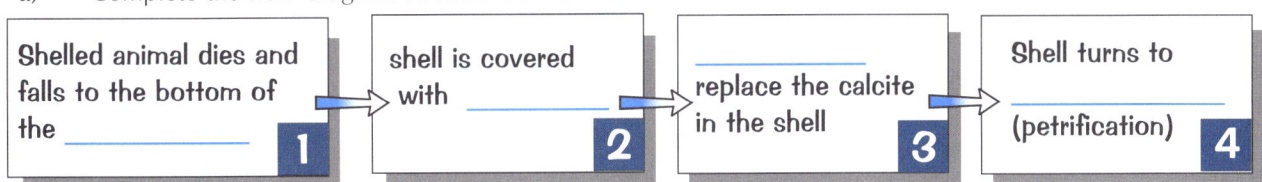

| Shelled animal dies and falls to the bottom of the _____ **1** | shell is covered with _____ **2** | _____ replace the calcite in the shell **3** | Shell turns to _____ (petrification) **4** |

b) i) Why is the soft body of the shell fish animal not fossilised?
   ii) Why is the hard shell so well fossilised?

c) What conditions must be present if fossils are to be formed?

d) Preserved organisms have been found in peat, ice and amber. The absence of which element has contributed to their preservation?

Q3) Coal comes from fossilised trees that have been buried and preserved. Normally when trees die, they decay and release their minerals back into the ground.

a) Why did some trees not decay, but become fossilised as coal instead?

b) How do we know that coal is fossilised wood?

Q4) Choose the correct word or words from inside the brackets to complete the sentences.

a) In order for decay to occur, oxygen (is / is not) needed.
b) Most fossils occur from hard parts of animals because they decay (quickly / slowly).
c) The best fossilisation occurs (under the sea / on land).
d) The (higher / lower) in a rock sequence a fossil is found, where the sequence has not undergone any movement, the older it is.

Top Tips: Fossils give us great evidence about what prehistoric creatures looked like and how long ago they lived. Remember, there are **three** ways that an organism can be fossilised — and **three** ways that the **whole** organism can be preserved.

Section Five — Genetics and Evolution

Evolution

Q1) Use the following words to complete the blanks.

*adaptations   characteristics   changed   Darwin   degenerate   environment   food
evolution   existence   extinct   fittest   nature   organisms   survival   natural*

Evolution is about how living things have _____ over millions of years. Lamarck and _____ had different ideas about how this happened. Lamarck believed that new structures appeared when there was a need for them and those that are not used _____. He also proposed that changes acquired in the lifetime of organisms were then passed on to the offspring. Darwin on the other hand proposed that organisms with the best _____ to their _____ survive and have offspring which inherit those adaptations. Useful characteristics become more common. Less well adapted organisms die out.

All _____ over reproduce, so individual organisms have to compete, particularly for _____. Disease and predation cause large numbers of organisms to die. This is called the struggle for _____. This struggle leads to the _____ surviving. In other words, those individuals with the most suitable _____ are the most likely to survive. So, _____ selects the characteristics that are going to aid _____. This is called _____ selection. These gradual changes are the mechanism by which _____ occurs.

Q2) Place the sentences in order to explain the evolution of the giraffe.

~ *mutation* resulted in some giraffes having longer necks than others.
~ *all* giraffes had *short* necks.
~ *natural selection* resulted in longer necked offspring surviving.
~ the giraffe population had individuals whose necks *varied* in length.
~ only *long* necked giraffes *survived* the competition for food.

Q3) The diagram shows the earliest occurrence and abundance of fossil vertebrates.

a) What were the *first vertebrates* to evolve?
b) The dinosaurs became extinct about 60 million years ago. What *evidence* is there of this in the diagram?
c) Which were the *last vertebrates* to evolve?
d) How do fossils help us to *understand* evolution?
e) Although the diagram shows evolution as being continuous, there are many missing links in the fossil record of many animals.

How can we *explain* these missing links?

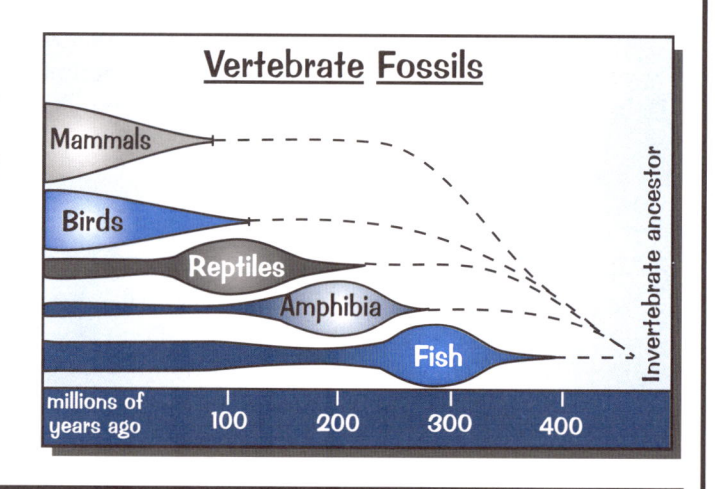

Vertebrate Fossils

Mammals, Birds, Reptiles, Amphibia, Fish — Invertebrate ancestor

millions of years ago: 100   200   300   400

Top Tips: Evolution is how living things **gradually** change over **millions of years** — think about how natural selection shapes the evolution of different animals.

Section Five — Genetics and Evolution

Natural Selection

Q1) Use the following words to complete the blanks.

alleles   disease   environment   favourable   offspring
natural   die   species   survive   variation

There is a wide range of _____ within particular _____ because of differences in their genes. Predation, _____ and competition (often for food) cause large numbers of individuals to _____. Individuals that survive are those that are most suited to their _____. Those individuals that survive pass on their genes (and therefore their characteristics) to their _____. This process is known as _____ selection. Natural selection can alter the frequency of particular _____ in a population. Alleles determining _____ characteristics increase in frequency. This is because alleles which enable individuals to _____ are passed on to the next generation.

Q2) The peppered moth is normally light in colour. Occasionally, a black variety appears. Insect eating birds like the thrush prey on these moths.

a) i) How does a black moth appear in a population of light coloured moths?
   ii) How is the population of these moths kept constant?

b) In 1848 the first black variety was noticed in Manchester. By 1895, 98% of the moth population of Manchester was black. During this time, the environment also became darker as a result of increasing pollution. Why did the number of black moths increase so dramatically between 1848 and 1895?

c) Today, in industrialised areas, the population of dark moths is almost 100%. In Scotland and South-West England the reverse is true. Why does this happen?

d) Why is the black variety not a new species?

e) What is the name for the process that determines the survival features of a population?

Peppered Moth

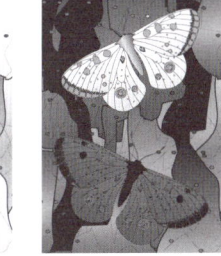

White and Black peppered moths on tree bark in unpolluted area

White and Black peppered moths on tree bark in polluted area

Q3) Complete the sentences by choosing the correct words from inside the brackets.

a) The frequency of alleles which determine useful characteristics (decreases / increases) in a population.
b) Factors like disease cause a population to (decrease / increase).
c) Organisms that are the best survivors are those that are (best suited to their environment / strongest).
d) Survivors pass their genes on to their (offspring / partner).
e) Natural selection is the process by which (evolution / mutation) takes place.
f) In order for changes to occur in the characteristics of a population, (mutation / predation) must take place.

Top Tips: Natural selection — top theory. The **environment** selects characteristics that make individuals **survivors**. Survivors can **pass on** their **genes** to their children, who then pass them on to theirs and so on, and on — that's how evolution **works**.

Section Five — Genetics and Evolution

Section Six — The Environment

Population Sizes

Q1) There are twelve sycamore trees in a wood. Their environment is quite sunny, with plenty of nutrients in the soil. They share the wood with many other plants and animals.

a) What is the population of sycamore trees?

b) What is the habitat of the sycamore trees?

c) Match the terms to the correct definitions:

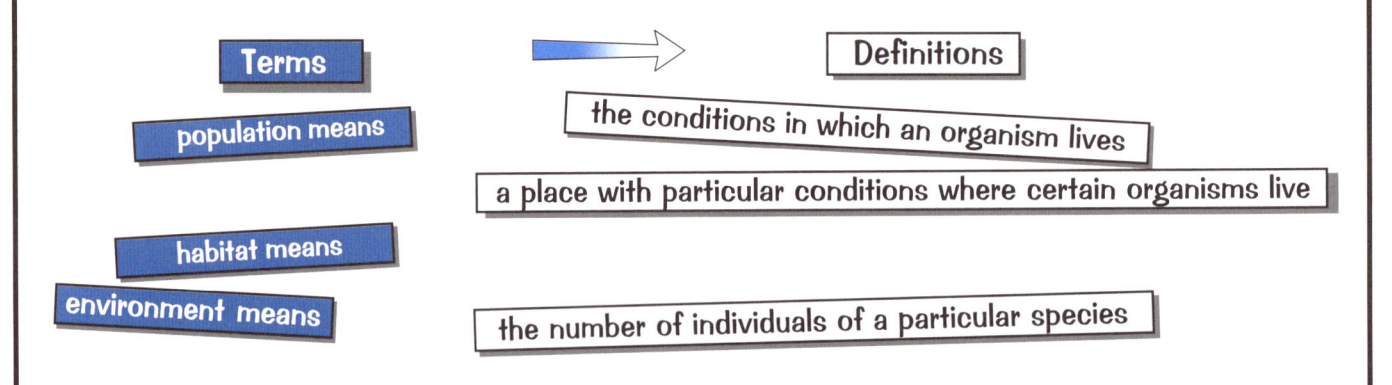

Terms
- population means
- habitat means
- environment means

Definitions
- the conditions in which an organism lives
- a place with particular conditions where certain organisms live
- the number of individuals of a particular species

Q2) The cane toad was brought to Australia in 1935.

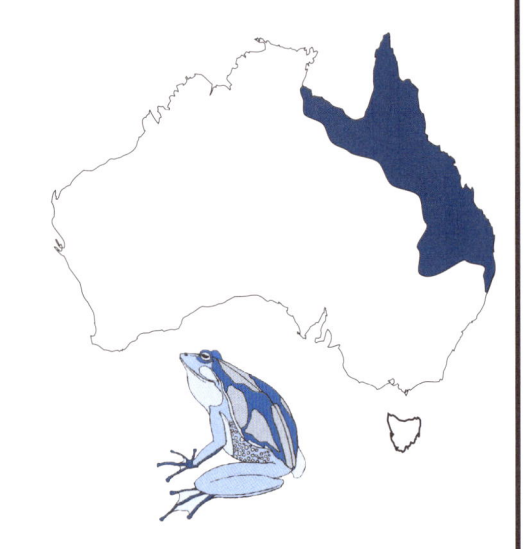

It grows up to 24cm long, and can lay up to 40,000 eggs in one season. It is highly poisonous to other animals, and most native tadpoles cannot live in the same water as cane toad tadpoles. The map on the right shows how far it has spread — and it is still on the march.

Suggest reasons why the cane toad has been so successful in Australia.

Q3) The North American grey squirrel was introduced into Britain in 1876.

Until then, the red squirrel was the only squirrel in Britain. The maps on the right show approximately where these squirrels could be found. The map on the left is from 1990, and the one on the right is from 1940.

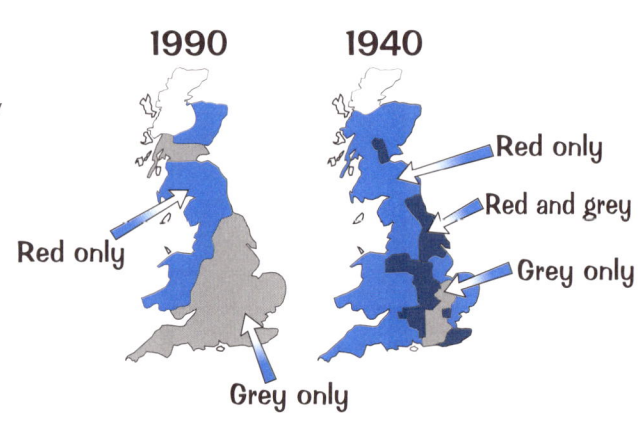

1990 — Red only, Grey only

1940 — Red only, Red and grey, Grey only

a) Describe the changes in the distribution of the squirrels.

b) Suggest reasons for these changes.

Population Sizes

Q4) The graph below shows the change in the numbers of a species of predator and its prey over time.

a) What do the words predator and prey mean? Give two examples of a predator and its prey.

b) What do you notice about the changes in the numbers of predator and prey with time? Explain why these changes happen.

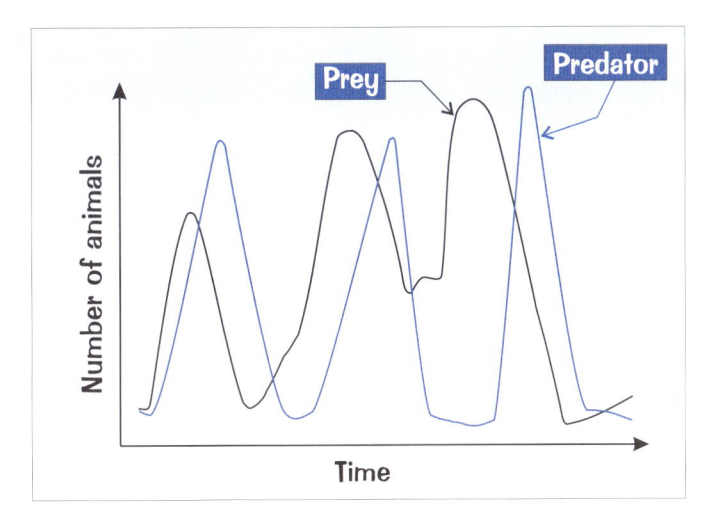

Q5) The number of mice in a wood was estimated at the same time each year for thirteen years. The results obtained are shown in the chart on the right.

a) A road was built through the middle of the wood at the end of year 8. What effect has this had on the number of mice in the wood? What effect will this road have on the study in future years?

b) Suggest two reasons why the number of mice in the wood fell between years 4 and 5 of the study.

c) Suggest two reasons why the number of mice in the wood rose between years 6 and 7 of the study.

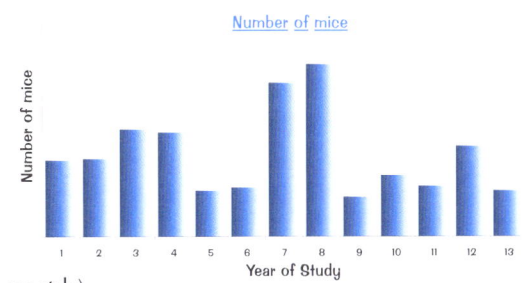

(Don't just write down the opposite of your answers to part b).

Q6) Draw a table with the headings shown on the right.

In the "factor" column list the things that can affect the size of a population of organisms. In the "examples" give an example of this factor at work. (Try to think of plant examples as well as animal examples). One line has been done for you as an example.

Factor	Examples
Competition for water	Weeds and wheat

Top Tips:
Population size is actually just **common sense** if you remember that organisms **thrive** if: they've got the **things they need** (water, light, food, etc); they're **better** at getting those things than the **competition**; they don't get **eaten** and they don't get **ill**. Remember that, and it won't get too complicated.

Section Six — The Environment

Communities (Adapt and Survive)

Q1) The graph on the right shows the average daytime temperature (line) and rainfall (bars) on the northern edge of the Sahara desert. Although it can be over 57°C in the day, at night the temperature can fall below 0°C. Sometimes it does not rain for years.

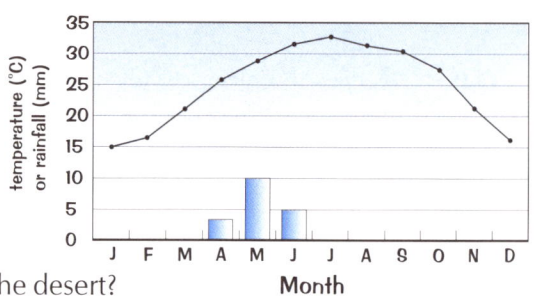

a) From this information, what is the environment like in the desert?

b) You possibly thought that the desert is just lots of sand. Just 15% of the Sahara desert is covered by sand dunes, the rest is stone plateaus or gravel surfaces. What problems will animals and plants living in a desert face? What will happen to them if they are not adapted to the desert?

Q2) The Sidewinder is a snake which lives in deserts.

It moves sideways across the sand by throwing its body into a series of S-shapes, always keeping a loop of the S-shape off the ground, with two other parts touching. Explain why it does this.

Q3) Many desert animals, such as the kangaroo rat, spend the day in a burrow and come out at night.

What are the advantages and disadvantages of doing this?

Q4) Camels are probably the best-known animals in the desert.

There are two types, the Bactrian camel (right) and the Arabian camel or dromedary (left).

a) Describe the features that the camels have in common which make them adapted for desert conditions.

b) It has been discovered that a shaved camel loses nearly twice as much body water as an unshaved camel. Suggest why losing its hair could cause this difference.

c) Humans need to maintain a fairly constant body temperature, but camels can tolerate a big change in their body temperature. They can allow it to go from about 34°C to 41°C during the day, and then they cool off during the night. This means that during the day they do not need to use methods of cooling that humans do. How is this advantageous to the camel?

Q5) The following features are adaptations of desert plants to allow them to survive the environment.

Study each of these features carefully. For each feature, decide what condition in the environment the plant has adapted to, and explain how the adaptation helps the plant to survive in the desert.

a) The seeds of flowering desert plants can lie dormant in the soil for years until the rain allows them to germinate, grow, and flower quickly.
b) Some plants have long roots which reach deep underground.
c) Some plants have shallow roots which spread just under the surface.
d) Succulent plants store water in their leaves, stems, and roots.
e) Some plants drop their leaves during a dry spell. They usually have small leaves.
f) Some plants take in and store carbon dioxide at night. During the day their stomata are closed.
g) Many plants have modified leaves which form thorns, and photosynthesis occurs in the stems.

Section Six — The Environment

Communities (Adapt and Survive)

Q6) The graph below shows the average daytime temperature (line) and rainfall (bars) in the Arctic. The temperature can fall to -80°C and the wind can blow at over 300 km/h. In the winter, it is dark all the time, but in the summer the sun shines all the time.

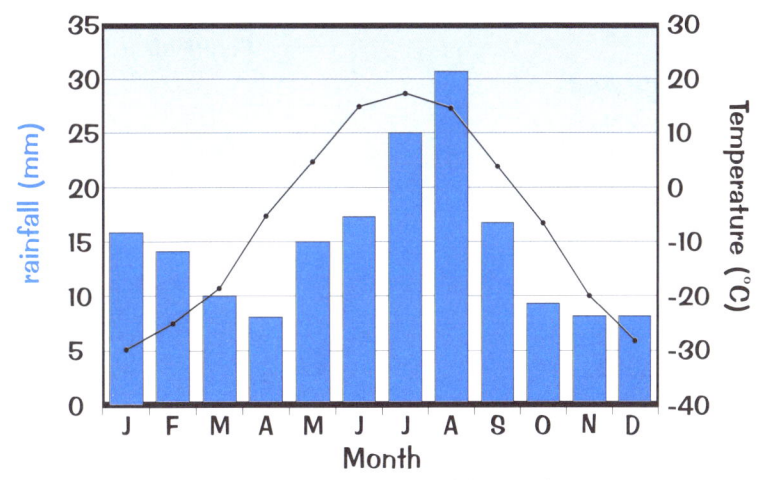

a) From this information what is the environment like in the Arctic?

b) It's not all sea-ice in the Arctic. There is a lot of barren land too, known as the tundra. The plants there often grow very close to the ground, and have small leaves. Suggest why the plants grow like this.

c) What problems will animals face living in the Arctic? Suggest some adaptations that would allow animals to live successfully in the Arctic.

Q7) Lemmings are small rodents that live in the tundra.

They have a rounded body about 12cm long. Their fur is light brown, and they have small ears that are hidden by fur. Lemmings live in burrows. Explain how the lemming is adapted to life in the Arctic.

Q8) Polar bears and walruses are probably the best known animals in the Arctic. Both have large bodies, with thick layers of fat under the skin. The polar bear has fur that looks white in the light. The walrus has long tusks and tough brown skin. Male walruses often fight each other.

a) Suggest why polar bears and walruses do not live in burrows.

b) Explain how polar bears and walruses are adapted to life in the Arctic.

Q9) The snowshoe hare has white fur in the winter and reddish-brown fur in the summer.

Suggest a reason for this change.

Q11) Desert foxes have very large ears, whereas Arctic foxes only have very small ears.

Suggest a reason for this difference (it is not to do with hearing or hiding).

Top Tips: Obviously, animals and plants **not** suited to the environment will be **less likely** to survive than those which **are**. By **natural selection** creatures have evolved **features** that help them to cope. The camel and polar bear examples are good ones to remember because the features are **shared** by lots of other animals in **similar environments**.

Section Six — The Environment

Acid Rain

Q1) The table on the left shows the amount of acid rain gases from different sources.

The percentage contributions of nitrogen oxides have been plotted on the graph below.

Acid Rain Gas	Source	%
Sulphur dioxide	Industry	10
	Other	8
	Domestic	5
	Power stations	34
Nitrogen oxides	Road transport	22
	Power stations	13
	Other	5
	Industry	4

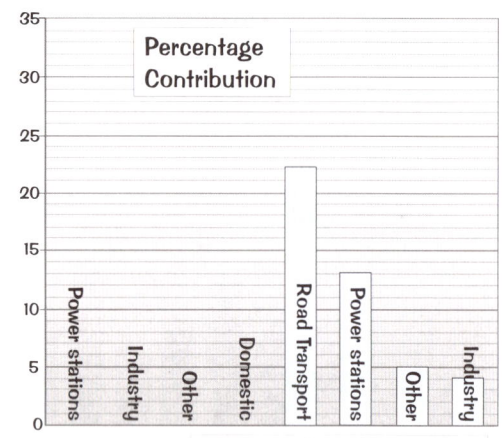

a) Complete the graph to show the percentage contributions of sulphur dioxide from the different sources.

b) Which source produces the most sulphur dioxide?

c) Which source produces the most nitrogen oxides?

d) Which source produces the most acid rain gases?

Q2) Answer these questions about the formation of acid rain:

a) What gases dissolve in clouds to make acid rain?

b) What acids can be found in acid rain?

Q3) Acid rain can react with limestone and marble statues and stonework on buildings, causing them to be eroded. For a long time, it was not clear that acid rain was damaging trees. The map on the right shows how much damage has been done to trees in Europe. The circles show how much acid rain damage there is, starting with the most in the centre, and becoming less further out.

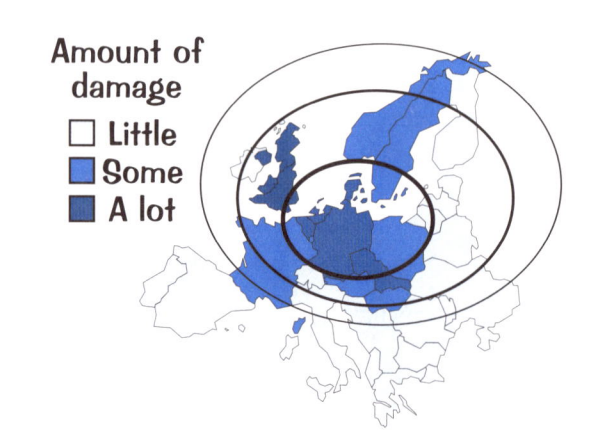

a) Britain, Germany and France produce a lot of acid rain gases, but the Scandinavian countries in the north do not. Suggest why Scandinavia has quite high levels of acid rain and damaged trees.

b) Discuss how much the evidence in the map supports the idea that acid rain damages trees.

Section Six — The Environment

Acid Rain

Q4) Research has shown that acid rain can damage trees, especially conifers like spruce and pine, causing their leaves to fall off. It also reacts with minerals in the ground, such as aluminium, magnesium and potassium, causing them to dissolve and be washed away underground.

a) Suggest what will happen to a tree that loses some of its leaves due to acid rain.

b) Aluminium is toxic to trees, but is usually insoluble. Explain how acid rain could poison trees.

c) Magnesium is found in chlorophyll. What would you expect to happen to plants growing in areas where acid rain is falling? Explain your answer.

d) The roots of trees in acid soils can grow poorly. What effects will this have on these trees?

e) Draw a diagram to summarise the effects of acid rain on trees.

Q5) As acid rain falls into rivers and lakes, they become increasingly acidic. Water flowing off the land contains high levels of aluminium and mercury released by the acid rain.

a) What will happen to the water plants in acidified lakes and rivers?

b) Small crustaceans at the bottom of the aquatic food chain die if the pH falls below about 6. What will happen eventually to the other animals in the lake if the pH falls below 6?

c) The soluble aluminium can react with sulphuric acid to make aluminium sulphate. This clogs the gills of fish with sticky mucus. Suggest the likely effect of this on the fish.

d) In some parts of Europe, fish caught from acidified lakes are condemned as unfit for human consumption. Suggest a reason for this.

Q6) A lot of money is now being spent to combat acid rain because of its economic effects as well as its environmental costs. Suggest three economic effects of acid rain.

Q7) There are two main ways to combat acid rain. First, the acid in the environment can be neutralised. For example, powdered lime (calcium oxide) can be added to lakes and soils. This reacts with the acids and raises the pH closer to 7. The lakes have to be treated regularly, however. Secondly, the release of acid gases at source can be avoided. For example, the "flue gases" coming out of power stations can be treated with limestone (calcium carbonate). This reacts with sulphur dioxide and produces gypsum (calcium sulphate). This can be used in plasterboard and for filling in quarries.

a) Why do lakes have to be treated more than once? What problems does this treatment cause?

b) What are the advantages and disadvantages of treating the flue gases as described above?

Top Tips: There are two key bits here — the causes and the effects of acid rain. You'll need to know where the two main acid rain gases come from and the acids they form (be prepared to give a **word equation**). You really should know **at least two** effects of acid rain.

Section Six — The Environment

The Greenhouse Effect

Q1) The temperature on the surface of the Moon ranges from -175°C to 125°C, with an average temperature of about -20°C.

The difference between the temperature on the surface of the Moon and that on the Earth is due to the greenhouse effect. Copy and complete the sentences below about the greenhouse effect, choosing the correct words from the coloured pairs:

"Energy from the Moon / Sun passes through the Earth's atmosphere / surface and cools / warms the Earth's surface. Heat energy from the Earth's surface is radiated into space / the ground but some of it is absorbed / reflected by gases in the atmosphere. This cools / warms the atmosphere, which is good / bad for life on Earth. However, excess CO_2 / O_2 produced by burning fossil fuels is causing the earth to warm up too much which may cause flooding and drought."

Q2) Only some of the gases in the atmosphere, called greenhouse gases, are good at absorbing heat energy. These include carbon dioxide and methane, which both occur naturally in the atmosphere.

a) Name a natural source of carbon dioxide.

b) Since the Industrial Revolution began in the 19th century, humans have been burning fossil fuels. Name a greenhouse gas released by burning fossil fuels.

c) Study the top graph on the right, which shows the amount of carbon released from burning fossil fuels since 1850. Describe the graph — how has the release of carbon from fossil fuels changed? Suggest why this change happened.

d) Study the bottom graph on the right, which shows the amount of carbon dioxide in the atmosphere since 1850. Describe the graph — how has the amount of carbon dioxide in the atmosphere changed? Suggest why this change happened.

e) There are natural processes that can absorb the carbon released as carbon dioxide from fossil fuels. Name one of these processes.

f) Explain what the changes in the amount of carbon dioxide in the atmosphere could do to the temperature of the Earth.

g) Suggest how changes in the Earth's temperature ("global warming") could cause a change in sea level.

h) Explain what you think might happen if the amount of carbon dioxide in the atmosphere continues to rise. Make sure you consider the possible effect on low-lying areas of the world.

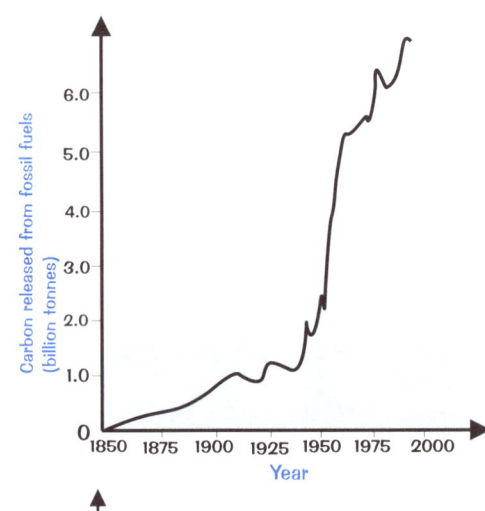

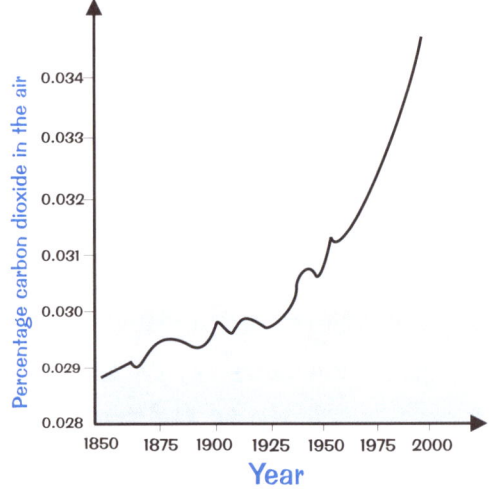

Top Tips: You've got to understand the factors that lead to increased greenhouse effect and global warming. The greenhouse effect is good for life on Earth because it keeps us nice and warm, but getting too warm will muck up the climate and melt the ice caps.

Section Six — The Environment

Farming and its Problems

Q1) The list below shows some of the things that have allowed modern farming to keep up with the growth in population.

For each one, explain how it has helped increase food production.

| Artificial fertilisers | Artificially selected animals and plants | Mechanisation |

Q2) More use of machinery (mechanisation) has caused the average size of fields and farms to increase greatly. This has been achieved by felling trees and removing hedges between smaller fields.

a) Why are larger fields needed for machinery such as combine harvesters, tractors and ploughs?

b) What problems are caused to wildlife communities when trees and hedges are removed?

Q3) In some parts of the world, large areas of forests have been cut down to make way for farms.

a) What problems might cause some countries to remove large areas of forest in order to provide more farmland?

b) Photosynthesis causes carbon dioxide to be removed from the atmosphere and to be locked up as wood. What will happen to the uptake of carbon dioxide from the atmosphere in deforested areas? What will happen to the production of oxygen in these areas?

c) Frequently, trees are burnt after being cut down, producing carbon dioxide.
How will your answers to part **b)** affect the impact of doing this?

d) Trees that are not burnt may be allowed to decay by the action of microbes.
Explain how this will contribute to the release of carbon dioxide into the atmosphere.

Q4) The sentences below are steps in a lake becoming eutrophic, but they are muddled up.

a) Sort them into the correct order and write them down.

- Fish and other aquatic animals die of suffocation.
- The microbes take more oxygen from the water for their respiration.
- Excess fertilisers leach from the soil and are washed into the lake.
- The number of microbes that feed on dead organisms increases.
- There is increased competition between the plants, and some die as a result.
- Water plants in the lake start to grow rapidly.

b) In the corrected sequence, why should water plants grow more quickly?

c) What resources are the water plants competing for? Which resource is probably in excess?

d) If there are more plants in the lake, you might expect more oxygen to be produced by photosynthesis. Why does the oxygen content of the water go down instead?

Normally, the action of decomposers such as bacteria is welcomed because it allows scarce nutrients to be recycled for use by other organisms in the community, as in the nitrogen cycle.

e) Why is the action of decomposers such a problem in the case of a eutrophic lake?

f) Describe some environmental and economic consequences of eutrophication.

g) Suggest two courses of action that might be taken to rescue a lake which is becoming eutrophic.

Section Six — The Environment

Farming and its Problems

Q5) Untreated sewage has the same effect as dead vegetation in the process of eutrophication.

   a) What part does raw sewage play in eutrophication?

   b) In many parts of the world, the discharge of raw sewage is increasing. Why is this happening?

   c) In addition to eutrophication, what other hazards are there in discharging sewage into lakes, rivers and seas?

Q6) Many timber-producing areas are some distance from the nearest road. Logs are towed over a river or lake to the sawmills. Some get stuck, become waterlogged and then sink.

   Describe what might happen to a lake as a result.

Q7) Answer these questions about pesticides:

   a) What is a pesticide? Give an example of a pesticide. Why are pesticides useful to farmers?

   b) In a study of an aquatic food chain in a small pond, it was found that many of the animals contained a fat-soluble pesticide called Kilzemall. The results are shown below. Describe, and explain, the trend in the concentration of Kilzemall going up the food chain.

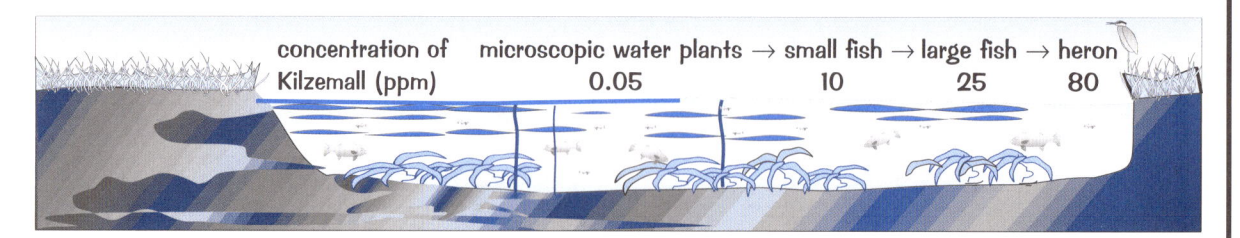

concentration of Kilzemall (ppm)	microscopic water plants	→ small fish	→ large fish	→ heron
	0.05	10	25	80

   c) Kilzemall was designed to kill insects in wheat fields and not insects in water. Suggest how the pesticide got into the pond.

   d) In later studies, scientists were astonished to discover that polar bears and penguins contained high amounts of Kilzemall in their bodies. Suggest how the pesticide managed to get into their bodies. Remember: polar bears and penguins only meet in zoos, and farmers are not likely to be doing any farming at the poles.

   e) Modern pesticides are tested in many ways to ensure their safety. Explain why we should be concerned about the health of organisms exposed to pesticides.

Top Tips: This boils down to **three** themes: fertilisers, pesticides and deforestation. You need to understand how **each** damages the environment. Don't muddle up **fertilisers** and **pesticides** — they cause harm in different ways. Sadly, its the price we pay for cheap, plentiful food.

Pyramids of Number and Biomass

Q1) The blank pyramid below could be a pyramid of numbers or a pyramid of biomass.

Copy the diagram. On the left-hand side of your diagram, label the arrows to show which step refers to the primary, secondary and tertiary consumers (the producer has already been labelled for you).

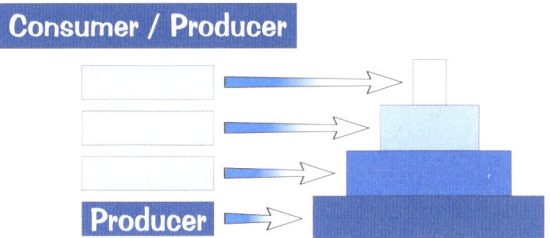

Q2) Draw pyramids of numbers for the following food chains. Make sure you label each step with the name of the organism and how many of them there are.

a) microscopic water plants (1 million) → water fleas (100,000) → trout (50) → kingfisher (1)

b) oak tree (1) → caterpillars (500) → birds (5)

c) Ideally, the width of each bar would be drawn to scale, so that the trout bar in part **a)** would be fifty times wider than the kingfisher bar. This is usually not possible. Explain why.

d) If you have done part **b)** correctly, it will not look very pyramid-shaped.
Why can a pyramid of numbers have an unusual shape like this?

e) Draw a pyramid to show the following short food chain: wheat → human. Decide on a suitable width for the wheat bar (thousands of plants might be needed to feed one person). In tropical countries, a disease called schistosomiasis can be a big problem. It is caused by a parasitic worm, about 1cm long, which lives in the blood vessels and feeds on blood. A person might be infected by dozens of these worms. Add a labelled bar to your pyramid of numbers. Explain why this pyramid is not pyramid-shaped.

f) Think of another food chain that will produce a pyramid of numbers that is not pyramid-shaped. Draw and label the pyramid, and write down the food chain along side it. Explain why your pyramid has its unusual shape.

Q3) Pyramid information:

	Carrots	Rabbits	Foxes
A	1	100	4000
B	1	4000	100
C	100	1	4000
D	100	4000	1
E	4000	1	100
F	4000	100	1

a) What information does a pyramid of numbers give?

b) In the food chain, carrot → rabbit → fox, which row in the table on the right represents the most likely numbers of each organism?

c) What do you notice about the size of the organism as you look from left to right along this food chain?

d) Which pyramid of numbers below most closely matches the correct answer to part **b)**?

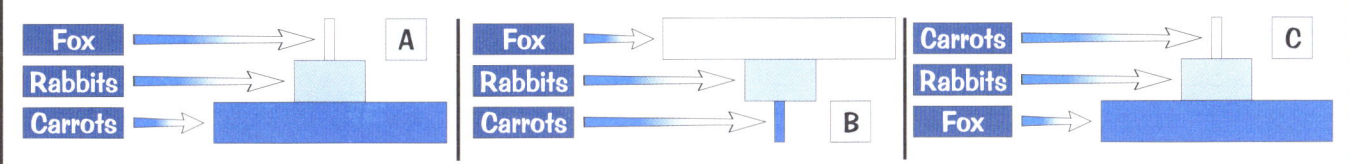

e) What do you notice about the size of the organism and the width of its bar on the pyramid of numbers in the correct answer to part **d)**?

Section Six — The Environment

Pyramids of Number and Biomass

Q4) Explain what is meant by the word biomass.
What information does a pyramid of biomass give?

Q5) One of the food chains in the North Sea is: phytoplankton → zooplankton → small fish → cod.

The biomass of each of the organisms in the food chain was estimated from samples and experiments. It was found that for every 1kg of cod, there was 100kg of phytoplankton, 80kg of zooplankton and 10kg of small fish. In each case, the masses are dry masses.

a) What does dry mass mean? Why does it allow fairer comparisons to be made between the biomass of different organisms?

b) Draw a pyramid of biomass for this food chain. Draw it to scale, and make sure that you label each bar with the name of the organism and its biomass in kg.

c) In some pyramids of numbers and biomass, the top bar can be shown as a vertical line. Explain why this is sometimes necessary.

d) Between which two organisms in this food chain is the most mass lost? How much mass?

e) Between which two organisms in this food chain is the greatest proportion of mass lost?

f) Suggest reasons why the biomass is less at each trophic level than the one before it.

g) The wet mass of a small fish averages about 1.5kg, and that of adult cod averages about 7.5kg. Assuming that both types of fish have the same proportion of water in their bodies, how many small fish feed one cod?

Q6) Look at these pyramids:

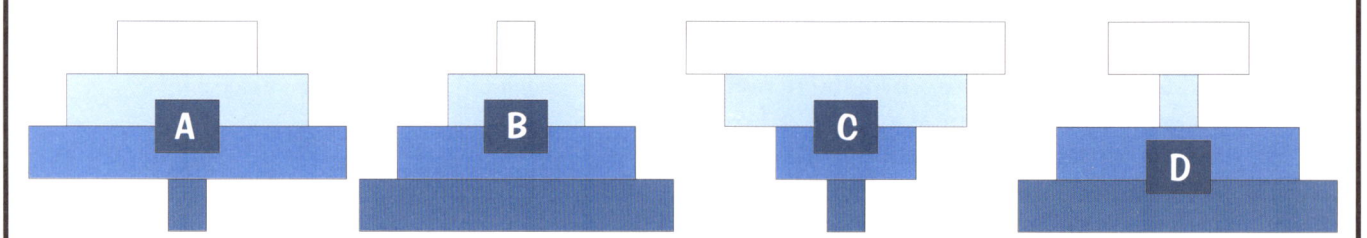

Explain which of the pyramids above could represent:
a) The pyramid of numbers for a community that relies on a large producer.
b) The pyramid of biomass for a woodland community.
c) The pyramid of numbers for a food chain that ends with parasites such as fleas.
d) The pyramid of numbers for a marine community in which the producers are tiny algae.

Top Tips: Remember it takes a lot of food from the level below to keep one animal alive. Pyramids of biomass always get narrower the higher you go, but pyramids of numbers can be any shape — you have a hundred fleas on one dog, but they still weigh less than the dog.

Section Six — The Environment

Energy Transfer

Q1) Photosynthesis uses energy to produce the sugars needed for respiration.

   a) What type of organism can photosynthesise?
   What type of energy is absorbed to drive photosynthesis, and from where does it come?
   Write down the word equation for photosynthesis.

   b) All living organisms respire. Write down the word equation for respiration. Energy is released by respiration. What is this energy used for? Give more than one answer.

   c) Where did the energy released by respiration originally come from?

Q2) The diagram below shows the fate of energy, captured by photosynthesis in barley plants, as it passes through pigs on its way to humans.

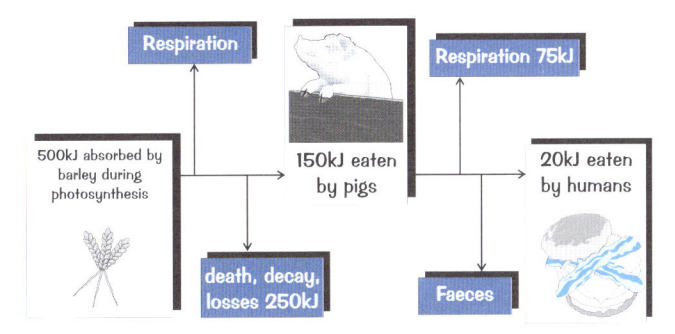

[Diagram: 500kJ absorbed by barley during photosynthesis → Respiration; death, decay, losses 250kJ; 150kJ eaten by pigs → Respiration 75kJ; Faeces; 20kJ eaten by humans]

   a) Work out how much energy is lost from the barley plants by respiration.

   b) Work out how much energy is lost from the pigs in faeces.

   It's difficult to stop the pigs producing faeces, but if the amount of respiration by the pigs could be reduced, more energy would pass to the humans.

   c) For what purposes do the pigs use energy released by respiration?

   d) Suggest ways that the amount of respiration by the pigs could be reduced, giving reasons for your answers.

   e) More people could be fed if they ate the barley, instead of letting the pigs eat it and then eating the pigs. Work out how many times more people might be fed this way.

   f) Apart from respiration by the barley and the pigs, there are two other sources of energy loss. What are they? Suggest how the energy lost in these ways could be reduced.

Q3) It is often suggested that if everyone became a vegetarian, ten times more people in the world could be fed.

   a) Use your knowledge of energy transfer in food chains to explain this idea.

   b) In practice, fewer extra people would be fed in this way. Suggest two reasons for this.

Top Tips: These pages give you the reason you have biomass pyramids. Energy, from the sun, works its way up the food web, but 90% gets lost at each stage. Energy and material are always lost in waste materials and energy is lost through respiration just by being alive.

Section Six — The Environment

The Carbon Cycle

Q1) Word equations and symbol equations are often the clearest way to write down a concept.

a) Write down the word equations for photosynthesis and respiration in plants.
The substances involved are carbon dioxide, glucose, oxygen and water.

b) Which process releases energy, and which one needs energy?
Where does each process occur?

c) Which process will release a carbon compound into the atmosphere, and which one will remove carbon compound from the atmosphere? Which carbon compound is involved?

d) The diagram below represents part of the carbon cycle.

Copy it, and fill in the missing words and process names.
Leave plenty of space to add more processes to your diagram.

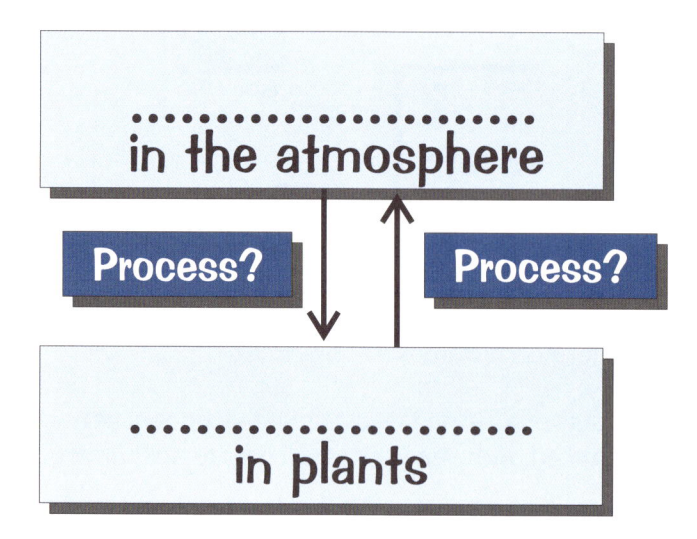

```
............
in the atmosphere
        ↓    ↑
   Process?   Process?
        ↓    ↑
............
in plants
```

e) Look at the two processes. Describe the similarities and differences between them.

Q2) Plant cell walls contain cellulose fibres.

Cellulose consists of thousands of glucose molecules joined together. However, the way in which they are joined means that the enzymes in most animals are not able to break down cellulose. Ruminants, like cows, have bacteria in their digestive system that can break down cellulose. Fungi are also able to break down cellulose.

What would happen if there were no bacteria and fungi capable of digesting cellulose?

The Carbon Cycle

Q3) Bacteria and fungi can break down solid waste materials from animals.

They can also break down materials in dead animals and plants. This is known as decomposition or decay.

a) What general word is used to describe bacteria and fungi that break down dead material?

b) What is the benefit to the bacteria and fungi of digesting these materials?

c) What carbon compound will be returned to the atmosphere as a result of their activities?

d) What substances will they release into the soil?

e) Why are bacteria and fungi important for the recycling of carbon in the carbon cycle?

Q4) Copy and complete these sentences about decomposition and decay by microbes. Choose the correct word from each of the underlined pairs.

"Microbes digest materials faster when they are in cool / warm conditions which are moist / dry. Many microbes work better if there is more oxygen / nitrogen in the environment."

Q5) Humans make use of microbes to treat sewage before discharging it into rivers.

a) What is sewage? Why should we want to treat it before discharge?

b) Suggest suitable conditions for the microbes to break down sewage efficiently.

Humans also make use of microbes in garden compost heaps.

c) Why is compost better suited for the garden than the original ingredients?

d) What sorts of materials are suitable for making compost? What do we use compost for?

Top Tips: The Carbon Cycle — another beautiful example of **nature's harmony**, and another **diagram** to learn. There's only **one** way carbon dioxide gets from the atmosphere into the plant and animal biomass — photosynthesis. The plants and animals get **eaten** or turned into **useful stuff** and finally get **burnt** or **rot**, releasing carbon dioxide back into the atmosphere.

Section Six — The Environment

The Nitrogen Cycle

Q1) Microbes can break down proteins in dead plants and animals.

They can also break down proteins in faeces and urea in urine. In some cases, putrefying bacteria break down these compounds in the absence of oxygen to form terribly smelly amines (often with a "fishy" smell). Usually, microbes break down proteins and urea to form ammonia and ammonium compounds.

a) What is the name given to bacteria which break down dead material?

b) Nitrifying bacteria in the soil convert ammonia into nitrates.

What use are nitrates to plants?

c) The diagram below represents part of the nitrogen cycle.
Copy it, filling in the missing words.
Leave space for some more processes.

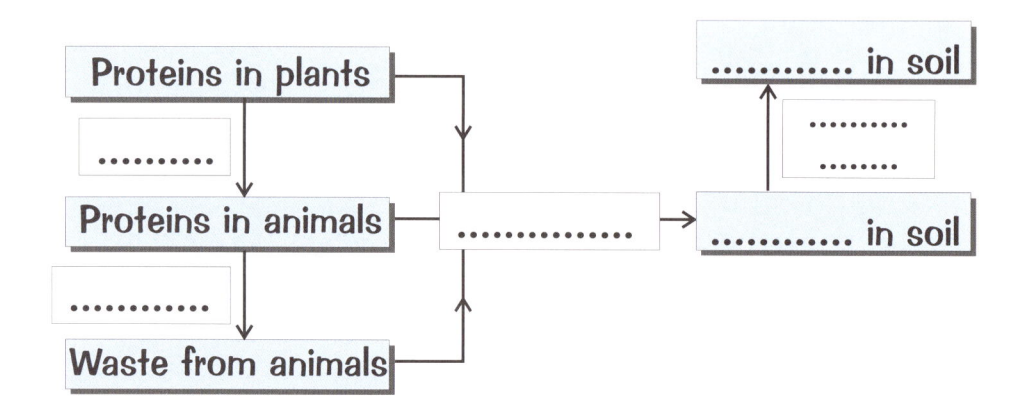

```
Proteins in plants ──┐                    ............ in soil
       │             │                           ↑
   .........         │                      .........
       ↓             ↓                      .........
Proteins in animals ──→ ............. ──→  ............ in soil
       │             ↑
   .........         │
       ↓             │
Waste from animals ──┘
```

Q2) Denitrifying bacteria in the soil can convert nitrates in the soil into nitrogen gas.

a) Add a labelled arrow and box to your nitrogen cycle to show the action of denitrifying bacteria.

b) Add another labelled arrow to show the action of nitrogen-fixing bacteria in the soil.
Add a labelled arrow to show how nitrates get into plants.

c) Write a summary of the role of microbes in the nitrogen cycle.
Name each type of bacterium, what it does and where it is found.

d) What could happen if denitrifying bacteria were more active than decomposers, nitrogen-fixing bacteria and nitrifying bacteria? Would it matter if they were less active?

Top Tips: The nitrogen cycle **is** harder than the carbon cycle, and it's easy to get confused by the **d**ifferent microbes involved. You need to understand it if you are after a good grade, so go through it **carefully** step by step so you can **complete**, **label** and **interpret** a diagram and explain what happens to the nitrogen in each stage. Learn and enjoy.

Section Six — The Environment

ANSWERS

These are for checking, NOT COPYING, be warned.

Biology

Higher Level

Answers

Cells P.1 → P.6

Page 1 — Cells:

1) **a)** Reproduction / Sensitivity / Excretion.
   b) Reproduction – producing offspring / Sensitivity – responding to things in the environment / Excretion – getting rid of waste from chemical reactions.

2) **a)** Reproduction **b)** Growth **c)** Nutrition
   d) Sensitivity + growth + movement.

3) Movement — Changing position or posture
   Growth — Oak trees develop from acorns
   Reproduction — A plant makes and releases seeds
   Respiration — Releasing energy from food:

4) In the order they appear: reproduce; move; grow; respiration; nutrition; excreted; sensitivity.

Page 2:

1) **a)** Chlamydomonas.
   b) Has a cell wall and a chloroplast.

2) nucleus, cytoplasm, cell membrane, mitochondria. (any three)

3) **a)** See diagram:
   b) Chloroplasts.
   c) Photosynthesis.
   d) Chlorophyll.
   e) Support and strengthen the cell.

4) Nucleus, cell membrane, cell wall, vacuole, sap, cytoplasm, nucleus, chloroplasts.

5) **a)** A tail, vacuole.
   b) Any two of cytoplasm, nucleus, membrane, mitochondria.

6) **a)** Blood cells are found in the circulatory system. Brain cells are found in the nervous system and the uterus is found in the reproductive system.
   b) A glandular tissue is a tissue which produces substances / chemicals / secretions (eg a tissue that makes enzymes, hormones).

Page 3:

1) Nucleus, cytoplasm, membrane. The egg's function is for reproduction and the carrying of genetic information from the parents.

2) **a)** A = sperm cell, B = nerve cell, C = leaf cell.
   b) A = reproduction/fertilisation, B = carries nerve signals, C = photosynthesis/making food.
   c) A = tail for swimming, lots of mitochondria for energy, vacuole containing enzymes for penetrating egg cell,
   B = long for taking messages to all parts of the body, myelin sheath for speeding up transmission, branching dendrites at end so it can be connected to more than one cell,
   C = chloroplasts containing chlorophyll for trapping light, otherwise fairly transparent to allow the passage of light.

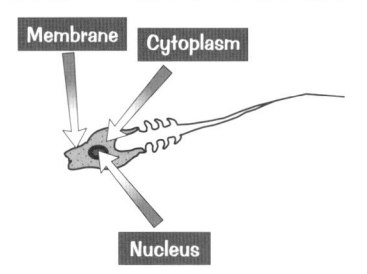

3) **a)** See diagram:
   b) Any example, e.g. bone cell which provides support to the body.

4) **a)** They have a projection/extension — increases surface area for absorption of water / minerals.
   b) Sap vacuole, cell wall.

5) **a)** Their walls are thin (only one cell thick).
   b) Carbon dioxide, waste substances.

6) Immunity / fighting disease — engulfing bacteria, producing antibodies, producing antitoxins.

7) **a)** Adapted for a certain function.
   b) i) The shape increases the surface area for diffusion and allows the cell to bend in narrow capillaries.
   ii) Provides more space to carry haemoglobin.

Pages 4, 5, 6:

1) **a)** The red ink from inside the Visking tubing _diffuses_ into the water; it moves from a high to a low concentration of _ink_ particles.
   b) Water moved into the Visking tubing by osmosis from a high concentration of water (lower concentration of sugar) to a lower concentration of water (higher concentration of sugar).

2) Sea water has a high concentration of salt, which draws water _out_ of the plant by osmosis (particularly the roots).

3) **a)** D **b)** O **c)** D **d)** O
   e) O **f)** O **g)** D **h)** D

4) Prune A — swells because it gains water by osmosis. The skin acts as a partially permeable membrane.
   Prune B — stays shrivelled/shrivels more, because it loses water/ does not gain water.

5) (Strong) concentration of salt in boat; water moved out of potato cells into space containing salt by osmosis. The membranes of potato cells act as partially permeable membranes. Water lost from the potato cells is replaced by water from the sink.

6) water molecules, high water, low water, osmosis, partially permeable, diffusion.

7) **a) i)** Osmosis.
   ii) Guard cells have a greater concentration of solute than the surrounding cells — this causes water to move into them from the surrounding cells.
   b) i) Oxygen, carbon dioxide. **ii)** Diffusion.

8) **a)** A — shrinks because it loses water by osmosis.
   B — gets larger/longer because it gains water by osmosis.
   b) Concentration of sugar was the same as that inside potato cells.

9) **a)** Osmosis.
   b) i) Respiration. **ii)** Diffusion.
   c) i) Carbon dioxide. **ii)** Diffusion into water.

Section Seven — Answers

Plants P.6 → P.13

d) Their cytoplasm has the same concentration as the sea.
10) a) i) Water (with sugar). ii) Inside the fruit. iii) Osmosis.
b) Diffusion.

Page 7 — Plants:

1) a) A = flower; B = stem; C = roots.
   b) Leaf.
   c) A = reproduction,
      B = hold plant upright + transport food, water and minerals,
      C = anchorage and absorb water and mineral salts.
2) See table:

Name of plant	Possible type of habitat	Leaf adaptation	Reason for adaptation
Burdock	Woodland, shaded areas	Large leaf	Large area to absorb light
Cactus	Desert	Reduced size, spiny leaves	Loses less water, protection from animals
Marram Grass	Sand dunes, dry area, exposed area	Curling, stomata on inside surface	Reduces water loss

3) a) To anchor the plant and absorb water and minerals.
   b) Have root hairs.
4) flower, roots, water, mineral salts, xylem, stem, leaves.

Pages 8, 9:

1) a) i) Transport: water, food (sugar) and provides support for leaf.
      ii) Xylem for water transport, Phloem for sugar transport.
         Xylem and Phloem for support.
   b) i) Stomata. ii) Amount of water in (OR turgidity of) guard cells. iii) To reduce water loss.
   c) i) Palisade cell. ii) To make food (sugar) / photosynthesis.
      iii) Has many chloroplasts / has cylindrical shape.
   d) i) (Spongy) mesophyll cell.
      ii) Gases can diffuse through spaces.
   e) Reduce/stop water loss.
2) a) Lower surface is on the water, and the plant gets more gases (CO_2 + O_2) from the air / very difficult to get gases from water.
   b) Carbon dioxide.
   c) Large surface area of leaf.
3) a) Veins.
   b) Phloem cells.
   c) Sugar / sucrose (accept glucose).
   d) Palisade / mesophyll (the palisade is part of the mesophyll)
4) A — i), B — iii), C — ii), D — iv).
5) a) Prevents water loss / reduces water loss.
   b) i) Reduces water loss / evaporation by reducing the circulation of air around the stomata.
      ii) To prevent leaf losing too much water / to reduce evaporation.
   c) The hairs also serve to reduce air flow around the leaves, reducing the rate of transpiration / evaporation from the surface.
   d) The sunken surface again reduces the flow of air around the stomata, so reduces the rate of evaporation / transpiration. This would help prevent the plant drying out in its desert habitat.
   e) You would expect the waxy cuticle to be thicker.

6) a) The green cells have choroplasts; white cells do not.
   b) Chlorophyll.
7) palisade, chloroplasts, chlorophyll, mesophyll, carbon dioxide, xylem, veins, waxy cuticle, stomata, guard cells.

Pages 10, 11:

1) a) i) Evaporation. ii) Diffusion.
   b) Stoma.
   c) Amount of water in (OR turgidity of) guard cells.
   d) The lower surface has more pores (so it loses less water).
2) a) Some used in photosynthesis and cell turgidity.
   b) Evaporation.
   c) Xylem.
   d) Minerals / nutrients.
3) a) To reduce water loss.
   b) The guard cells control the opening and closing of the stomata. The pores are open when the guard cells are turgid, but closed when they are flaccid (when they have lost water), thus reducing further water loss.
4) a) i) 'A'.
      ii) Similar number of stomata on both surfaces.
   b) Allow transpiration; allow gaseous exchange; control rates of transpitation / gaseous exchange.
   c) i) Any of these: light, temperature, humidity, wind movements.
      ii) Affects size of pore, according to whether the guard cell remains turgid (to keep the pore open), or becomes flaccid due to water loss (closing the pore).
5) a) B.
   b) Moving air causes more evaporation from leaf surface by carrying newly evaporated moisture away from the leaf surface (so that a concentration gradient is maintained).
   c) Curve A resembles the response on a hot day. This is because both higher temperatures and moving air increase evaporation.
6) a) The lower surface will colour the cobalt chloride paper first because of the larger number of stomata which will lose more water.
   b) Transpiration / evaporation.
   c) Soil / rain.
   d) Any one of the following: less light, colder, more humid, still air.
7) a) Evaporation / capillary action / capillarity.
   b) i) Decreases.
      ii) Increases only if heat is generated / no change.
      iii) Increases.
      iv) Decreases.
   c) Both have pores.
   d) Pore size is controlled in leaves.
8) a) To reduce evaporation / transpiration.
   b) To increase humidity / reduce evaporation.
9) transpiration / evaporation, xylem, leaves, stomata, guard, lower, evaporation, temperature, greater, wilt, cuticle, thicker.

Pages 12, 13:

1) a) i) Xylem. ii) Transports water and minerals.
   b) i) Phloem. ii) Transports sugar.
   c) Vascular bundle.
2) a) i) They are living cells. ii) They are dead cells.
   b) Food (sugar) could not travel past the heated area/phloem cells could not transport food when heated (damaged/killed).
   c) Swelling would occur in the spring. This is because the food stored in the roots is moving up the stems where it's needed to grow new leaves etc.
3) a) The cells are perforated to allow the movement of substances from cell to cell.

Section Seven — Answers

Plants P.13 → P.16

  b) They are hollow so that movement of their contents can occur.
  c) Roots, stems, storage organs, shoot tips, root tips.
  d) Any two of: respiration / storage / making structures (growth) / growth at shoot tips or root tips / repair of damaged tissues.
  e) The transported food consists of sugar (accept 'glucose' or 'glucose / sucrose') and also other food substances like fatty acids and amino acids.

4) a) To stop the sugar leaving the grapes.
  b) So that the grapes can swell with water.
  c) Burst / skin cracks.

5) a) Photosynthesis.
  b) Sugar / glucose / starch.
  c) Phloem cells.
  d) Sugar / sucrose.
  e) Roots, fruits, tubers, shoot tips, root tips, etc.

6) a) i) Osmosis. ii) Evaporation (accept diffusion).
  b) Xylem cells.
  c) Stomata.
  d) Transpiration stream.

7) a) Being waterproof, lignin stops xylem cells from losing water.
  b) Large space(s) in the end wall.
  c) Minerals.

8) a) Wood doesn't need to be alive for xylem to transport water.
  b) i) Phloem. ii) Dissolved food (glucose / sucrose / sugar / amino acids etc).
  c) White flower turns pink / red.

9) a) Sugar or equivalent.
  b) Phloem.

10) xylem, stem, stream, transpiration, minerals, sugar, photosynthesis, respiration, starch, vascular, cytoplasm, living.

Pages 14, 15:

1) a) Clockwise from top left —
    oxygen is released into the **air / atmosphere**,
    (sun)light for energy is absorbed by **chlorophyll / chloroplasts**,
    water from the soil,
    carbon dioxide from the **air / atmosphere**.
  b) Photosynthesis.
  c) Starch / sugar / glucose.

2) a) See diagram:
  b) i) Iodine solution. ii) Blue / black.
  c) So there was no starch at the start of the experiment. To see where starch was produced.
  d) chlorophyll is needed for photosynthesis, light is needed for photosynthesis.

3) See table:

	Photosynthesis	Respiration
Raw materials used	water and carbon dioxide	carbohydrate/sugar/glucose and oxygen (in aerobic respiration)
End products	oxygen + glucose	carbon dioxide+water (+energy)
Purpose of process	To make food/sugar/glucose	To release energy from food (to do useful work)

4) a) The environment is getting lighter and CO_2 is used for photosynthesis.
  b) & c) See graph:

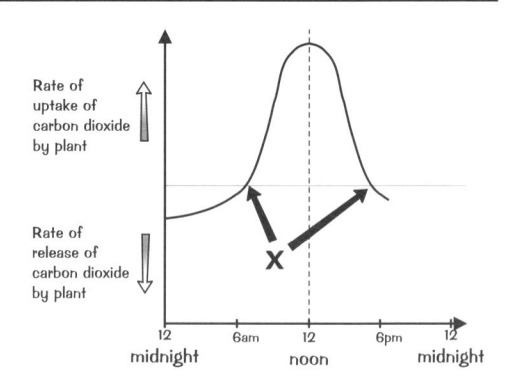

6) a) Lack of oxygen.
  b) Carbon dioxide.

7)

Leaf	Has starch	Turns blue / black
A		✓
B		
C	✓	✓
D		

8) Word equation:

$$\text{Carbon dioxide + water} \xrightarrow[\text{chlorophyll}]{\text{light/solar energy absorbed by}} \text{glucose + oxygen}$$

Chemical equation:

$$6CO_2 + 6H_2O \xrightarrow[\text{chlorophyll}]{\text{light/solar energy absorbed by}} C_6H_{12}O_6 + 6O_2$$

9) a) Temperature / concentration of carbon dioxide.
  b) Curve drawn higher up than but parallel with other two curves (but coinciding with them at the origin).
  c) The influence that most restricts the rate of a reaction.

10) a) C and D.
  b) i) Carbon dioxide. ii) Respiration.
  c) i) There was less carbon dioxide. ii) Photosynthesis.

Page 16:

1) a) i) Stems, leaves, roots, seeds, fruits (also tubers, bulbs, corms, etc.).
    ii) Starch (stems, leaves, roots, tubers, bulbs, corms), lipids (seeds), sucrose/glucose (fruits).
  b) Prevents swelling with water (by osmosis).
  c) It makes the fruit attractive to animals which eat it and spread the seeds.
  d) Photosynthesis.
  e) Respiration.
  f) (Two of) lipids / amino acids / proteins / starch / cellulose.

2) a) 'a'. b) Osmosis. c) Water moves through holes in the Visking tubing to an area of lower water concentration. The holes are too small to allow the passage of glucose molecules.
  d) Insoluble / osmosis does not take place / does not cause swelling with water. e) Lipid.
  f) Leaf, stem, root, tuber, bulb, corm, etc.

3) Glucose, starch, insoluble, stems, sucrose, lipids, proteins, cellulose, respiration, larger, active.

Human Biology Part One   P.17 → P.21

Pages 17, 18:

1) Alex and Georgina's idea's.
2) a) i) Down. ii) The bottom cells are inhibited by the accumulation of auxin. iii) Gravity and moisture + light.
   b) i) Up. ii) Bottom cells elongate faster due to the accumulation of auxin. iii) Gravity and light.
   c) Growth hormone/auxin.
   d) Makes them elongate.
3) shoots, gravity, roots, moisture, hormones, auxin, growth, roots, seedless, fruits, growth, bushier.
4)

Chemical Involved	How is it used?	What effect does it have?
Rooting hormone	Shoots are dipped into it	Promotes root growth on shoots
Weedkiller / (growth) hormone	Sprayed on broad-leaved weed plants	Kills broad-leaved plants
(Growth) hormone	Sprayed on unpollinated flowers	Produces fruit without any pips

5) a) Grow them in the dark / cover the tip of the shoot / give them an equal amount of light all the way round (and it would help to plant them upright).
   b) The shoots are getting more light from the left. He should block off all the light/give them even light/cover the tip.
6) a) First and second plants grow straight, third grows towards the light, fourth grows straight and taller than the others, and will also look less healthy.
   b) First and second get an even amount of light/hormones evenly affected; in the third, light causes the hormone to accumulate on the left. In fourth, no growth hormone is destroyed by the light, so plant grows faster (but would be thinner).
7) a) If growth hormones are applied to _unpollinated_ flowers, seedless fruits are produced.
   b) Selective weedkillers act on plants by _disrupting_ the growth of the plant.
   c) Cutting the tips of plants makes them grow _bushier_.
   d) Fruits can be made to _ripen_ when they are sprayed with hormones.

Pages 19, 20:

1) Food is first broken down in the mouth. The food is chewed and shredded into smaller pieces by the teeth. This is called mechanical digestion. The salivary glands make saliva, which is secreted into the mouth. The food is mixed with a carbohydrase enzyme in saliva called amylase. This begins to break down starch into sugar. This is called chemical digestion. At this stage, the food is broken down into pieces that are small enough to be swallowed. The saliva lubricates the food to make it slip down the oesophagus easily. The smaller pieces of food provide a large surface area for the amylase to work on more effectively.
2) Labelling the parts of the digestive system: A — liver, B — small intestine, C — large intestine, D — mouth, salivary glands and oesophagus, E — stomach, F — pancreas, G — gall bladder.
3) Matching parts to functions, in the correct order:
   Small intestine makes protease, lipase and carbohydrase enzymes. Breakdown products of digestion are absorbed into the blood here.
   Stomach produces hydrochloric acid and protease enzymes.
   Oesophagus (gullet) connects the mouth to the stomach.
   Large intestine absorbs water and stores faeces.
4) a) The food does not go through the salivary glands, pancreas, gall bladder, liver (also the teeth).
   b) The muscular parts are: oesophagus, stomach, small intestine, large intestine (also the jaws, and various sphincters).
5) The "wrong way" means that the food has gone down the trachea (windpipe). The "right way" means that the food has gone down the oesophagus (gullet). When we swallow, the food pushes the soft pallet upwards which stops food getting up the nose. The epiglottis is a flap of skin that drops over the entrance to the trachea when we swallow ensuring that the food goes down the oesophagus and not the trachea.
6) a) A is longitudinal muscle. B is circular muscle.
   b) Peristalsis.
   c) Peristalsis involves rhythmic contractions and relaxations of the circular muscles. This squeezes the food through the intestines. The bolus of food needs to be large enough for this to work efficiently — dietary fibre helps here.
7) The stomach expands to contain the food we swallow. The stomach muscles contract rhythmically to churn the food with gastric juice to produce a creamy suspension called chyme.
8) a) Villi. One on its own is called a villus.
   b) See diagram: (Epithelium, Capillaries, Lacteal)
   c) The villi increase the surface area of the internal surface of the small intestine to about 140m^2 — hundreds of times greater than if the surface were smooth. This helps absorption of digested food.
   d) The intestines are highly folded and coiled to fit into the abdomen. The great length of the intestines helps to increase the surface area for absorption of food and water.

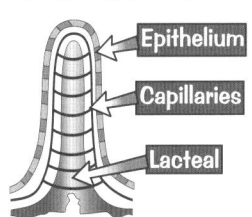

Page 21:

1) _A catalyst_ is a substance that increases the rate of a chemical reaction, but is not used up during the reaction. It can be used over and over again to speed up a reaction.
   An enzyme is a substance which acts as a biological catalyst. Enzymes are proteins that will only catalyse certain reactions, and work best over a narrow range of temperatures and pH.
2) Digestion is the process in which large food molecules are broken down into smaller molecules which are soluble and can be absorbed into the blood.
   Digestive enzymes are the biological catalysts that speed up the breakdown of large food molecules into smaller molecules.
3) Carbohydrase catalyses the breakdown of starch into sugar (maltose).
   Protease catalyses the breakdown of protein into amino acids.
   Lipase catalyses the breakdown of fat into fatty acids and glycerol.

Section Seven — Answers

Human Biology Part One P.21 → P.23

4) a) Hydrochloric acid.
   b) The pH of the stomach contents is about pH 2. Hydrochloric acid is a strong acid so you would expect a low pH.
   c) Hydrochloric acid kills most of the microbes taken in with the food. It also provides the correct pH for the protease enzymes there to work effectively.

5) a) Carbohydrase enzymes are produced by the salivary glands, the pancreas and the small intestine.
   b) Starch is digested in the mouth (and the oesophagus during swallowing) and the small intestine.
   c) Salivary amylase works best in slightly alkaline conditions (its optimum pH is about pH 7.4). The strongly acid conditions of the stomach will be far below the optimum pH for amylase, and digestion of starch will stop. Some digestion of starch may continue inside a bolus of food until the acid reaches the inside of the bolus.
   d) Stomach, pancreas and the small intestine.
   e) Protein is digested in the stomach and the small intestine.
   f) Lipase is produced by the pancreas and the small intestine.
   g) Fat is digested in the small intestine.

6) a) Emulsify means to break down droplets of liquid into smaller droplets, allowing the smaller droplets to spread through another liquid in which they cannot dissolve.
   b) The surface area of fat increases when it is emulsified.
   c) Bile emulsifies fats. This provides a larger surface area of fats for lipase enzymes to work on, so increasing the rate of digestion.

7) Completed flow chart.

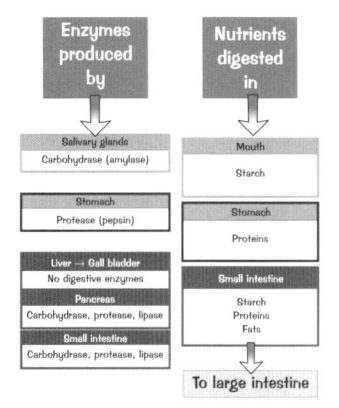

   Enzymes produced by
   - Salivary glands: Carbohydrase (amylase)
   - Stomach: Protease (pepsin)
   - Liver → Gall bladder: No digestive enzymes
   - Pancreas: Carbohydrase, protease, lipase
   - Small intestine: Carbohydrase, protease, lipase

   Nutrients digested in
   - Mouth: Starch
   - Stomach: Proteins
   - Small intestine: Starch, Proteins, Fats
   - To large intestine

8) When food enters the mouth, starch is digested into sugar (maltose) by carbohydrase produced in the salivary glands. When the food reaches the stomach, digestion of starch stops, but protein is digested into amino acids by protease produced in the stomach. When the food reaches the small intestine, starch is further digested into sugar by carbohydrase produced in the pancreas. Protein continues to be digested into amino acids by proteases produced by the pancreas and small intestine. Fats are digested into fatty acids and glycerol by lipase which is produced by the pancreas and small intestine. Bile is produced by the liver and released by the gall bladder. Bile emulsifies the fats to provide a larger surface area for lipase to work on.

Pages 22, 23:

1) Starch is digested to form smaller molecules called sugar.
   Protein is digested to form smaller molecules called amino acids
   Fat is digested to form smaller molecules called fatty acids and glycerol.

2) a) The sand does not dissolve. Small particles of sand form a suspension in the water; larger particles fall to the bottom to form a sediment.
   b) The sugar dissolves in the water.
   c) When the mixture is filtered, the sand gets trapped by the filter paper and forms a residue.
   d) When the mixture is filtered the sugar solution passes through to form a filtrate.
   e) Filtration is where an insoluble solid is separated from a liquid in which it is suspended by applying it to a porous substance, such as filter paper. The porous substance traps the insoluble solid, and the liquid goes through it. Insoluble substances like sand can be filtered; soluble substances like sugar cannot.

3) a) Note: Structural proteins such as keratin (found in hair and nails) and membrane proteins are insoluble in water.

Soluble	Insoluble
Protein	Protein
Amino acids	Fat
Fatty acids	Starch
Glycerol	
Sugar	

   b) Fat, starch and some proteins (e.g. keratin), can be separated from water by filtration. This is because they do not dissolve in water and so cannot pass through the filter paper.
   c) The products of digestion are soluble, and therefore cannot be filtered.

4) a) The sugar passed through the walls of the Visking tubing by diffusion.
   b) The starch molecules were too large to pass through the pores of the visking tubing and were therefore not in solution.
   c) The student could speed up the process of diffusion by: Warming the water to increase the speed of movement of the sugar molecules. Increasing the concentration gradient, e.g. by using more concentrated sugar solution or a greater volume of water, stirring the water to reduce the concentration of sugar just outside the bag, or by replacing the water during the 30 minutes. Increasing the surface area, e.g. using a larger bag to hold the small volume of water but making it flatter.

5) a) The products of digestion are absorbed into the bloodstream in the small intestine.
   b) Dietary fibre cannot be digested, (and a lot of it is insoluble. It's therefore not absorbed by the digestive system).
   c) Excess water is absorbed in the large intestine.
   d) The large intestine also stores faeces (indigestible waste) before it leaves through the anus.
   e) If too much water is absorbed, the faeces become hard, and you get constipation.
   f) If too little water is absorbed, the faeces become very soft and you can get diarrhoea.

6) a) "Diffusion is the _passive_ movement of particles _down_ a concentration gradient from a _high_ concentration to a _low_ concentration. Diffusion through membranes is _faster_ when the membrane is thin and has a _large_ surface area."

Human Biology Part One   P.23 → P.27

b) The small intestine is very long (about 6m) to provide a large surface area for the movement of substances through the wall of the intestine. The wall of the intestine also has millions of finger-like projections called villi, which further increase the surface area many times. The surface epithelium of the villi is very thin allowing substances to pass quickly through it.

c) There is a dense network of capillaries in each villus. The capillary wall is also very thin, allowing the products of digestion to pass very quickly into the bloodstream.

Page 24:

1) a) Starch.
   b) Iodine solution turns blue — black when added to starch.

2) a) The starting mixture should turn blue — black, showing that starch is present.
   b) If Benedict's reagent turns red, it shows that a reducing sugar is present.
   c) Iqbal should have tested the starting mixture with Benedict's reagent in case it already contained sugar. He should also have tested the mixture at the end with iodine solution to see if the starch had gone. If the experiment worked, you would expect to see no change with the Benedict's reagent at the start (stays blue), and no change with the iodine solution at the end (stays brown — although this does depend on the amounts of starch and amylase used).
   d) Iqbal ought to set up a control tube with starch suspension only and no amylase.

3) John's instructions should read:

   The Biuret Test.
   The biuret test is used to detect **protein** in food.
   1. Put some food in a test tube and add some **dilute sodium hydroxide solution**.
   2. Give it a shake and add some **copper sulphate solution** (this is blue).
   3. If it goes **purple**, there is **protein** present.

Page 25:

1) The two main components of the circulatory system are the heart and the blood vessels.

2) The circulatory system's main functions include; transporting nutrients and oxygen to the cells in the body, transporting wastes away from the cells in the body, distribution of hormones and heat around the body. It is called the circulatory system because blood circulates around the body.

3) Labels from the diagram:

Blood vessels	Number	Organs	Letter
Pulmonary vein	1	Intestines	C
Aorta	2	Kidneys	D
Vena cava	3	Liver	B
		Lungs	A

4) The pulmonary artery branches into two because we have two lungs – one branch for each lung.

5) Veins carry blood from other organs towards the heart; arteries carry blood from the heart towards the other organs. The hepatic portal vein does not go directly back to the heart, but takes blood rich in dissolved food molecules to the liver, for processing and storage.

6) a) When the smooth muscles contract, the diameter of the artery decreases.
   b) This is called vasoconstriction.
   c) Prolonged stress can cause increased blood pressure (hypertension). It may also help the plaque-forming process in the arteries and so increase the risk of heart attack.

7) a) Exercise increases the heart rate and stroke volume. The heart rate increases the most.
   b) Study of the table shows that :
      Cardiac output = Heart rate x Stroke volume.
      So : Cardiac output = 100 x 110 = 11000cm^3 per minute.
   c) An increased cardiac output is needed when we exercise to get more blood to the exercising tissues, e.g. the muscles. As the muscles are respiring at a greater rate than at rest, more glucose and oxygen is needed by them. There are more waste products to be removed by the blood too.
   d) Fit athletes often have very efficient hearts that can deliver a greater volume of blood with each beat, i.e. a greater stroke volume. Therefore, their heart rate does not need to be as great as a non-athlete to deliver enough blood to the tissues of their bodies.

Pages 26, 27:

1) a) There are four chambers in the human heart.
   b) The upper chambers are called atria. Singular: atrium.
   c) The lower chambers are called ventricles.
   d) Deoxygenated blood returns from the body to the right side of the heart. (Which is on the left hand side of the diagram because it shows the heart from the front.)
   e) Oxygenated blood returns from the lungs to the left side of the heart. (On the right of the diagram.)
   f) The valves prevent the backflow of blood.
   g) The right side of the heart pumps blood to the lungs to be oxygenated. The left side of the heart pumps oxygenated blood to all parts of the body, including the heart itself, but **not** the lungs.

2)

Label	Part of heart
A	Right atrium
B	Right ventricle
C	Left atrium
D	Left ventricle

3)

Label	Blood vessel
1	Vena cava
2	Pulmonary artery
3	Aorta
4	Pulmonary vein

4) The vena cava carries deoxygenated blood to the heart.
   The pulmonary vein carries oxygenated blood away from the lungs.
   The pulmonary artery carries deoxygenated blood to the lungs.
   The aorta carries oxygenated blood to the rest of the body.

5) a) The right side of the heart only has to pump blood to the lungs, but the left side has to pump blood to the rest of the body, so the walls of the left side must be thicker to achieve this. The atria only have to pump blood into the ventricles, but the ventricles have to pump blood from the heart to the lungs and the rest of the body and so must be thicker.

Human Biology Part One P.27 → P.29

b) The walls of the heart are made from muscle (called cardiac muscle). This is expected because the heart works by contracting and relaxing, which muscles do.

c) If a coronary artery became blocked, oxygenated blood would not get to the heart tissues supplied by that artery. This could cause a heart attack.

d) Deoxygenated blood in the right ventricle can mix with oxygenated blood in the left ventricle, and so the blood leaving the heart for the rest of the body contains insufficient oxygen. This gives the skin a bluish tinge, as the blood circulating is not fully oxygenated.

6) a) Correct sequence of events, right side of the heart: The vena cava brings blood from the body to the heart. Blood pours into the right atrium. While the right ventricle is relaxed, blood flows into it through the open tricuspid valve. The atrium contracts to finish filling the ventricle with blood. The ventricle contracts, squeezing the blood inside. The tricuspid valve shuts to stop blood going back into the atrium. The walls of the ventricle push the blood out of the heart through the pulmonary artery. The semi-lunar valves stop blood flowing backwards into the ventricle.

b) Correct sequence of events, left side of the heart: The pulmonary vein brings blood from the lungs to the heart. Blood pours into the left atrium. While the left ventricle is relaxed, blood flows into it through the open bicuspid valve. The atrium contracts to finish filling the ventricle with blood. The ventricle contracts, squeezing the blood inside. The bicuspid valve shuts to stop blood going back into the atrium. The walls of the ventricle push the blood out of the heart through the aorta. The semi-lunar valves stop blood flowing backwards into the ventricle.

c) Flow chart of common events:

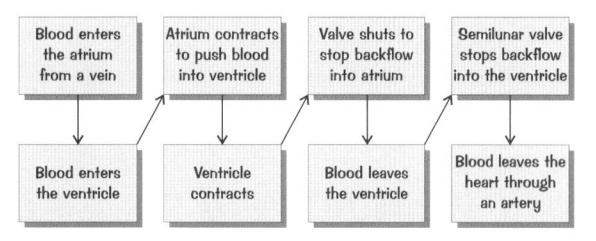

[Flow chart: Blood enters the atrium from a vein → Atrium contracts to push blood into ventricle → Valve shuts to stop backflow into atrium → Semilunar valve stops backflow into the ventricle; Blood enters the ventricle → Ventricle contracts → Blood leaves the ventricle → Blood leaves the heart through an artery]

Page 28:

1) *Arteries* carry blood *from* the heart at *high* pressure. *Veins* carry blood *to* the heart at *low* pressure.

2) a) [Diagram of artery and vein cross-sections labelled: Lumen, Endothelium, Elastic fibres and smooth muscle, Fibrous coat]

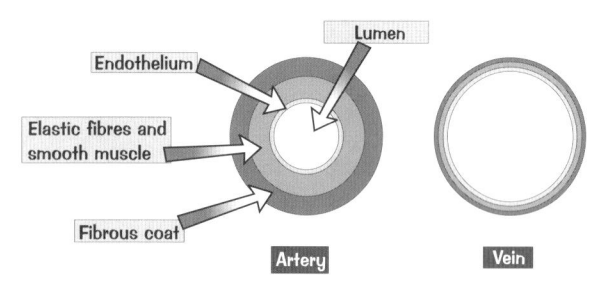

b) *Similarities*: Both vessels have a lumen surrounded by an endothelium, elastic fibres and smooth muscles, and a fibrous coat.
Differences: For a given diameter of blood vessel, arteries have a narrower lumen and thicker walls than veins do.

c) Arteries must carry blood at high pressure. The thick, muscular and elastic walls allow them to stand up to the high pressures produced by the heart. They can return to their original diameter after the surge of blood at high pressure. Veins only need to carry blood at low pressure. They do not need such thick walls, but the large lumen helps to maintain the blood flow.

3) a) & e) See diagram:

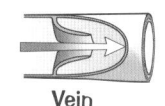

[Diagrams of Vein and Artery]

b) The extra structure in the vein is a semi-lunar valve.
c) The semi-lunar valve prevents blood flowing backwards.
d) Semi-lunar valves can also be found at the exits to the ventricles in the heart.
e) Arrow added to diagram of vein as above: blood flowing from left to right in the diagram pushes the walls of the valve against the wall of the capillary; if blood tries to flow back the other way, it fills the two halves of the valve with blood so closing it tightly.
f) Blood is kept moving in veins (vessel A) by the contractions of muscles around large veins, especially in the arms and legs.
g) Contractions of the heart keep blood moving in the arteries (vessel B).
h) In both cases, muscles are involved in keeping the blood moving.

4) a) Capillaries allow cells to receive the substances they need from the blood, including water, oxygen and dissolved nutrients. They also allow cells to pass waste products into the blood, including carbon dioxide and other excretory products.
b) The wall of the capillary is very thin, often just one cell thick. This allows substances to pass into the cells from the blood, and out of the cells into the blood, quickly by diffusion.

Page 29:

1) a) Layer A is plasma.
b) Layer B contains white cells. Layer C contains red cells. Layer B also contains platelets.
c) About 45% of blood is made up of cells.

2) a) The function of red blood cells is to transport oxygen.
b) The biconcave disc shape increases the surface area available for absorbing oxygen.
c) Haemoglobin. Haemoglobin combines with oxygen to form oxyhaemoglobin. This can split up again to release oxygen. Haemoglobin can also combine with carbon dioxide in areas of high carbon dioxide concentration.
d) The cytoplasm of red cells can contain more haemoglobin if there is no nucleus.

3) Carbon monoxide can suffocate you. It bonds very strongly to haemoglobin, and prevents the red cells carrying sufficient oxygen for the body's needs. As it is odourless and colourless, it is not easy to detect carbon monoxide (special detectors can be fitted in houses to warn of its release). Gas fires need to be checked to ensure that they are burning efficiently and not emitting dangerous levels of carbon monoxide.

4) Platelets help in the clotting of blood at the site of a wound. This prevents blood loss and entry of micro-organisms into the body.

Human Biology Part One   P.29 → P.33

5) a) Labelled diagram:
   A Nucleus
   B Cytoplasm
   C Cell membrane
   b) White cells protect us against infection by: engulfing microbes, producing antibodies, producing antitoxins.
   c) White cells can also be found in the bone marrow, lymph nodes and the spleen.

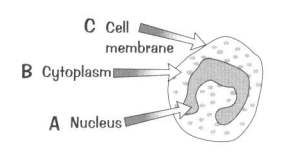

6) Plasma transports all of the listed substances, with the exception of oxygen (transported by the red cells).

7) Completed summary table:

Red cells	Platelets	White cells	Plasma
Transport of oxygen	Helping to clot blood at the site of a wound	Protection of the body from infection by: engulfing microbes, producing antibodies, producing antitoxins	Transport of red cells, white cells, platelets, dissolved mineral salts, products of digestion, carbon dioxide, urea, water, antibodies, antitoxins, hormones

Pages 30, 31:

1) "The breathing system takes _air_ into and out of the body. This allows _oxygen_ to pass from the air into the bloodstream, and _carbon dioxide_ to pass out of the bloodstream into the air".

2) a) The heart would normally be found in the space at X.
   b) Matching letters to labels (some are used twice):

Letter	Label
A	Trachea
B	Rib
C	Lung
D	Intercostal muscles
E	Diaphragm
F	Intercostal muscles

Letter	Label
G	Pleural membrane
H	Bronchus
I	Bronchiole
J	Alveoli
K	Rib

3) a) The ribs form the rib cage which protects the lungs from external damage.
   b) The diaphragm separates the lungs from the abdomen.
   c) The pleural membranes make the inside of the chest cavity slippery. This protects the outside surface of the lungs as they rub against the ribs when we breathe.

4) Correct order : trachea → bronchi → bronchioles → alveoli.

5) a) The trachea is also called the windpipe.
   b) The rings of cartilage support the trachea and bronchi. They keep these air passages open when we breathe in (the air pressure inside the air passages falls when we breathe in).
   c) There is one bronchus for each lung (so two bronchi in total).
   d) A bronchiole is a smaller air passage formed when the bronchi divide. The bronchioles themselves divide further producing smaller and smaller bronchioles.
   e) An alveolus is a tiny air sac found at the end of bronchioles, where gas exchange occurs.

6) a) Breathing in: The muscles between the ribs contract. This pulls the ribcage upwards. The diaphragm muscles contract. This causes the diaphragm to flatten. The volume of the thorax increases. The pressure inside the thorax goes down. The pressure inside the thorax gets less than atmospheric pressure. Air is pushed into the lungs from outside to make the pressures equal.
   b) Breathing out: The muscles between the ribs relax. This lets the ribcage go downwards. The diaphragm muscles relax. This causes the diaphragm to bend upwards. The volume of the thorax decreases. The pressure inside the thorax goes up. The pressure inside the thorax gets more than atmospheric pressure. Air is pushed out of the lungs to make the pressures equal.

7) The diaphragm must contract very quickly during a hiccup.

8) The alveoli provide an enormous surface area over which diffusion can take place. The walls are moist, allowing gases to dissolve so that they can diffuse through the walls of the alveoli. There is a dense network of capillaries surrounding the alveoli. The walls of the capillaries are also only one cell thick, and gases can diffuse easily through them into and out of the bloodstream.

9) See table:

GAS	% in inhaled air	% in exhaled air
oxygen	21	16
carbon dioxide	0.04	4
nitrogen	78	78

10) Respiration equation:
    glucose + oxygen → carbon dioxide + water + energy transferred

Pages 32, 33:

1) The correct function of respiration is to release energy from cells. Plants do respire.

2) a) glucose + oxygen → carbon dioxide + water + energy transferred.
   b) $C_6H_{12}O_6 + 6O_2 \rightarrow 6CO_2 + 6H_2O$ + energy transferred.
   c) Glucose and oxygen are needed for respiration. They are transported to the cells in the bloodstream. Glucose comes from food (digested in the digestive system and absorbed through the walls of the small intestine into the bloodstream). Oxygen comes from air (inhaled into the lungs and absorbed through the walls of the alveoli into the bloodstream).
   d) Carbon dioxide and water are produced by respiration. Carbon dioxide and water diffuse from the cells into the bloodstream through the walls of the capillaries. They will then diffuse from the bloodstream into the alveoli (in the lungs) again through capillaries, and are then passed out of the body as exhaled air. Water also leaves the body in urine, faeces and sweat.
   e) Energy is produced by respiration.

3) a) _Similarities_ : Both release energy, both need glucose.
      Differences : Aerobic respiration requires oxygen, anaerobic does not. Aerobic produces carbon dioxide and water, anaerobic only produces lactic acid.
   b) Aerobic means "with air"; anaerobic means "without air".
   c) Aerobic respiration releases 19.2 times more energy than anaerobic respiration does (note the units are not both kJ).
   d) Aerobic respiration produces 19 times more ATP molecules per molecule of glucose than anaerobic respiration does, because aerobic respiration releases just over 19 times more energy than anaerobic respiration does.

Human Biology Part One   P.33 → P.35

4) a) David's muscles are unable to keep on contracting because they are using up more oxygen than his body can supply. When the oxygen supply has been used up, his muscles begin to respire anaerobically which produces lactic acid. The build up of lactic acid in his muscles is the cause of the pain he feels and the reason he is unable to continue clenching.

b) With his hand lowered, David's hand muscles receive more blood than when it is raised. This brings more oxygen to the respiring muscle cells, and takes away the waste products of respiration more effectively. This allows the muscles to contract more often before the amount of lactic acid formed by anaerobic respiration reaches a painful concentration.

5) Because yeast contains enzymes.

6) a) Aerobic respiration.

b) When Kathryn begins to run, her muscles contract more frequently. This additional muscular activity needs energy from respiration. More oxygen is needed to allow aerobic respiration to continue at a greater rate than when she was resting, so oxygen uptake increases.

c) There is a limit to how much air can be taken in by breathing, how much gaseous exchange can take place in the lungs, and how much oxygen can be transported to the respiring cells by the blood.

d) During the race, more energy is required for muscular contraction than can be supplied by aerobic respiration alone, so anaerobic respiration occurs. The product of anaerobic respiration is lactic acid, and this builds up in her body.

e) After the race, less energy is needed for muscular contraction. The additional oxygen being taken in can be used to oxidise the lactic acid to carbon dioxide and water. This continues until it is all oxidised, with the rate of oxygen uptake gradually returning to normal.

f) The oxygen debt is the volume of oxygen needed to oxidise all the lactic acid produced by anaerobic respiration. Depending on fitness, the oxygen debt can be up to 20 litres of oxygen (dm^3).

Pages 34, 35:

1) a) Stimuli. Singular: stimulus.
b) Receptors.
c) If we can detect, and respond to, changes in the environment we can, for example, avoid danger and catch food.

2) a) Matching sense organs to senses:

Sense organ	nose	tongue	ears	eyes	skin
Sense	smell	taste	hearing/balance	sight	temperature/touch

b) Matching senses to stimuli:

Stimulus	chemicals	light	position	sound	pressure	temperature change
Sense	smell/taste	sight	balance	hearing	touch	temperature

c) Completed table:

Sense organ	Stimulus	Sense
nose	chemicals	smell
tongue	chemicals	taste
eyes	light	sight
ears	sound	hearing
ears	position	balance
skin	pressure	touch
skin	temperature change	temperature

3) A nerve impulse is an electrical signal that passes along a nerve fibre, in only one direction.

4) a) The stimulus is the heat of the hot object.
b) The response is the movement of the finger.
c) The effector is the arm muscle.
d) [Diagram of reflex arc showing Stimulus → Receptor → Sensory neurone → Relay neurone (section through spinal cord) → Motor neurone → Effector → Response, with Back and Front labelled]

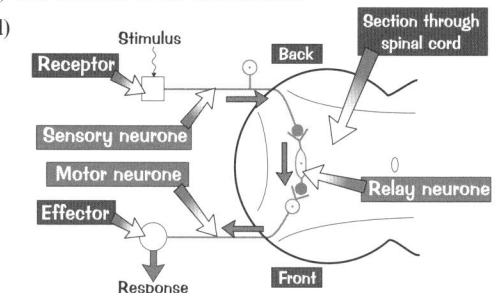

e) The neurones connect the receptor to the effector.
f) Correct reflex arc: stimulus → receptor → neurones (coordinator) → effector → response.
g) The reflex arc shows that nerve impulses from a reflex action do not have to pass through the brain. Therefore reflex actions are involuntary and much quicker.

5) Tap on leg → stretch receptor → impulse passes along sensory neurone → impulse passes through relay neurone → impulse passes along motor neurone → leg muscle contracts → leg straightens.
Grit in eye → touch receptor in eyelid → impulse passes along sensory neurone → impulse passes through relay neurone → impulse passes through motor neurone → tears secreted by tear gland in eye → eyes water to remove the grit.

6) a) A sensory neurone carries a nerve impulse from a receptor to the spinal cord. A motor neurone carries a nerve impulse from the spinal cord to the effector, e.g. muscle.
b) Diagram B represents a sensory neurone. There is a sensory nerve ending on the left, and the cell body is attached to the nerve fibre, rather than being at one end.
c) [Diagrams A and B of neurones, each labelled with Cell Body and Nerve fibre (axon); B also labelled with Sensory nerve ending]

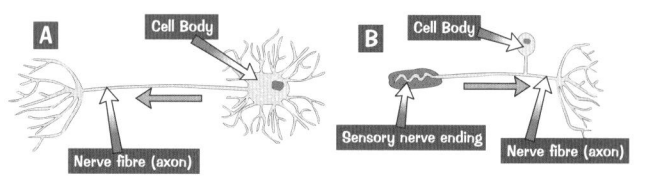

d) Motor neurone: X is connected to an effector, such as a muscle or gland.
Sensory neurone: X is connected to a connector (relay) neurone.
e) Key features: Long nerve fibres (axons) to connect distant parts of the body. Many branching nerve endings to make many connections with other nerves or with muscles and glands.

7) A reflex action is an *automatic* response to a *stimulus*. It happens very *quickly* and *does not involve* the *brain*. Reflex actions allow us to coordinate body activity by *nervous control*.

8) a) X: brain Y: spinal cord Z: nerves/neurones.
b) The central nervous system.
c) Nerve impulses can travel in both directions in the spinal cord, but remember that they can only travel in one direction in individual nerve fibres.

Human Biology Part Two   P.35 → P.39

d) Functions of the brain: to receive impulses from all the sensory organs in the body, to send off motor impulses to glands and muscles, to correlate impulses from various sensory neurones, to coordinate activities in the body, to store information. The brain is not involved in reflex actions. These continue without involving the brain, but there may be connection to the brain to allow us to sense that we have, for example, moved our leg in response to a tap on the knee.

9) a) Synapses are found between neurones. Synapses allow the nerve impulse to be passed from one neurone to another.

b) The bubbles of chemical crossing the synapse carry the message across the gap between the two neurones (the nerve impulse itself does not cross).

c) The presence of mitochondria suggests that energy from respiration is needed for the synapse to function.

d) Neurones have an insulating fatty sheath around them, so the electrical impulse cannot pass directly. The need for a chemical to cross the gap between the two neurones allows a degree of control in the transmission of the nerve impulse from one neurone to another.

Pages 36, 37:

1) a) & b) Completed table:

Label	Name
A	Suspensory ligaments
B	Iris
C	Cornea
D	Pupil
E	Lens
F	Ciliary muscles
G	Retina
H	Optic nerve
X	Blind spot
Y	Fovea
Z	Sclera

2) Correct part and function:
Ciliary muscles — pull the lens for focusing. *Cornea* — lets light into the eye and begins focusing. *Iris* — controls the amount of light entering the eye. *Lens* — focuses light onto the retina. *Optic nerve* — sends signals to the brain. *Pupil* — lets light through to the lens. *Retina* — light-sensitive layer - sends signals to the optic nerve. *Suspensory ligaments* — holds the lens in place.

3) a) The light travels through the conjunctiva, cornea, aqueous humour, the pupil, the lens and the vitreous humour. It will also partially travel through the retina (the black choroid layer beneath it absorbs the residual light).

b) Light hits, but cannot travel through, the iris and the sclera. It will also hit the suspensory ligaments, ciliary muscles and the blind spot (optic nerve with blood vessels).

4) a) The black circle at the centre of the iris is the pupil.

b) Muscle A: radial muscles; Muscle B: circular muscles.

c) Diagram 2 shows the eye in bright light. This is because the pupil is very small, restricting the amount of light entering the lens.

d) In diagram 1, the circular muscles are relaxed, and the radial muscles have contracted.

e) In diagram 2, the radial muscles are relaxed, and the circular muscles have contracted.

f) In bright light, the circular muscles of the iris contract and the radial muscles relax. This makes the diameter of the pupil smaller, allowing less light through to the lens. In dim light, the radial muscles contract and the circular muscles relax. The diameter of the pupil increases allowing more light in.

g) Other muscles involved with the eye include the ciliary muscles. These pull the lens to allow focusing. Shown on the diagram, but not labelled, are the extrinsic muscles that move the eyeball around in the eye socket.

5) a) A thin lens is needed to focus light from a distant object. A thick lens is needed to focus light from a nearby object.

b) The light rays are bent the most in the diagram with the thick lens.

6) a) The cornea and lens are able to change the direction of light.

b) The lens of the eye is able to focus both distant and nearby objects.

7) a) The lens must be thick here because light from a nearby object must be bent more to be focused onto the retina.

b) The natural shape of the lens is fat.

c) If the ciliary muscles relax, the suspensory ligaments will be pulled and will become taut. The lens will be pulled into a thin shape.

d) The thin lens will be able to focus distant objects.

e) Diagram of focusing light from a distant object: the light should bend both when entering the lens and when leaving it.

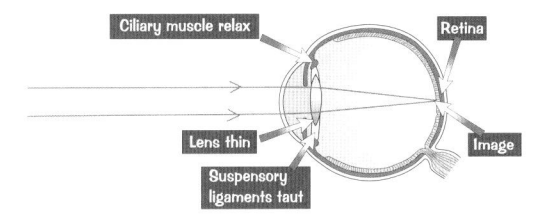

Pages 38, 39 — Human Biology Part Two:

1) chemicals, hormones, glands, bloodstream

2) a) pancreas.
b) glucagon.
c) ovaries.
d) pituitary.
e) stimulates release of the egg.

3) a) glucose,
b) insulin,
c) liver, glycogen.
d) insulin, liver,
e) Glucagon is produced in the pancreas and travels to the liver. This causes the liver to convert glycogen back into glucose in the blood, restoring normal blood sugar level.

4) 1 – C, 2 – D, 3 – A, 4 – E, 5 – B.

The many Types and Functions of Hormones

5) *Hormones* are chemicals made and released by glands and carried in the blood stream to affect specific target organs. Ductless (endocrine) *glands* produce and release hormones. *Insulin* is the hormone produced by the pancreas which instructs the liver to convert excess glucose into glycogen and store it. *Glucagon* is the hormone again made by the pancreas which instruct the liver to do the opposite – convert glycogen to glucose and increase the sugar level of the blood. *FSH* is Follicle Stimulating Hormone which stimulates egg maturity. *Oestrogen* is the female sex hormone produced by the ovaries.

6) *Glucose* is a simple sugar. Molecules of glucose can join together form starch. *Glycogen* is the storage product of glucose in the liver. The *pancreas* is a digestive organ producing enzymes and also contains the endocrine gland producing insulin and glucagon. The *liver* is one of the most important organs of the body but one of its main functions is to convert excess glucose and store it as glycogen. The *ovaries* are the female reproductive organs which produce ova (eggs). The *pituitary* is the "master gland" which controls all the other glands.

Human Biology Part Two   P.39 → P.44

7) **a)** See diagram:

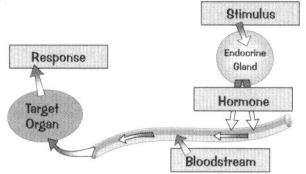

b) Chemical (Hormones): slower message, act for a long time, act more generally, longer term reaction.
Nerves: fast message, act for a short time, act in a precise area, immediate reaction.

Page 40:

1) See diagram: Pancreas
2) **a)** Insulin, glucagon, (adrenaline).
   b) The diabetic cannot produce insulin and store excess glucose as glycogen.
   c) The level of glucose would be higher.
3) **i)** Injection of insulin.
   ii) Diet with little sugary or high carbohydrate food.
4) **i)** Affects brain cells – can lead to fainting or more seriously coma.
   ii) Glucose is excreted by the kidney, not stored.
5) None / little because a diabetic person has no / or little insulin and so cannot transform glucose into glycogen, unless insulin has been injected.
6) **a)** The pancreas produces insulin which causes the liver to change glucose into glycogen and so makes the blood glucose level normal again.
   b) The pancreas produces glucagon which causes the liver to change glycogen into glucose, releasing it into the blood and making the blood glucose level normal again.
7) **a)** Rapidly increased activity could cause the use of most of the glucose for respiration, rapidly reducing the blood-sugar level.
   b) The hormone glucagon is then produced to allow glycogen to be changed to glucose in the liver and return the blood glucose level to normal.
8) No, because insulin is a protein and would be digested while it's in the digestive system before entering the blood.
9) As the hormone insulin is a protein the enzymes pepsin and trypsin would digest it.
10) **a)** Glucose.
    b) Add Benedicts solution to urine in a test tube, boil, and watch for a precipitate forming. If sugar is present the precipitate is usually orange. If it is absent no colour change is observed.
11) _Pancreas_ — an important gland, _Diabetes_ — a disease, _Glucose_ — energy-giver, _Glycogen_ — storage compound, _Insulin_ — another hormone, _Glucagon_ — a hormone.

Pages 41:

1) Menstruation.
2) Ovulation.
3) **a)** The menstrual cycle.
   b) Fertilisation of an egg, or menstruation and the repetition of the cycle.
4) 1.

5) **a)** progesterone, break, down, menstruation.
   b) oestrogen, thicken, blood, vessels, fertilised egg.
   c) progesterone, uterus lining, 28, fertilised egg
6) Yes.
7) About 2 weeks (14 days) after the beginning of menstruation.
8) The egg is only alive and in the correct area for fertilisation for a short period of time.
9) No. They are all present in an immature state at birth but become mature one by one during menstruation.

Pages 42:

1) The menstrual cycle.
2) The uterus lining thickens and the blood supply increases if it has to receive a fertilised egg (ovum).
3) Usually no more than one.
4) **a)** Ovulation. **b)** Progesterone. **c)** Menstruation.
5) _ova_ — eggs; _ovary_ — organ which produces eggs and their hormones; _puberty_ — the change which occurs as the male and female sex organs develop; _ovulation_ – the release of an egg from the ovary; _Fallopian tube / oviduct_ — the tube which leads from the ovary and which the egg travels along; _uterus_ — the main sex organ where the foetus develops; _cervix_ — the opening to the uterus; _vagina_ — the entrance to the female sex organs; _menstruation_ —the monthly flow of blood from the lining of the uterus; _menstrual cycle_ — the cycle of 28 days which starts with menstruation.

Pages 43, 44:

1) Glands
2) The bloodstream.
3) The ovaries and the pituitary.
4) **i)** causes egg to mature and ovaries to produce oestrogen.
   ii) stops production of FSH and stimulates the release of LH.
   iii) Luteinising Hormone (LH).
   iv) ovary.
5) **a) i)** FSH **ii)** Oestrogen **iii)** LH
   b) Pituitary
   c) Progesterone
6) See diagram:

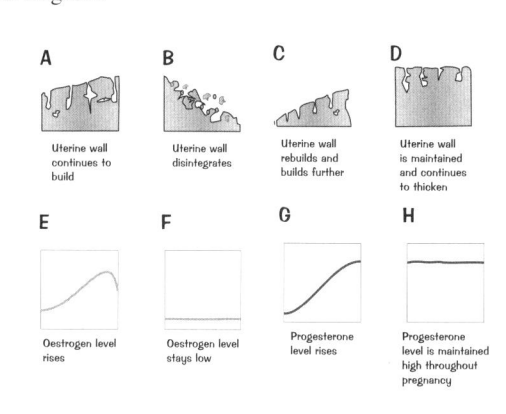

7) **a)** Oestrogen.
   b) Progesterone.
8) The site where hormones have their effect.

Human Biology Part Two P.44 → P.49

9) **Effects : A** – Causes egg development and stimulates oestrogen production; **B** – Maintains uterus lining.
   Hormones : 1 – Oestrogen; **2** – LH (Luteinising Hormone)

10) a) Progesterone and Oestrogen. (or just progesterone.)
    b) It would increase it.
    c) Egg development and release would be stopped.
    d) Yes. Levels of the hormones would fall back to normal after a period of time.

11) Yes. Oestrogen inhibits production of FSH so that no eggs mature. Levels of FSH fall so no more oestrogen is produced.

12) a) FSH.
    b) It causes more eggs to mature.

13) a) Progesterone.
    b) To maintain a good blood supply to provide all the necessary requirements for foetal development and remove all waste products.

14) An increasing oestrogen level stops the production of FSH and causes the production of LH.

15) a) FSH.
    b) Oestrogen.
    c) Getting the correct dosage can be difficult (sometimes too many eggs can be released), the treatment is expensive and can be disruptive.

Pages 45, 46:

1) a) Bacteria, viruses.
   b) Warm / moist conditions.
   c) They can make us ill (can name examples)

2) a) Bacteria.
   b) Virus.

3) See table:

	Bacteria	Viruses
1	About 1/1000mm	About 1/10,000mm
2	Can produce toxins	Can produce toxins
3	Cell wall	------------
4	------------	Coat of protein
5	Cytoplasm	------------
6	Can reproduce rapidly	Can reproduce rapidly
7	Contain DNA	Contain DNA
8	Slime capsule	------------

4) a) Diffusion.
   b) Chlorine.

5) Two of : contact with infected people, unhygienic conditions, broken skin.

6) i) warm ii) good food supply iii) moist.

7) A disease-causing micro-organism.

8) Bacteria, viruses, fungi.

9) Fungus.

10) See table:

Disease	Type of microbe (bacteria, virus, fungus) which carries it	How it is spread (air droplets, infected water, food contamination)
Common cold	Virus	Air droplets
Measles	Virus	Air droplets
Cholera	Bacterium	Infected water
Polio	Virus	Air droplets, infected water
Whooping cough	Virus	Air droplets

11) A sneeze contains thousands of droplets of water from the mouth and nose. As these droplets contain viruses, the cold virus may infect another person.

12) Any 4 of the following: by air droplets, by dust, by cuts or scratches, by touch, by animals.

13) a) Heat and drought.
    b) They form a thick protective coat around themselves (a spore) and become dormant, for a long time if necessary. When conditions are good again the spore bursts open, and the bacteria are released.

14) Bacterial – take antibiotics ; Viral – wait for your body to overcome it. There's no treatment.

15) Household hygiene includes cleaning and disinfecting the bathroom and work surfaces (eg. in the kitchen), keeping raw meat separate from other foods and cooking food properly.

Page 47:

1) Any of : unbroken skin, clotting of the blood to seal the wound, white cells (phagocytes to ingest bacteria, lymphocytes to produce antibodies), mucus and cilia in respiratory tract, acid in stomach.

2) a) Lymphocyte
   b) Red blood cells (erythrocyte).
   c) Phagocyte

3) Red blood cell (erythrocyte).

4) Lymphocyte

5) Phagocyte. Antibodies bind to pathogen. Phagocyte attracted to pathogen and ingests / engulfs it. Pathogen destroyed by digestive enzymes.

6) a) Epidermis
   b) The epidermis is waxy and impermeable to water and pathogens.
   c) A gap in the skin eg. a cut, allows pathogens to enter more easily.

7) a) Plasma and platelets.
   b) i) Blood clotting prevents pathogen entry.
      ii) Blood clotting prevents too much blood loss.

Pages 48, 49:

1) Solvents, Tobacco and Alcohol

2) a) Production of another drug by another living thing, e.g. penicillin — drug from the fungus of Penicillium
   b) Chemicals are combined and used as a drug to affect behaviour or help a human.

3) a) Slow down the brain and make you feel happy
   b) Stimulants.
   c) Coffee, tea or caffeine.
   d) Painkiller / analgesic.

4) Any 2 of the following: they can damage your health, they can impair your senses and affect your behaviour, they can lead to excess spending on drugs, they may lead to addiction where people are dependent on the drug

5) a) Cannot do without the drug.
   b) Painful symptoms when drug use is stopped or withdrawn.

Section Seven — Answers

Human Biology Part Two   P.48 → P.52

6) a) Chemicals which can dissolve substances.
   b) People breathe in the fumes given off by the solvent in the glue.
   c) The liver, kidneys, brain and lungs.
   d) Specifically, sores around the eyes, mouth and an irritable nature. There are also more severe symptoms such as convulsions and unconsciousness.

7) a) Any two of heroin, morphine and aspirin.
   b) Deterioration in personal life, severe addiction and difficult withdrawal, turning to crime to finance the habit, risk of contracting diseases transmitted by shared needles and other drug related effects such as hallucinations.

8) a) Arouses the body. High energy.
   b) Depression, lower resistance to disease.
   c) Hallucinogens.
   d) Depression and dizziness.
   e) Painkillers.
   f) Unconsciouness, coma and breathing failure.

9) A – 3, B – 5, C – 1, D – 2, E – 4, F – 6.

10) a) 1 – liver, 2 – kidneys, 3 – brain, 4 – lungs, 5 – heart.
    b) Solvents – liver, lungs, brain, kidneys, heart.
       Alcohol – brain, liver.
       Tobacco – lungs, heart.
       Stimulants – brain, heart.
       Sedatives – brain.

11) a) Chemical (physical) and psychological.
    b) Anything from headaches, fevers and shakes to nausea, hallucinations and severe depression.

12) nervous, Caffeine, mild, headaches, amphetamines, hallucinations, personality changes, depression, hallucinogen, energy, overheating, dehydration, heroin, crime, withdrawal, overdose, paints, glues, behavioural, lungs, brain, liver, kidneys.

Page 50:

1) a) The nervous system.
   b) It affects behaviour by slowing down the nervous system and can give the individual more confidence.

2) Liver and brain.

3) a) 90cm^3 of alcohol. *Working:*
      2 double whiskies = (2×10) 20cm^3
      3 glasses of wine = (2×10) 30cm^3
      1 pint of beer = (2×10) 20cm^3
      20 + 30 + 20 = 90cm^3
   b) The body is free of alcohol between 9 pm and 12 midnight as it requires 9 hours for the liver to process 90cm^3 of alcohol at 10 cm^3/hr.

4) Alcohol dilates the blood vessels of the skin and allows more heat loss from the blood.

5) Alcohol slows down the reactions.

6) Liver

7) A hardened drinker who needs large quantities of alcohol just to keep going from day to day.

8) Alcohol stops the heavy drinker feeling hungry and so they may suffer from deficiency diseases because they only eat small amounts of food and do not get the required vitamins. Also alcohol destroys some vitamins.

9) The more alcohol that is taken the poorer the driver's judgement becomes. His/Her reactions are slower and this results in an increased risk of them causing an accident.

10) The larger person has a greater mass of water in their body – the alcohol will be more dilute and so have a lesser effect.

11) Heart disease, cirrhosis of the liver, stomach ulcers, pneumonia, cancer of the digestive system (any three).

12) relaxation, stress, slows, inhibited, liver, brain, depression.

Page 51:

1) Nicotine.
2) Tar and Carbon Monoxide.
3) Lung Cancer.
4) Bronchitis and Emphysema.
5) Carbon monoxide combines with the haemoglobin in the red blood cells and makes the blood less efficient at carrying oxygen. The heart works harder to deliver sufficient oxygen to the tissues which causes strain on heart.
6) Blocks arteries, specifically the coronary artery.
7) It is a cough caused by smoke affecting the lining of the air tubes which then increase their mucus production and induce coughing.
8) Breathing in other people's smoke.
9) Any four of : nose, throat, chest irritation, breathing difficulties, coughing, red and runny eyes, runny nose, headaches, increased risk of lung cancer.
10) They could produce small weak babies possibly suffering from asthma.
11) Diagram (a) shows normal lung alveoli diagram (b) shows emphysema in the alveoli. The lining in the walls of the alveoli break down and this reduces the surface area where gaseous exchange can take place.
12) a) Tar in cigarette smoke make the cells inside the lungs divide more than normal. They can carry on dividing and form a lump called a tumour – lung cancer.
    b) A growth develops in the bronchial tubes which blocks them and makes breathing very painful.
13) addictive, coats, lungs, foreign, bacteria, emphysema, bronchitis, lung cancer, heart, blood vessels, depression.

Pages 52, 53:

1) To keep the body's internal environment relatively constant.
2) Hormones
3) a) Carbon Dioxide and Urea.
   b) Carbon Dioxide is produced by respiration, excreted by the lungs. Urea is produced by the break down of proteins (deamination), excreted by the kidneys.
4) a) A – Brain / B – Lungs / C – Stomach / D – Pancreas / E – Bladder / F – Kidneys / G – Liver / H – Skin.
   b) F, G and H.
   c) (Hypothalamus of the) brain.
5) Ion, sugar and water content of the blood and body temperature.

Genetics and Evolution P.52 → P.59

6) **a)** Nervous System.
   b) i) Blood vessels near the surface of the skin enlarge (dilate) making blood flow near the surface of the skin and lose heat to the surroundings.
   ii) Sweating (from the sweat glands). Its evaporation causes cooling as heat is used to evaporate the sweat.
   c) Salt/Ions.
   d) i) Blood vessels near the surface of the skin become smaller (constrict) and prevent heat being lost.
   ii) The metabolic rate increases and this produces extra heat. We shiver which is caused by involuntary contraction of our muscles.

7) **a)** The pancreas and the liver.
   b) Insulin and glycogen.
   c) One hormone inhibits or stimulates another hormone which may inhibit or stimulate the first hormone.
   d) If blood-sugar is high, then the pancreas produces more insulin and this instructs the liver to change glucose to glycogen. If too much glucose is changed to glycogen then blood-sugar drops which makes the pancreas stop producing insulin and start producing glucagon. The liver then turns glycogen into glucose and releases it into the blood.

8) **a)** ADH (Anti-Diuretic Hormone).
   b) Pituitary.
   c) Hypothalamus
   d) Following the path of the diagram:
   i) dilute, much, decreases, less, less, large, dilute.
   ii) concentrated, little, increases, more, more, small, concentrated.

9) **a)** Ultrafiltration.
   b) Ions, glucose, urea.
   c) Reabsorption. Glucose.
   d) Urine – urea, waste ions, excess water.

Page 54:

1) **a)** Removal of urea, adjustment of ion content of the blood and adjustment of the water content of the blood.
   b) To get rid of waste made by the body.

2) **a)** A — kidney / B — renal vein / C — renal artery / D — ureter / E — bladder / F — urethra.
   b) Renal artery carries oxygenated blood and the renal vein carries de-oxygenated blood.

3) **a)** Nephron (kidney tubules)
   b) A blood capillary.
   c) a – 1, b – 7, c – 5, d – 6, e – 2, f – 3, g – 4, h – 8, i – 9, j – 10.

Page 55:

1) **a)** continuous
   b) light intensity / wind exposure
   c) Genetically

2) **a) i)** mass, intelligence, height, hair colour, fitness **ii)** eye colour
   b) i) all continuous features **ii)** eye colour
   c) Fitness
   d) Fitness — exercise; Intelligence — education; Hair colour — sunlight; Height and Mass — diet.

3) **a) i)** a and c **ii)** They are the only two that have all the same features not affected by the environment. (roll tongue, brown hair and brown eyes)
   b) i) ability to tan; hair colour **ii)** Sex, tongue rolling, eye colour.

4) See table:

Characteristic (Human)	Type of Variation		Affected by Environment	
	Continuous	Discontinuous	Yes	No
Birth weight	✓		✓	
Skin colour	✓		✓	
Blood group		✓		✓
Hand span	✓		✓	
Eye colour		✓		✓
Haemophilia		✓		✓

5) Discontinuous, range, inherited, environmental.

Pages 56, 57:

1) **Across**: 3 — Sperm Cell 6 — Male 8 — Gamete 11 — Chromosome 12 — Genotype 14 — Recessive.
   Down: 1 — Cell 2 — Allele 4 — Paired 5 — Clone 7 — Heterozygous 8 — Gene 9 — Zygote 10 — Meiosis 13 — Ova.

2) **a)** Haploid
   b) Fertilisation
   c) 46
   d) 112
   e) Meiosis
   f) Mitosis
   g) Sex Cell

3) **a)** A and a or B and b
   b) i) A and B **ii)** a and b
   c) Brown. It has the dominant gene.

4) **a)** dominant
   b) gamete
   c) genotype
   d) DNA
   e) diploid
   f) mitosis
   g) homozygous
   h) gamete
   i) clones
   j) variation

5) Heterozygous → Aa,
   Gamete → ovum,
   Chemical making up chromosomes → DNA,
   Part of the DNA → Gene.

6) **a) i)** Appearance **ii)** Genes present
   b) Children/first generation
   c) i) 2:2 or 1:1 **ii)** 2:2 or 1:1
   d) TT, Tt, tt
   e) tall and dwarf

7) DNA, chromatids, centromere, gene, alleles, dominant, recessive, homozygous, heterozygous

Pages 58, 59:

1) **a)** nucleus
   b) 46 or 23 pairs
   c) DNA

2) Nucleus, chromosomes, diploid, sex, haploid, genes, DNA, protein, cytoplasm, divide

3) **a) i)** nucleus
   ii) cytoplasm

Genetics and Evolution P.59 → P.65

b) See diagram:

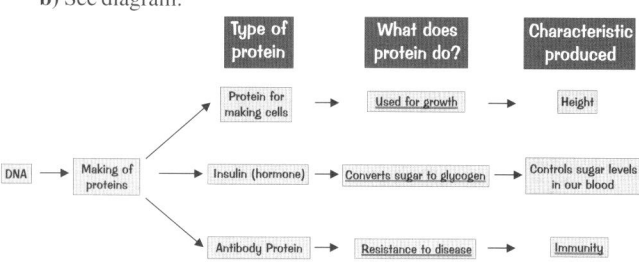

```
                          Type of        What does           Characteristic
                          protein        protein do?         produced
                      ┌─ Protein for  →  Used for growth  →  Height
                      │  making cells
DNA → Making of ──────┼─ Insulin (hormone) → Converts sugar to glycogen → Controls sugar levels
      proteins        │                                                   in our blood
                      └─ Antibody Protein → Resistance to disease → Immunity
```

c) Characteristics change. Different proteins or altered proteins are produced

d) have different genes/DNA for making proteins

8) a) male has XY, female XX
   b) all chromosomes are part of a pair
   c) i) 46 / 23 pairs ii) nucleus
   d) i) DNA ii) double helix iii) genes

Pages 60, 61:

1) asexual, exact, two, parent, reduction, gametes

2) a) meiosis
   b) mitosis
   c) mitosis
   d) meiosis
   e) mitosis

3) a) A = mitosis, B = meiosis.
   b) everywhere except sex cells
   c) i) anthers/stamens and ovaries/ovules ii) testes and ovaries
   d) i) 46   ii) 23

4)
Organism	Number of chromosomes in a body cell	Number of pair of chromosomes	Number of chromosomes in each gamete	Haploid number	Diploid number
Fruit Fly	8	4	4	4	8
Kangaroo	12	6	6	6	12
Rye Plant	20	10	10	10	20
Chicken	36	18	18	18	36
Mouse	40	20	20	20	40
Humans	46	23	23	23	46
Crayfish	200	100	100	100	200

5) **Diagram A -**
   1) DNA all spread out in long strings.
   2) Identical strands of DNA coil up together to form twin-armed chromosomes.
   3) Chromosomes line up along centre, cell fibres pull them apart.
   4) Membranes form around the two sets of chromosome threads - these are the nuclei of the two daughter cells.
   5) The threads unwind into long strands of DNA - process starts again.

   Diagram B -
   1) Reproductive cell (in testis or ovary) containing 23 pairs of chromosomes.
   2) Two new cells form, each cell containing one chromosome from each of the 23 pairs. New cells contain a mix of the father and mother chromosomes, but half the full complement.
   3) The two new cells split mitosis-style with the chromosomes themselves splitting.
   4) Gametes (Sperm cells or egg cells) are produced.

Pages 62, 63:

1) a) See diagram:

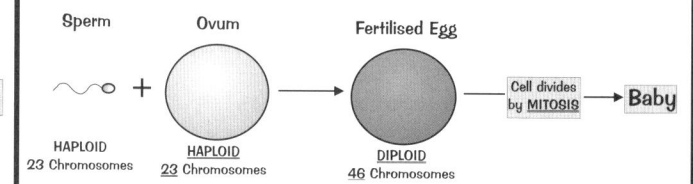

```
Sperm          Ovum              Fertilised Egg
 ～○    +      ○         →         ●         → Cell divides → Baby
                                                 by MITOSIS
HAPLOID        HAPLOID             DIPLOID
23 Chromosomes 23 Chromosomes      46 Chromosomes
```

   b) i) testes ii) ovaries
   c) gametes
   d) zygote
   e) fertilisation
   f) oviduct / Fallopian tube

2) a) See diagram:
   b) i) testes ii) ovaries
   c) i) sperm cells that contain genes/genetic material
      ii) egg cells that contain genes/genetic material
   d) i) homologous ii) 23

3) gametes, fertilisation, meiosis, variation, egg, children, sperm, ova, testes, ovaries, chromosome, diploid.

4) *diploid* — full chromosome complement; *fertilisation* — fusion of gametes; *gamete* — a sex cell; *haploid* — half the full chromosome complement; *ova* — female sex cells; *ovaries* — produces female sex cell/egg; *zygote* — fertilised egg

5) male gamete — sperm; fusion of gametes — fertilisation; cell division for gamete production — meiosis; half the chromosome number — haploid; cell division for zygote development — mitosis. a fertilised egg — zygote; an egg cell — ovum;

6) a) meiosis.
   b) gametes.
   c) homologous.
   d) haploid.
   e) ovum.

Page 64:

1) a) Part of a chromosome that determines a characteristic/manufacture of a protein.
   b) Naturally during replication or through agents such as radiation or chemicals.
   c) i) yes/possible ii) gene *may* be passed on to offspring

2) chromosome, naturally, replication, nucleus, divide, mutations, ionising, mutagens, carcinogens, harmful, sex, mitosis, neutral, beneficial, antibiotics, genetic.

3) a) Resistance in bacteria/any suitable example, cancer/any suitable example
   b) they are neutral/neither benefit nor harm individuals

Page 65:

1) a) get more lethal alleles as you increase ionising radiation
   b) i) Changes them.
      ii) one of two genes that controls a particular characteristic
   c) X-Rays, UV light, chemical mutagens. The Side-effects of the X-Ray.

Genetics and Evolution   P.65 → P.69

2) See diagram for part **a**):

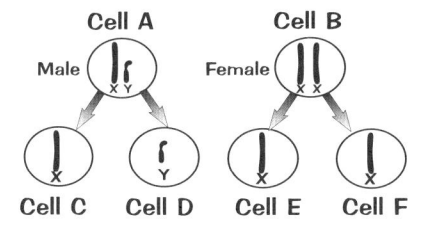

Cell A — Male (XY) → Cell C (X), Cell D (Y)
Cell B — Female (XX) → Cell E (X), Cell F (X)

  b) A in testes, B in ovaries
  d) male = sperm cells, female = egg cells
  e) meiosis
  f) A = 46 B = 46 C = 23 D = 23 E = 23 F = 23
  g) A and B are diploid. C, D, E and F are haploid

3) **a)** See diagram:

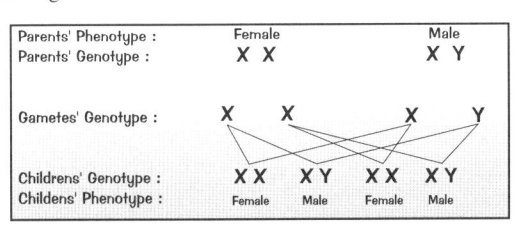

Parents' Phenotype :	Female		Male	
Parents' Genotype :	X X		X Y	
Gametes' Genotype :	X	X	X	Y
Childrens' Genotype :	XX	XY	XX	XY
Childens' Phenotype :	Female	Male	Female	Male

  b) 50:50 / 2:2 / 1:1
  c) No, every time a woman conceives there is a 50:50 chance of a boy/girl being born.
  d) See diagram:

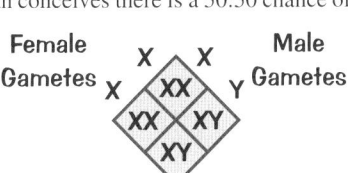

Female Gametes X, X ; Male Gametes X, Y → XX, XY, XX, XY

4) **a)** X or Y
  b) X
  c) i) Man's gamete.
      ii) sex of the child depends on whether an X or Y bearing sperm fuses with the egg

Pages 66, 67:

1) **a)** Both alleles are the same.
  b) Because B is a dominant gene, b is recessive.
  c) They determine the same characteristic, i.e. colour.
  d) i) First generation of offspring. **ii)** Two different alleles.
  e) i) B **ii)** It 'dominates' or masks a recessive allele
  f) i) The genes present. **ii)** Appearance/physical characteristics.
  g) i) See diagram: **ii)** Phenotypes: 3 black, 1 brown. Genotypes: BB, Bb, bb. **iii)** 3 black : 1 brown **iv)** F2

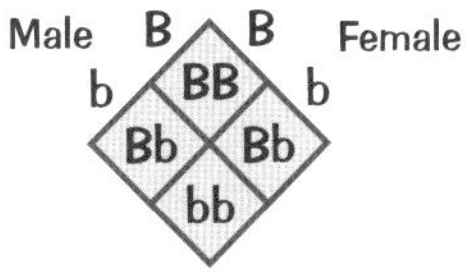

Male B, b ; Female B, b → BB, Bb, Bb, bb

2) **a)** B — brown and b — blue / any sensible choice.
  b) See diagram:

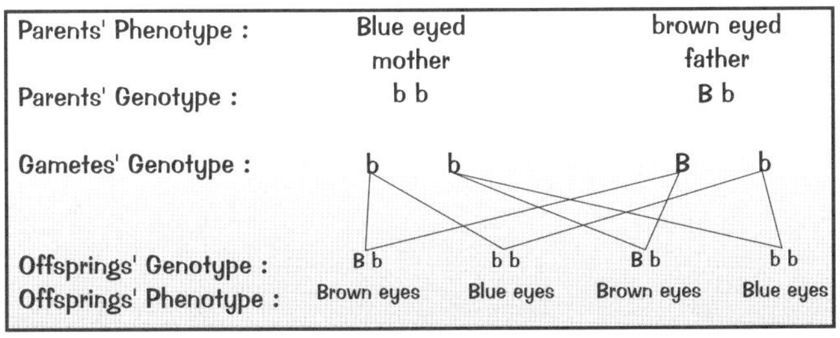

Parents' Phenotype :	Blue eyed mother		brown eyed father	
Parents' Genotype :	b b		B b	
Gametes' Genotype :	b	b	B	b
Offsprings' Genotype :	Bb	bb	Bb	bb
Offsprings' Phenotype :	Brown eyes	Blue eyes	Brown eyes	Blue eyes

  c) Mother (bb), ½ offspring (bb)
  d) Brown eyed parents may carry the gene for blue eyes, blue eyed child inherits one recessive blue eyed gene from each parent.

3) monohybrid, height, alleles, recessive, homozygous, heterozygous, phenotype, genotype, F1, F2.

4) **a)** D - dark , d - auburn / any suitable choice
  b) i) Dd **ii)** dd **iii)** Dd and dd **iv)** Dd **v)** dd

5) **a) i)** Male. **ii)** Non-taster.
  b) i) T and t / any suitable letters **ii)** tt
    iii) non-taster - must have 2 recessive genes.
  c) i) Tt. **ii)** Is a taster but passes on a gene for non-tasting.
  d) i) All non-tasters (white boxes and circles) **ii)** 4, 11, 15, 16 or 17
  e) See diagrams for the two cases

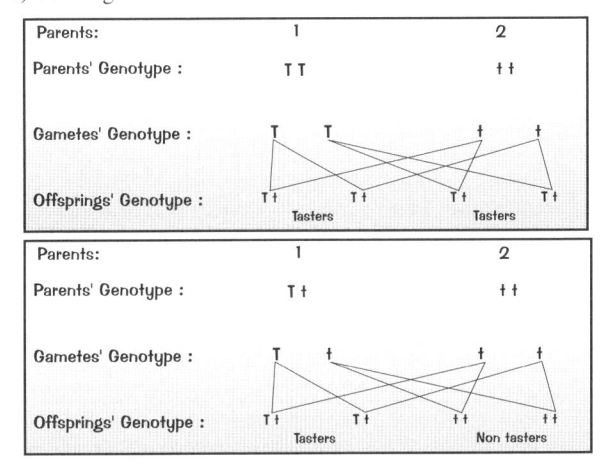

Parents:	1		2	
Parents' Genotype :	T T		t t	
Gametes' Genotype :	T	T	t	t
Offsprings' Genotype :	Tt	Tt	Tt	Tt
	Tasters			Tasters

Parents:	1		2	
Parents' Genotype :	T t		t t	
Gametes' Genotype :	T	t	t	t
Offsprings' Genotype :	Tt	Tt	tt	tt
	Tasters			Non tasters

6) **a) i)** TT (tall) tt (dwarf) **ii)** Tt
  b) i) 1 TT : 2 Tt : 1 tt **ii)** 3 tall : 1 dwarf
    iii) dwarf (tt) one offspring (TT) **iv)** both parents (Tt) and 2 offspring (Tt)
  c) Any from flower colour, texture of seeds, pod shape, flower position, seed coat colour, seed shape or other suitable answer.

Pages 68, 69:

1) Genetic, recessive, membranes, mucus, lungs, digestive, allele, both, carriers

2) Carrier - Cc; normal - CC; sufferer - cc

3) **a) i)** both parents, two children (Cc) **ii)** 1/4 children (cc) **iii)** 2/4 children (CC and cc) **iv)** parents and 2/4 children (Cc)
  b) Carry recessive alleles, but are not sufferers.
  c) See diagram:

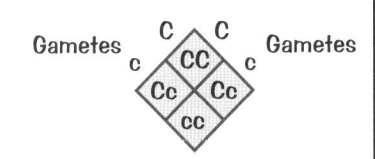

Gametes C, c ; Gametes C, c → CC, Cc, Cc, cc

4) **a)** Cystic fibrosis is an *inherited* disease.
  b) Cystic fibrosis is caused by a *recessive* allele
  c) Children can inherit the cystic fibrosis disease when *both* of their parents have the recessive allele.
  d) Sufferers of cystic fibrosis have breathing problems due to the *excessive production of mucus*.
  e) The allele for cystic fibrosis is found *equally in men and women*.

Section Seven — Answers

Genetics and Evolution   P.69 → P.74

5) **a)** Father = Cc, Mother = CC.
   b) No
   c) i) No **ii)** each one has a 50% chance of carrying the disease.
   d) 50%
   e) 50%
   f) i) No **ii)** He could have the same genotype whether one or both parents were carriers.

6) **a)** See diagram:

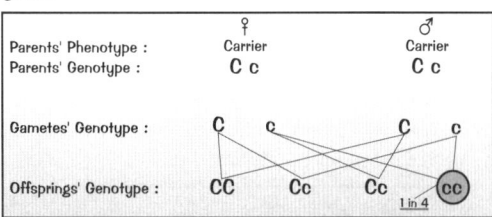

   Parents' Phenotype: ♀ Carrier   ♂ Carrier
   Parents' Genotype: C c   C c
   Gametes' Genotype: C c   C c
   Offsprings' Genotype: CC Cc Cc cc (1 in 4)

   b) No
   c) They have a recessive allele but do not suffer from the disease.

7) Genotype for a carrier = Cc; Produced in the lungs of sufferers = mucus; The normal, homozygous, dominant condition = CC; Has the cystic fibrosis allele but no ill-effects = carrier, Cc; One in four chance of a child having this genotype from two carrier parents = CC, cc.

Pages 70, 71:

1) Red, recessive, carrier, malaria, protected, blood, alleles, oxygen.

2) **a)** Since the carriers of the sickle cell allele are more immune to malaria, more people with this allele will survive in malaria infected areas. Hence the high distribution of the allele in these areas.
   b) i) They are protected against malaria.
   ii) Their offspring may develop the disease.

3) **a)** See diagram:

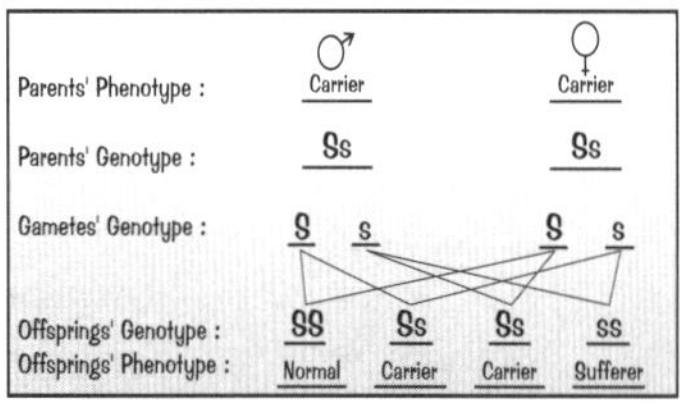

   Parents' Phenotype: ♂ Carrier   ♀ Carrier
   Parents' Genotype: Ss   Ss
   Gametes' Genotype: S s   S s
   Offsprings' Genotype: SS Ss Ss ss
   Offsprings' Phenotype: Normal Carrier Carrier Sufferer

   b) i) 1 in 4 (25%).
   ii) They are deprived of oxygen (because red cells stick in their capillaries).
   c) i) Lack of iron / haemoglobin in blood.
   ii) Protection from malaria.

4) Dominant, one, allele, nervous, disease, mental

5) **a)** 1 in 2 (50%)
   b) i) They don't have carriers - disease usually appears in childhood. **ii)** Symptoms don't appear until after age 40 when sufferer has already had children.

6) Interbreeding in small community / with close relatives.

7) **a)** See diagram:

   Parents' Phenotype: Father Sufferer   Mother Normal
   Parents' Genotype: Hh   hh
   Gametes' Genotype: H h   h h
   Offsprings' Genotype: Hh Hh hh hh
   Offsprings' Phenotype: Sufferer Sufferer Normal Normal

   b) 1 in 2 (50%)

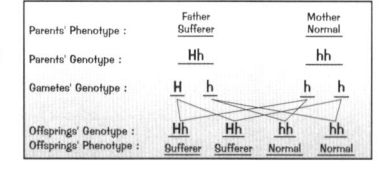

Page 72:

1) People, varieties, characteristics, breed, selective, milk, ears, colour, alleles, variety

2) **a)** Pointed ears, long tail, long hair, sticking up ears, pointed snout, etc.
   b) Have greater variety of alleles - haven't been selected for aesthetic purposes which sacrifice health.

   c) Basset hound: long back — back problems, floppy ears — get infections under ears. Bedlington: floppy ears — get infections under ears. Bulldog: narrow hips — cannot give birth easily, flat nose — has breathing problems. Shar-Pei: folded skin - get infections under skin, in-turned eyelids — sight problems. Other examples acceptable.
   d) The breed would eventually disappear.

3) **a)** The process where people breed animals with the best characteristics is called _artificial_ selection.
   b) Selective breeding _decreases_ the number of alleles in a population
   c) Farmers often selectively breed to _increase_ yields of food produced.
   d) Selective breeding involves _sexual_ reproduction.
   e) Breeding characteristics like floppy ears into dogs is _disadvantageous_ to the dog.

Pages 73, 74:

1) **a)** Asexual
   b) i) Have same genes / or similar. **ii)** Clones
   c) i) Grow quickly / Need less space / Can grow all year round / New plants are disease free / All plants have the same requirement / Easier to harvest.
   ii) Reduce gene pool / Vulnerable to diseases.
   d) Cuttings

2) **a)** Asexual
   b) Identical
   c) Different
   d) i) New plants are produced quickly, identical to parent plant.
   ii) Less variety, reduction in gene pool.

3) **a)** Plants that are produced by cuttings grow into new plants by _mitotic_ cell division.
   b) Tissue cultures are a useful way of producing large numbers of _identical_ plants from a small number of cells.
   c) Genetically identical plants are produced by _asexual_ reproduction.
   d) Growing plants from tissue cultures _decreases_ the gene pool.
   e) Cloning techniques are also used in producing identical animals by splitting embryo cells _before_ they specialise.

4) genetically, asexual, mitosis, cuttings, tissue, identical, cells, splitting, embryo, host, naturally.

5) **a)** Mitosis.
   b) Because they are genetically identical.
   c) i) Fast, identical to parent. **ii)** Reduces variety / gene pool.
   d) i) Cloning.
   ii) Can quickly produce offspring with exactly the same wool.

6) Cell division which produces identical cells — mitosis.
   Genetically identical individuals — clones.
   Reproduction which produces variation in plants — sexual.
   Reproduction which produces identical plants — asexual.
   Cell division producing variation in daughter cells — meiosis.

Section Seven — Answers

The Environment P.75 → P.79

Page 75:

1) a) Different rock layers exposed / rocks are broken open.
   b) They were once below the oceans.
   c) More likely for animals to be covered by sand / mud under sea: decay slowly in these conditions.
   d) Soft parts decay easily / hard parts do not decay easily.

2) a) 1 – Sea, 2 – Sand, 3 – Minerals, 4 – Rock.
   b) i) Decays quickly
      ii) Decays slowly, body parts replaced by minerals.
   c) Anaerobic / cold / dry / acidic (conditions preventing decay).
   d) Oxygen

3) a) Conditions for decay absent / not enough oxygen.
   b) Can see annual rings / plant structures / or named structures, eg xylem.

4) a) In order for decay to occur, oxygen <u>is</u> needed.
   b) Most fossils occur from hard parts of animals because they decay <u>slowly</u>.
   c) The best fossilisation occurs <u>under the sea</u>.
   d) The <u>lower</u> the rock layer a fossil is found in the older it is.

Page 76:

1) changed, Darwin, degenerate, adaptations, environment, organisms, food, existence, fittest, characteristics, nature, survival, natural, evolution.

2) All giraffes had short necks, mutation resulted in some giraffes having longer necks than others, the giraffe population had individuals whose necks varied in length, natural selection resulted in longer necked offspring surviving, only long necked giraffes survived the competition for food.

3) a) Fish.
   b) Number of reptile in diagram declining 60 million years ago.
   c) Mammals
   d) They show changes and development of organisms over millions of years.
   e) Fossilisation is rare / did not occur.

Page 77:

1) variation, species, disease, die, environment, offspring, natural, alleles, favourable, survive.

2) a) i) Mutation. ii) Predation / amount of food / disease.
   b) Black moths were camouflaged from their predators and not eaten as much.
   c) In polluted / industrial areas, black moths survive. In cleaner areas (Scotland and Southwest) light moths survive.
   d) It can breed with a light moth and produce fertile young.
   e) Natural selection.

3) a) The frequency of alleles which determine useful characteristics <u>increases</u> in a population.
   b) Factors like disease cause a population to <u>decrease</u>.
   c) Organisms that are the best survivors are those that are <u>best suited to their environment</u>.
   d) Survivors pass their genes on to their <u>offspring</u>.
   e) Natural selection is the process by which <u>evolution</u> takes place.
   f) In order for changes to occur in the characteristics of a population <u>mutation</u> must take place.

Pages 78, 79 — The Environment:

1) a) The population of sycamore trees is the number of trees in the wood, which is 12.
   b) The habitat of the sycamore trees is the wood.
   c) Terms to definitions: Population means the number of individuals of a particular species. Habitat means a place with particular conditions where certain organisms live. Environment means the conditions in which an organism lives.

2) The cane toad has been successful because it has no natural predators. The native animals that do try to eat it are poisoned and die. The native frogs cannot breed where the cane toad breeds. It can produce many eggs in one season.

3) a) In 1940, the red squirrel was found over most of Britain. It co-existed with the grey squirrel in England in the Midlands, the North East and South East, and in Central Scotland. The grey squirrel existed on its own only in central Southern England. In 1990, the grey squirrel was the only squirrel in most of England, and also in Central Scotland. The red squirrel could still found in parts of Wales and Scotland, although its range in Scotland was less than in 1940.
   b) The grey squirrel seems to have a competitive advantage over the red squirrel. This may be because the grey squirrel has a more varied diet than the red squirrel. There may be differences in the reproductive success between the two squirrels. As the red squirrel's range in Scotland has been reduced (and elsewhere, though not shown on the map) even where there was no grey squirrel, it is possible that some other factor is affecting red squirrels and that grey squirrels are simply migrating into habitats vacated by the red squirrels.

4) a) Predators are animals which kill and eat other animals. Prey are the animals eaten by predators. Examples could include foxes (predators) eat rabbits (prey), etc.
   b) The numbers of predator and prey go up and down regularly. The number of predators increases after the number of prey increases, and falls after the number of prey decreases. This is because the population is usually limited by the amount of food available. If the population of prey increases, more food is available for its predators and so their population may increase. As the population of predators increase, they eat more of the prey and so the population of prey decreases. This means less food for the predators, and so their population decreases again. As there are now fewer predators, the population of prey increases again.

5) a) The road seems to have severely reduced the number of mice in the wood. The road has cut the study area in two. This will make it difficult to compare the results from later years with those from earlier years, as the size of the wood has been reduced. It is possible that new habitats have been created as a result, and old ones will have been destroyed.
   b) The number of mice in the wood might have fallen due to: increased predation from other animals, e.g. owls, a reduction in the amount of available food, increased competition for the available food or space from another species, there may have been a very harsh winter between years 4 and 5, mice may have migrated out of the wood, a new disease.
   c) The number of mice in the wood might have risen due to: decreased predation from other animals, e.g. owls, an increase in the amount of available food, decreased competition for the available food or space from another species, there may have been a very mild winter between years 6 and 7, other mice may have migrated into the wood from elsewhere.

6) Possible table:

Factor	Examples
Competition for water	Weeds and wheat
Competition for light	Trees and grass
Competition for nutrients	Sycamore and oak trees
Competition for food	Blackbirds and thrushes
Competition for space	Weeds and carrots
Predation	Mice eaten by owls
Grazing	Grass eaten by cows
Amount of food available	Mice for owls to eat
Disease	Myxomatosis in rabbits

Section Seven — Answers

The Environment P.80 → P.82

Pages 81:

1) **a)** The temperatures are very high on average, especially in June, July and August. There is very little rainfall during the year, with most falling in May, so for most of the year it is likely that there will be very little water. There are extremes of temperature during the day, from very cold at night to very hot during the daytime.
   b) The sand, rocks and gravel will make it difficult for plants to take root. Rain is likely to soak away or evaporate quickly, so there will be little water except when it rains. The sand may be difficult to move over. If plants and animals do not adapt they will perish.

2) The Sidewinder's movements help to keep it cool by keeping some of its body off the hot sand. Different parts of the body are in contact at different times as it moves. It also allows the sidewinder to get a grip in the sand.

3) Burrows are likely to be cool during the day, allowing the animals to come out at night when it is cooler on the surface. Prey will be hidden from predators (and predators will be hidden from their prey). As it is cooler underground, the animals may be able to conserve moisture. However, it is unlikely that there will be any food in the burrow, and the animals will need to forage at night. It may be difficult to find food in the dark, and predators may be hunting then, too.

4) **a)** Can store very large amounts of water, very little urine or sweating as they can tolerate big changes in body temperature, large feet to spread their weight over the soft sand, large surface area with all fat stored in the hump to help lose body heat, sandy colour for camouflage.
   b) The hair is insulating the camel against heat gain and water loss.
   c) As they do not need to maintain a constant temperature, they can save water which would have been lost through sweating to cool down.

5) **a)** The plants are able to continue their species without trying to grow when there is insufficient water.
   b) The plants can reach down to where there may still be water/minerals, etc.
   c) The roots can absorb surface water, e.g. if there is light rain or early morning dew.
   d) Plants can continue to live even when there is no ground water.
   e) Leaves are a potential source of water loss through transpiration, and so water can be conserved this way.
   f) Water can be lost by evaporation through stomata. This is reduced if the stomata are only open at night when it is cooler.
   g) The thorns put off grazing animals that might try to eat the plants or get at their stored water.

6) **a)** There are extremes of temperature in the Arctic; it can be quite warm in summer, but the temperature is below freezing for most of the year. There can be strong winds, which would make it seem much colder. There is relatively little rainfall, with most falling in the summer, so it is quite dry.
   b) Plants grow close to the ground to withstand the strong winds. Their small leaves will reduce water loss.
   c) The cold will be a major problem in the Arctic, and adaptations such as fur and lots of fat can be expected. Animals may also live in burrows to escape the cold and strong winds. Grazing animals might find it difficult to find food if the plants are low growing with small leaves.

7) Lemmings are small, so will lose heat quickly. They have fur and live in burrows to reduce their heat loss (their rounded bodies will keep their surface area to volume ratio down). Their ears are small and hidden by fur which again reduces heat loss. Their fur is light brown for camouflage in the tundra. They can hide from predators in their burrows.

8) **a)** Apart from being too big for a burrow, polar bears and walruses are large, so will have a small surface area to volume ratio. They will not lose heat as quickly as smaller animals and they do not need to hide from predators (so do not need to burrow).
   b) Polar bears are camouflaged against snow and ice. Their large size, fur and thick layers of fat will reduce heat loss. Walruses also have thick layers of fat to reduce heat loss. Their tough skin will protect them from tusks in fights.

9) The change in fur colour is likely to be for camouflage — white against snow in winter, and brown against earth and vegetation in summer.

10) Heat can be lost from the blood vessels in the ears by radiation. Large ears act like a radiator, and allow the desert fox to lose extra heat rapidly. Small ears will reduce heat loss from the Arctic fox.

Pages 82, 83:

1) **a)** Suggested graph or charts:

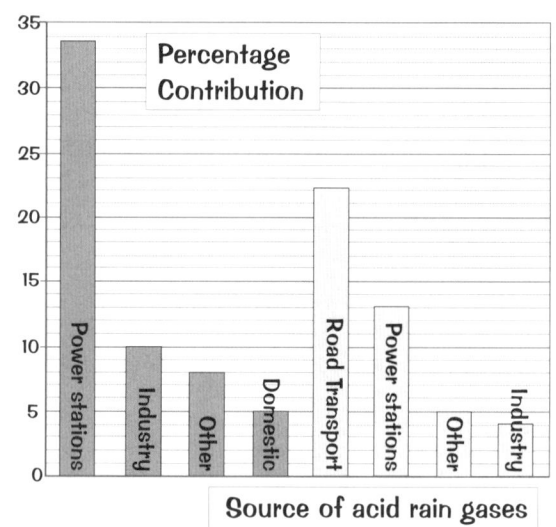

[Bar chart: Percentage Contribution — Source of acid rain gases. Power stations ~34, Industry ~10, Other ~8, Domestic ~5, Road Transport ~22, Power stations ~13, Other ~5, Industry ~4]

   b) Power stations produce the most sulphur dioxide (34%).
   c) Road transport produces the most nitrogen oxides (22%).
   d) Power stations contribute the most acid rain gases (47%).

The Environment P.83 → P.86

2) a) Nitrogen oxides, sulphur oxides and carbon dioxide.
   b) Nitric acid, sulphuric acid and carbonic acid.
3) a) The acid rain is blown to the Scandinavian countries from Great Britain by the wind.
   b) In Germany, where there is the most acid rain pollution, there is a lot of damage to trees. In countries with lower acid rain pollution, there is less damage to trees, for example the Scandinavian countries. Where there is least acid rain pollution, there is only little damage, e.g. Spain and Portugal. Great Britain has a lot of damage, although it does not have the highest acid rain levels (a lot of pollution is blown eastwards by the prevailing wind).
4) a) When the tree loses some of its leaves, it loses some of its ability to photosynthesise. As a result, it may grow slowly or die.
   b) Acid rain causes aluminium to dissolve. Once in solution, aluminium can be absorbed by the tree roots, and so will poison the tree.
   c) Magnesium will be washed out of the soil, so less will be available to the tree. As a result, less chlorophyll will be made, and so the tree cannot photosynthesise so well. It may grow slowly or die, and its leaves will look yellow.
   d) Trees will be unable to obtain enough water and minerals to grow properly. They will be more likely to fall down in high winds.
   e) Example diagram:

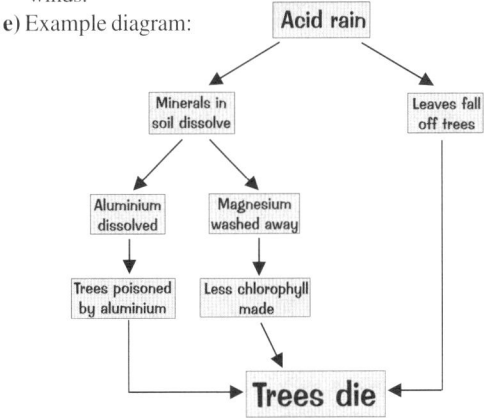

   Acid rain
   → Minerals in soil dissolve
       → Aluminium dissolved → Trees poisoned by aluminium
       → Magnesium washed away → Less chlorophyll made
   → Leaves fall off trees
   → Trees die

5) a) Water plants will be poisoned by the aluminium, and will lose leaves due to the acid.
   b) The crustaceans, and animals that depend upon them for food, directly or indirectly, will die.
   c) The fish will be unable to obtain enough oxygen and so will die.
   d) The fish contain high levels of mercury and aluminium washed in from the soil and absorbed from the water.
6) Economic effects: rusting buildings and vehicles that need repair / damaged buildings that need repair / crop damage / loss of forestry for timber / loss of fish for food.
7) a) Lakes need to be treated more than once because the acid rain continues to fall into them. Problems include adding extra calcium compounds to the lakes, organising the treatments, damage to the land because the lime will have to be quarried (carbon dioxide — a greenhouse gas — is released when limestone is roasted to make lime).
   b) *Advantages*: sulphur dioxide is stopped before it gets out / easier to treat a few power stations than lots of lakes, rivers and forests / "polluter pays" / useful materials as a by-product.
   Disadvantages: limestone must be quarried to do this (damages the landscape) / limited market for gypsum / will they be filling in the holes left when the limestone was quarried? / more expensive for the power station.

Page 84:

1) "Energy from the *Sun* passes through the Earth's *atmosphere* and *warms* the Earth's surface. Heat energy from the Earth's surface is radiated into *space* but some of it is *reflected* by gases in the atmosphere. This *warms* the atmosphere, which is *good* for life on Earth. However, excess CO_2 produced by burning fossil fuels is causing the earth to warm up too much which may cause flooding and drought."
2) a) Natural sources of carbon dioxide: Respiration, forest fires, volcanoes, rain reacting with limestone, spring waters.
   b) Carbon dioxide. (Sulphur dioxide is also released, and has a part to play in the greenhouse effect. However, its role is complex and does not appear in GCSE syllabuses.)
   c) The release of carbon from fossil fuels has increased dramatically with time, especially since 1950. This is probably due to increased use of oil for vehicles, and coal and natural gas for energy.
   d) The amount of carbon dioxide in the atmosphere has risen steadily since 1850. This is probably due to the release of carbon dioxide from fossil fuels.
   e) Carbon dioxide can be absorbed by plants for photosynthesis. It can dissolve in water. It can be incorporated into shells of sea creatures. It can eventually form rocks such as limestone.
   f) Carbon dioxide is a greenhouse gas. If there is more of it in the atmosphere, it should absorb more heat energy. The temperature of the Earth's atmosphere should rise as a result.
   g) As the temperature has risen, so has the sea level. This is probably due to ice melting at the poles and in glaciated regions.
   h) If carbon dioxide levels continue to rise, it would be expected that sea levels and temperature would rise as well. The rise in temperature will change the climate. The rise in sea level will cause flooding in low-lying areas of the world.

Pages 85, 86:

1) *Artificial fertilisers* ensure that there are sufficient minerals in the soil to support a high rate of plant growth. *Artificially selected animals and plants* provide increased yields of such products as milk, meat, wheat and rice. *Mechanisation* has allowed more land to be cultivated with fewer people.
2) a) Machines need the space to turn around. Hedges get in the way and leave areas that the machines cannot reach. Smaller farms do not generate enough income to pay for the machinery.
   b) When trees and hedges are removed, habitats are lost so reducing the number and diversity of wild animals and plants. Populations are split and may no longer contain enough individuals to continue.
3) a) In some countries the population has increased so much that new farmland is needed, so forests are cleared to make farmland. In addition, land may be used for cash crops such as beef and coffee to improve the export income of poor countries.
   b) The uptake of carbon dioxide will be reduced, and so will the production of oxygen.
   c) The carbon dioxide produced by burning will not be removed from the atmosphere, as there will be fewer trees to photosynthesise.

The Environment   P.8 → P.88

d) Microbes will release carbon dioxide due to respiration.

4) a) Correct sequence: Excess fertilisers leach from the soil and are washed into the lake. Water plants in the lake start to grow rapidly. There is increased competition between the plants, and some die as a result. The number of microbes that feed on dead organisms increases. The microbes take more oxygen from the water for their respiration. Fish and other aquatic animals die of suffocation.
b) The plants grow more quickly because they have received additional nitrates and phosphates.
c) The plants are likely to be competing for light and space. Nitrates, phosphates and water are likely to be in excess.
d) The oxygen content of the water goes down because additional decomposer microbes use the oxygen to respire.
e) In a eutrophic lake, the nitrates are not limited because they are being added to the community from outside. Eutrophication kills animals and eventually plants. Therefore, the microbes are not recycling the nutrient but causing increasing death followed by yet more decay.
f) Environmental consequences include reduction in the diversity of the community, water which is dangerous to health or undrinkable, the lake may silt up faster becoming too shallow. Economic consequences include loss of fisheries, weeds making it impossible to use the waterway (e.g. Lake Victoria), drinking water may need additional treatment to make it safe, lakeside resorts become unattractive to tourists.
g) A lake might be rescued by stopping further influx of fertilisers, pulling up overgrowing plants, flushing fresh water through if possible, aerating the water (direct oxygenation and agitation have both been tried).

5) a) Untreated sewage also provides food for microbes.
b) Increased population and overcrowding.
c) Raw sewage may contain viable live disease-causing bacteria.

6) The rotting timber may provide a source of food for microbes, leading to eutrophication (a similar situation exists with paper mills). The number of microbes that feed on dead organisms will increase. The microbes will take more oxygen from the water for their respiration, and so fish and other aquatic animals will die of suffocation.

7) a) A pesticide is a chemical designed to kill insects which damage crops. Pesticides include DDT (dichlorodiphenyltrichloroethane) and dieldrin. The use of pesticides increases crop yields by reducing crop pests.
b) On going up the food chain the concentration of *Kilzemall* increased. This was because each organism accumulated the chemical in its fat, and rather than it being eliminated from the body, it was passed to the next organism in the food chain where it accumulated even more.
c) The chemical might have blown into the pond during spraying or been washed into it by rain.
d) The pesticide may have been lifted into the atmosphere by winds and carried to the poles.
e) We eat plants and animals, and we need to be confident that they are healthy and don't contain damaging levels of hazardous chemicals.

Pages 87, 88:

1) Completed diagram:

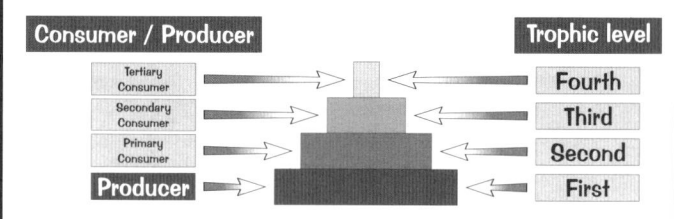

Consumer / Producer	Trophic level
Tertiary Consumer	Fourth
Secondary Consumer	Third
Primary Consumer	Second
Producer	First

2) a)
Kingfisher (1)
Trout (50)
Water fleas (100,000)
Microscopic water plants (1 million)

b)
Birds (5)
Caterpillars (500)
Oak Tree (1)

c) It is not always possible to draw the bars to scale because the numbers at each level can be very different. For example, it the kingfisher bar was 1mm wide, the microscopic water plants bar would be 1km wide!
d) A pyramid of numbers can have a non-pyramid shape if there is a single, large producer.
e)
Parasite (dozens)
Human (1)
Wheat plants (thousands)

Similar to answer for d), the parasites survive off a single large producer — a human.
f) Any suitable non-pyramidal example with relevant labelling and explanation.

3) a) A pyramid of numbers shows the numbers of organisms at each trophic level in a food chain.
b) Row F is the most likely to represent the numbers of organisms.
c) The size of the organism increases going from left to right along this food chain.
d) Pyramid A.

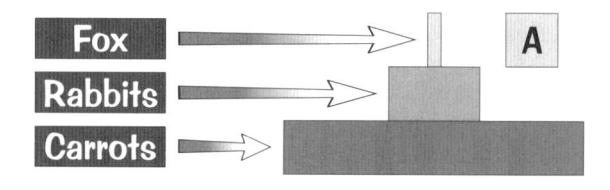

Fox
Rabbits
Carrots

A

e) The larger the organism, the narrower its bar.

Section Seven — Answers

The Environment P.87 → P.91

4) Biomass is the mass of living organisms at a particular trophic level. Pyramids of biomass show the mass of living organisms at each trophic level in a food chain.

5) a) Dry mass is the mass of an object after all the water has been removed. The amount of water in organisms can vary greatly between organisms, so the wet weight may not give a true picture of how much living material there is at each trophic level.
b) Pyramid:
(10cm for the phytoplankton works well).

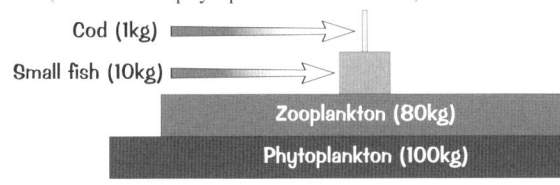

```
Cod (1kg)        ▬▭▷
Small fish (10kg) ▬▬▭▷
     Zooplankton (80kg)
     Phytoplankton (100kg)
```

c) If the biomass of the lowest trophic level is very large compared to the top level, a scale drawing will need a bar that is too small to draw accurately. A vertical line can be used then.
d) The most mass is lost zooplankton → small fish (70kg).
e) The greatest proportion is lost small fish → cod (90%).
f) Biomass is lost through waste materials and nutrients used for respiration.
g) 1kg of dry cod would eat 10kg of dry small fish.
Since both fish have the same proportion of water in their bodies, 1kg of wet cod would eat 10kg of wet small fish.
so 7.5kg of wet cod would eat 75kg of wet small fish.
So 1 cod would eat 75 ÷ 1.5 = <u>50 small fish</u>

6) a) Pyramid A — A large producer could support many herbivores, which then support fewer carnivores. + the first bar is small.
b) Pyramid B — Pyramids of biomass have the proper pyramid shape.
c) Pyramid D — Parasites are smaller than their hosts, so there will more of them, giving a wider final bar.
d) Pyramids B or D — The bottom bar would be the largest because many algae would be needed.

Page 89:

1) a) Plants photosynthesise. Light from the Sun is used to drive photosynthesis.
Equation: carbon dioxide + water → glucose + oxygen
b) *Equation*: glucose + oxygen → carbon dioxide + water
(+ energy transferred)
Energy released for growth, repair, heat, and movement.
c) Sunlight.

2) a) 500 – 250 – 150 = 100kJ
b) 150 – 75 – 20 = 55kJ
c) Energy from respiration is used for growth, repair, heat, and movement.
d) Reducing respiration: Restrict movement, e.g. by keeping them in a cage. This reduces muscular activity. Keep them indoors / in the warm / give them coats. This reduces the heat loss.
e) 150 ÷ 20 = 7½ times more people.
f) 1) Death, decay and other losses of plants. Possible ways to reduce losses: grow disease-resistant strains, compost the dead material, use pesticides.

2) Pig faeces. Possible ways to reduce losses: use the pig faeces as manure, use the faeces as fuel to warm the pig shed.

3) a) About 10% of the energy is transferred moving from one trophic level to the next. By cutting out a trophic level, 10 times more energy should get to humans, so 10 times more could be fed.
b) Not all the energy in plants is available to humans, e.g. roughage (which ruminants can use). More energy is used releasing nutrients from many tough plants than from meat. Meat may be a better source of some essential nutrients, e.g. amino acids.

Pages 90, 91:

1) a) Photosynthesis: carbon dioxide + water → glucose + oxygen
Respiration: glucose + oxygen → carbon dioxide + water
b) Respiration releases energy, photosynthesis needs energy. Respiration occurs in the mitochondria, photosynthesis occurs in the chloroplasts.
c) Respiration will release a carbon compound into the atmosphere, photosynthesis will remove a carbon compound from the atmosphere. Carbon dioxide is the compound involved.
d) Filled-in section of the carbon cycle:

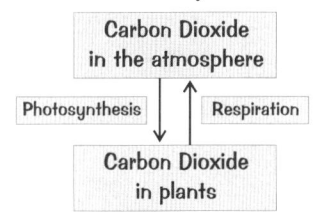

```
      Carbon Dioxide
      in the atmosphere
              ↑
Photosynthesis↓  Respiration
              ↑
      Carbon Dioxide
      in plants
```

e) Both processes involve carbon dioxide, glucose, oxygen and water. Both involve energy. Both take place inside cells. They seem to be opposites of each other, respiration releasing energy from glucose and photosynthesis using energy to make glucose. They occur in different parts of the cell.

2) If there were no bacteria and fungi capable of digesting cellulose, plant material would not decay completely and valuable nutrients might not be released. (The carbon could then only be recycled by burning).

3) a) Decomposers.
b) The bacteria and fungi obtain nutrients for respiration, and for growth and repair.
c) Carbon dioxide will be returned to the atmosphere (by respiration).
d) Minerals and nitrogen compounds.
e) Bacteria and fungi are important because they remove dead animals and plants, they release valuable minerals and nutrients from them. These minerals and nutrients are vital for the healthy growth of plants (without plants, the carbon cycle would cease).

4) "Microbes digest materials faster when they are in <u>warm</u> conditions which are <u>moist</u>. Many microbes work better if there is more <u>oxygen</u> in the environment."

5) a) Sewage comprises human faeces and urine, with varying amounts of water from homes and industry. It often contains harmful bacteria. It needs to be treated so that it cannot harm rivers, lakes and seas when it is discharged.
b) Suitable conditions: warm, wet, aerated (to get lots of oxygen). In some stages, beds of stones are used to give a large surface area.

Section Seven — Answers

The Environment P.91 → P.92

c) The minerals and nitrogen compounds in the original ingredients are not available to the plants, whereas in compost the cell walls have been broken down to release them. Some harmful chemicals will have been converted into harmless ones.

d) Damp plant remains such as grass clippings, carrot peel and tea bags are suitable for composting. Manure and newspapers can also be used. Compost is used as a fertiliser and soil improver.

Page 92:

1) a) Decomposers

b) Plants absorb nitrates through their roots, and use them to produce amino acids, proteins (and DNA).

c) Filled-in diagram:

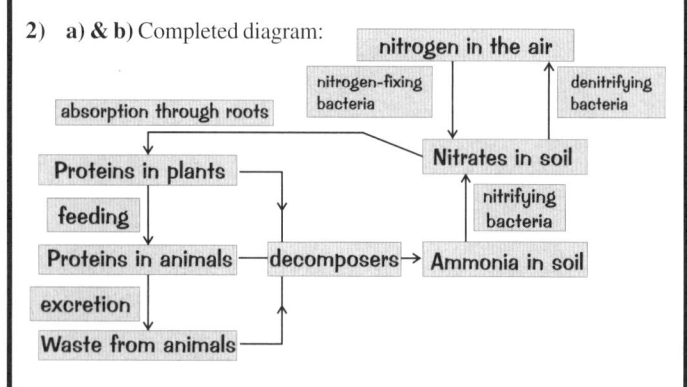

2) a) & b) Completed diagram:

c) Key points: Decomposers break down proteins and urea from plants, animals and animal wastes to form ammonia and ammonium compounds in the soil. Nitrifying bacteria in the soil convert the ammonia and ammonium compounds into nitrates in the soil. Denitrifying bacteria in the soil convert nitrates into atmospheric nitrogen gas. Nitrogen-fixing bacteria in the soil convert nitrogen into nitrates in the soil. Nitrogen-fixing bacteria in root nodules convert nitrogen into nitrates in the soil which are absorbed by the plant roots.

d) If denitrifying bacteria were more active than the others, all the nitrogen might end up in the atmosphere instead of in living organisms, which would then die as a result.

It would not matter if they were less active since returning nitrogen to the atmosphere is useless from the point of view of living organisms.